Punishment and Culture

Punishment and Culture

PHILIP SMITH

THE UNIVERSITY OF CHICAGO PRESS   CHICAGO AND LONDON

PHILIP SMITH is associate professor of sociology at Yale University and the author of *Cultural Theory: An Introduction* and *Why War? The Cultural Logic of Iraq, the Gulf War, and Suez,* the latter also published by the University of Chicago Press.

The University of Chicago Press, Chicago 60637
The University of Chicago Press, Ltd., London
© 2008 by The University of Chicago
All rights reserved. Published 2008
Printed in the United States of America

17 16 15 14 13 12 11 10 09 08   1 2 3 4 5

ISBN-13: 978-0-226-76609-6 (cloth)
ISBN-13: 978-0-226-76610-2 (paper)
ISBN-10: 0-226-76609-8 (cloth)
ISBN-10: 0-226-76610-1 (paper)

Library of Congress Cataloging-in-Publication Data

Smith, Philip.
    Punishment and culture : Philip Smith.
       p. cm.
    Includes bibliographical references and index.
    ISBN-13: 978-0-226-76609-6 (cloth : alk. paper)
    ISBN-13: 978-0-226-76610-2 (pbk. : alk. paper)
    ISBN-10: 0-226-76609-8 (cloth : alk. paper)
    ISBN-10: 0-226-76610-1 (pbk. : alk. paper) 1. Punishment. 2. Culture—Semiotic models.
I. Title.
GT6710.S65 2008
303.3′6—dc22

                                                                                    2007035707

♾ The paper used in this publication meets the minimum requirements of the American National Standard for Information Sciences—Permanence of Paper for Printed Library Materials, ANSI Z39.48-1992.

Contents

Acknowledgments

This book was written between 1992 and 2006, with most of the visible effort taking place in the final two years. For the whole period, however, intellectual tap roots were being put down in quiet and subterranean ways. At various points in time, research for the project was conducted at the Bibliothèque Nationale and the Bibliothèque de l'Histoire de Paris; at the École des Hautes Études en Sciences Sociales (EHESS), Paris; at the University of California, Los Angeles; Yale University; in the Department of History and Civilization at the European University Institute, Florence; in the Department of Criminology at Victoria University, Wellington; and at the University of Queensland, Brisbane. In diverse ways these institutions provided infrastructural, solidaristic and financial support. The library staff of these institutions helped with access to documents and archives. My wife, Philippa Smith, provided invaluable research assistance, especially for the chapter on the guillotine, during several intensive weeks in Paris working in the libraries and archives. Over the years discussions with Jeffrey Alexander, David Garland, John Pratt, Alexander Riley, Joachim Savelsberg, Barry Schwartz, Steven Sherwood, Arpad Szakolczai, Laurent Thévenot, and Jim Whitman, as well as with others too numerous to name, helped to develop the ideas expressed in this book. Nadine Casey assisted with the final printing and assembly of the manuscript. What can I say about Doug Mitchell at the University of Chicago Press that has not been said before? Doug understood the intent of this project from the start. Also at the Press Tim McGovern kept the wheels in motion that moved the product from manuscript to publication; Maia Rigas offered expert, detailed editing services; and Isaac Tobin came up with an outstanding design.

Chapter 2 was researched and drafted in 1992 and first appeared in 1996 after several periods of extra thinking. It has been further revised for this book. The original publication appeared as "Executing Executions: Aesthetics, Identity and the Problematic Narratives of Capital Punishment Ritual," *Theory and Society* 25, no. 2 (1996): 235–261 (copyright Kluwer Academic Publishers 1996). The material is reproduced here by kind permission of Springer Science and Business Media. Chapter 6 was researched in 1996 and written up over the following six years, being published in 2003 as "Narrating the Guillotine: Punishment Technology as Myth and Symbol," *Theory, Culture and Society* 20, no. 5 (2003): 27–51 (copyright Sage Publications Ltd. 2003). It too has been revised and for organizational reasons some paragraphs have been moved to chapter 7. It is reprinted by kind permission of Sage Publications Ltd. Taken as a whole, the book represents a deepening, thickening, consolidation, and generalization of the insights developed through writing these two earlier papers. The remaining chapters were written in 2005 and reworked in 2006 and again in 2007. Permission to reprint Andy Warhol's Little Electric Chair was provided by the Andy Warhol Foundation for the Visual Arts. Many thanks go to Amanda Burns of the Artists Rights Society for making the necessary arrangements. The Artists Rights Society also loaned the official slide from which the image used in this book was derived. The National Gallery in London is thanked for making available a digital file containing Canaletto's Ranelagh Rotunda painting and for giving permission to reproduce it here. The other images are my own scans and photos and are in the public domain.

This book owes much to my now twenty-year-long association with Jeffrey Alexander—eminent Durkheimian. It is dedicated to him with appreciation and in a spirit of solidarity.

CHAPTER ONE

The Penal Imagination

What exactly is the point of punishment? What is the inner logic of its curious methods? These two questions are at the heart of this book. Many think they already know the answers. They say punishment can be explained as the balancing of the scales of justice, the control of deviance, the expression of power, the deterrence of crime, or at least doing whatever is necessary to keep a lid on things. By the end of this study we will have come to a very different understanding, realizing that punishment in its generalities and specificities cannot be understood without reference to public meaning. Or, to be more precise, *meanings* that overlap and intersect in partly intended and partly accidental ways. These proliferate, sometimes in the mode of coherent formal statements but more often as a complex layering of insistent symbolisms and narrations. Although diverse they are not entirely random in their distributions, for as they scatter they mark out a peculiar kind of cultural terrain whose geometry is defined by the sacred and evil, the pure and polluted. Even where punishment looks most rationalized and bureaucratic these unruly meanings exert their insistent and surprising influence. They can toll the bell on the outmoded technique and ring in the new, fanning the flames of scandal and celebration alike. They play with our emotions and enable punishments to exert a sinister attraction, to become the object of fascination, fetishism, amusement, and dread. Never fully scientific nor merely technocratic and never quite closed off from public interest, punishment is always the locus of intense narrative activity and contestation within a wider civil discourse. Such will be my argument.

This is not the first book to explain punishment by identifying some underlying logic, rationality, or essence, but it is one in a very small minority that sees what we might think of as the "cultural life" of punishment as truly important in explaining the evolution and form of penal activity. Most scholars simply point to the juridical functions of formal sanctioning and to the explicit, official justifications for policy and procedure. They speak of retribution and deterrence, the rule of law and proportionality. Next there is reference to the ink on the pages of the statute and precedent books that outline appropriate measures. This is how most lawyers, legal historians, and legal philosophers talk. With a focus on the offence and the offender and available legally approved means, such an approach to explanation sits a little too close to common sense. This is the informed native's view and there are no surprises here. Indeed the perspective often comes close to tautology: the law is applied in this particular way because this is what we are supposed to do, to do otherwise would be illegal; the "rule of law" determines punishment activity; hanging disappeared in such and such a year because the law changed; prisoners are entitled to three meals a day because we have duty of care and so forth. We can also put aside as insufficiently arresting the word of another kind of insider, the policy analyst or applied criminologist. The vision in this case is of punishment as a series of validated efforts aimed at producing a better world through the regulation of unwanted activity. Here our vocabulary would involve words like efficiency, amenity, the common good, evidence, benchmarking, reasonableness, and reform. In this representation criminal justice activity is simply the exertion of a more or less well-intentioned practical reason as we look for sensible and humane ways to deal with enduring social problems, including not only crime control but also organizational needs for the just, affordable, and effective administration of punishment. Fair enough, we need good policy. But we also require good theory if we are to have some intellectual distance from the tyranny of such everyday preoccupations. As legal scholar Paul Kahn argues, it is high time for at least some practitioners and professors to turn away from normative questions relating to the workings of the law or efforts to justify or reform this or that policy. They might instead engage in a cultural analysis. For Kahn the first step is to undertake a thick description of the meanings of criminal justice, to make the law anthropologically distant and so to allow the study of the forms of "legal consciousness" without the prejudicial influence of any practical task at hand.[1]

The requirement for such a telescopic understanding has long been appreciated by critical theory, even if the call for a hermeneutics of justice has been largely rejected. We find it foreshadowed in the early work of Karl Marx and Friedrich Engels, who condemned the law in *The German*

Ideology as a system of property rights that supported bourgeois interests, subtly cloaking these in the language of legal universalism.[2] It was
developed in the work of the Frankfurt School theorists Georg Rusche
and Otto Kirchheimer, who saw punishment as a form of class oppression whose exact modality responded chiefly to the labor supply needs
of the economy. The line of thinking was continued thirty years later by
Louis Althusser's chilling description of criminal justice as part of a Repressive State Apparatus, the clockwork of legitimate thuggery that allowed capitalism to reproduce itself when faced with radical dissent. The
apotheosis comes with Michel Foucault's Nietzsche-influenced writings of
the 1970s outlining the crushing logic of discipline and normalization that
accompanied modernity. I turn to these in a few pages but can note here
that Foucault's enduring spirit can still be found in most contemporary
critiques by academics of the criminal justice system or of the broader
array of state interventions towards social control, such as the much-cited
discussion of "the new penology" by criminologists Malcolm Feeley and
Jonathan Simon or the dissection of race politics by Loïc Wacquant.[3]

Its ghost is also evident in the work of Zygmunt Bauman on the Holocaust and Nils Christie on the "crime control industry."[4] The argument
here is that modernity is a behemoth without compassion. A blind instrumental reason has gotten out of hand and the power to punish knows no
constraint of the heart. Horrors have eventuated precisely because meaning as value and ethical commitment has been stripped from social control process. The mode of explanation is one that talks of forms of power
and knowledge in the so-called carceral city; of the "net-widening" and
"mesh thinning" of surveillance and control systems; of the normalization
of harmless eccentricity by impersonal systems; the triumph of the prison-
industrial complex; of the rise of soulless hierarchical administrative and
managerial templates; of actuarial systems for risk management and of the
political imperatives for control over dangerous and unruly classes. This
is an intellectual territory where the modalities of punishment are stalked
by power and interests, whether those of concrete classes, elites, the state,
capital, or even—as we find in Foucault's work—the malevolent force
of some abstracted logic of "power" itself, a logic whose lifeblood is the
capillary triumph of instrumental reason. Whichever version we endorse,
the point is that punishment can now be explained away as an adjunct of
some form of legal-rational domination within the broader totality that is
modernity. So widespread is this belief that punishment today has become
a flagship field for theorists of wider societal disenchantment. Foucault's

Discipline and Punish has replaced Weber's *Protestant Ethic and the Spirit of Capitalism* as the seminal statement on how the organizing principles of society have radically changed over the past few centuries. Whether we read Foucault or Weber or those who drink from their cup, the point is the same. The spirit of our age is a distillation of a brutish bureaucratic nihilism, and its single malt showpiece is the prison.

I believe that this view is mistaken. Yet it is also laudable, for there is much that is appealing in the perspective of such a critical social science. Here we have a structuralist move of great intellectual power that situates punishment within the broader context of the social system. The critical theorists have grasped the nettle in claiming that social control has only an oblique relationship to conscious intent or public declaration or to the practical, sensible activities of lawmakers, judges, or reformers. Their product further attests that the "insider" view of the criminal justice practitioner, average law professor or policy analyst who is just one step removed from the fulcrum of practical reason, does not provide us with sufficient intellectual leverage. They understand that if we account for punishment in this local way we have a folk model rather than an explanation, one that reproduces the common sense categories of engaged experts. If we took it seriously, we would become like the anthropologist who used the shaman's incantations to explain a ritual. Hence there is also the important recognition in critical social science that punishment can be about latent rather than manifest social function and that the keys to understanding are to be recovered through an interrogation of the social as this intersects with the codes, policies, and institutions of criminal justice.

Yet for all these attributes critical social science is looking tired. What was an exciting paradigm revolution twenty or thirty years ago has become a normal science generating cloned books and articles on mass imprisonment, "at risk" youth, closed circuit television (CCTV) and so forth. The returns to effort for this kind of pessimistic culture diagnosis are diminishing with each additional publication. Just as Swedish design has become mainstream over the past thirty years, where there was once thinking outside the box we now have a flat-packed IKEA criminology. This allows readymade concepts to be bolted together to provide a simple, visually attractive and workable enough explanation in any field where formal social control is at hand. But to play further on this tempting metaphor would be mean-spirited and unnecessary. Much fine work is still being conducted, and so we must divert our energies to the heart of the matter. It is less profitable to argue that the critical theory approach has become devalued by mantra-like repetition than to press the case that this intellectual gem has long been fatally flawed by the claim that punishment is really about power and not poetics. We shall see later in this book how this has had serious consequences for its core business and has led to misinterpretations of historical process. For the present I can simply note that critical criminology has been caught off guard by some of the more empirically significant and theoretically intriguing developments in the contemporary social control environment. With unfortunate timing Foucault wrote the masterwork that inspired this intellectual movement in the early 1970s just as the tide was starting to turn on the form of "penal welfarism" he had subjected to such thorough dissection.[5] He had described and critiqued a complex of ideology and policy that placed at its vanguard a network of institutions of varying severity, believed in the reformability of deviants, privileged the state as a social agent, and accorded prestige to credentialed knowledge experts. A few years later this view was starting to look out of step with the times. Through the 1980s and 1990s criminologists were describing some puzzling changes. Public inputs into crime control seemed to be growing rather than shrinking as Foucault and standard critical theory predicted. There was dissatisfaction with experts and pressure for politicians to "do something" about deviants. Moreover, the public's thinking was looking nonrational. It had little to do with true risks of victimization, seemed to be driven by fear and myth, traded in stereotypes, and was oriented around concepts of vengeance rather than bureaucratic control. This upsurge in what is now known as "penal populism" called for a more culturally sensitive kind of analysis that could unpack the anxieties and imageries behind suburban outrage. Meanwhile, the welfarist experts seemed to be more interested in culture and more suspicious of bureaucracy and discipline than ever before. There was a renewed interest in restorative justice with associated tools such as conferencing, mediation, and reintegrative shaming. Here the focus was on generating intense and internalized social bonds, not atomism; on developing the personality rather than robotic, individualized conformists; on setting up authentic ritual encounters and enlisting the emotions rather than suppressing them. Issues of meaning, it seems, have returned to the agenda, and the Foucaultian "episteme" is itself now starting to look like the product of an era that has passed.

Partly spurred on by these and similar empirical shifts, a way towards a cultural analysis of punishment has been slowly forming in the past decade or so. This is less an intentional path exhibiting the merits of coordi-

nated engineering and careful design than a bush track that has been worn
by the successive feet of scholars, each on their own intellectual journey.
It is rough but nevertheless a route of sorts towards the purpose of *understanding* punishment rather than simply explaining it. Such progress has
been made on a number of fronts: the "cultural criminology" that draws
upon cultural studies, the new sociology of punishment, the literature on
moral panics and the media, and the work of social historians. Diverse
in inspiration and audience, these literatures share the perspective that
efforts to regulate deviants must be seen in more cultural terms as a pat-
terned set of meaningful or symbolic activities that are in need of hermeneutic analysis.[6] It has been established that we can read punishments
as didactic or communicative acts in which messages are sent. Such signals might denounce wrongdoing and celebrate justice, render clear the
structure of authority, or show commitment to moral values. We have also
come to understand that cultural inputs into punishment can reflect a
broader social ethos or a diffuse set of moral concerns without clear au-
thorship. For example, studies show that acceptable levels of retributive
violence have changed over time, as have understandings on the visibility
of punishment, or the appropriate quality of prison life, or even what a
prison should look like.[7] We have much better traction on the cultural
and institutional process through which those contemporary fears over
crime might find their indirect expression in penal policies.[8] Works by
symbolic interactionists have been rediscovered. These showed long ago
that cultural inputs can be detected in the ongoing practical activities and
processes of punishment, and in particular are incarnated in the informal
codes that govern institutional life.[9] Efforts have been made to read off
meanings from the routines and spatial arrangements of prisons, the oc-
cupational and administrative concerns of specialists, and the material or
governmental technologies through which social control is administered.[10]
The ability of punishment to change behavior has been shown to be con-
ditioned by wider meanings in criminal subcultures.[11] The death penalty
has been analyzed as a contested domain subject to and shaped by legiti-
mation struggles and responsive to the national and local cultures within
which it is situated.[12] Even within the critical theory trajectory there has
been change. Criminologists influenced by the cultural studies tradition
have begun to develop a "cultural criminology" that explores how power,
meaning, deviance, and criminalization intersect.[13] In short, there is a substantial body of literature suggesting that meanings within and without
the penal system influence the quantity and quality of punishment. These

meanings have been shown to be variable, contested, and frequently influential.

For all this achievement the expanding literature towards a cultural sociology of punishment is nebulous in form. If critical criminological theory has almost ceased to innovate it nevertheless has a lingua franca and some shared iconic theoretical referents, paramount among them Foucault's text. The less reductionist and more cultural field presents a body of work that is scattered and without any clear center of gravity. Turning to a hypothetical office bookcase labeled "Culture and Punishment: Resources," we will find one text offering insight into lynching in twentieth-century America, the adjacent volume recounting the institutional culture of some nineteenth-century Victorian prison, the next documenting the unruly procession from Newgate to the Tyburn Tree, something else on the meanings of captivity in literature, and then an examination of the rhetoric of the war on drugs and how this influenced three strikes legislation. This collection illustrates case study methodology, where fidelity to the concrete is the most prized virtue. Not surprisingly, it is dominated by historians. With their healthy suspicion of generalizing flights of fancy, they have given priority to accurately collecting and recounting the details of what happened, what people said, and what they probably thought. Theory tends to be an afterthought, systematic theory construction all but forbidden. So regrettably, and with a few exceptions, such detailed and impressive studies require retrofitting to the imperatives of generalizing social science. These books are less of a true "literature" marked by dense citational and empirical coreference around a core problem than a collection of interesting studies on diverse topics that have to be analytically reconstructed into a "literature" ex post facto through the exercise of the imaginative faculty. Placing books on our shelf and then shuffling them around until patterns form is a poor way to go about our business of constructing a more systematic cultural approach to punishment. This is a retrospective style of theory construction in which general, transposable lessons must be sought and plucked like plums from the pudding long after it has been baked.

In this book I suggest a far more radical approach to culture and punishment that begins with the articulation and application of some first principles. We should start with the vigorous intention of developing more universal, generalizable themes for a cultural criminology of punishment, not explaining a particular research site. If not a tessellated system, these principles should at least constitute a set of elementary claims and concepts revolving around a common theoretical nucleus. Such abstract models can then be illustrated, tested, proven to be of value through reference to multiple case studies, these selected as theoretically relevant sites of inquiry rather than valued for their intrinsic interest. Our trajectory towards this goal is to be defined by two scholars of the first order, Michel Foucault and Émile Durkheim. As David Garland realized long ago in a seminal essay,[14] although these are the two deepest thinkers on society and punishment they are not in concord. Indeed, their theoretical logics are almost diametrically opposed. For this reason they fortuitously provide the magnetic field within which we can orient our activity. Whereas Garland sketched the contours of disagreement with an even hand and in so doing opened up the intellectual space for a cultural sociology of punishment, my belief is that a more polemical approach is now required. And so to derive bearings for what follows, I describe Foucault largely as the pole to be avoided and Durkheim as that towards which we should point our compass. This will not be, however, the functionalist Durkheim familiar from textbooks and introductory lectures in criminology but rather what I have called elsewhere a "new Durkheim"[15] reconstructed in the light of contemporary cultural theory.

Foucault's Challenge

If Foucault is to appear here as a token enemy from time to time, the role does not indicate any lack of respect. To the contrary, his *Discipline and Punish* is seminal and so it provides the toughest challenge to the project of this book. It is with due deference that I throw down the gauntlet. There are many lessons to be taken from the great French philosopher. To begin, he demonstrates the intellectual benefits that come from fundamentally reworking a field through theoretical renewal rather than endless fact-finding missions. To the chagrin of some historians and the delight of others,[16] Foucault's landmark volume *Discipline and Punish* (1975) revolutionized the study of the evolution of punishment.[17] The means were simple: bold and unequivocal statements interpreting particular sites, a big picture view of what punishment was about, and backup in the form of a thick citation of evidence. Some of this was taken from historians both bourgeois and radical, but the majority was retrieved by reading original sources. Whereas the repeated collection of information in this or that study of punishment in the discipline of history had failed to ignite the intellectual powder keg, Foucault squeezed complex information into a shell of his devising, hooked it up to some ingenious theoretical wiring and finished with a fuse of stylistic flair. Then he managed to explode the field with this single bomb of some three hundred pages. Theory, you see, works in ways that facts cannot because it simplifies and concentrates as it explains. By imposing a metanarrative the move to generality trumps the concrete even as it respects the weight of the empirical.

Yet the question of approach aside, Foucault must remain a largely negative influence for our efforts towards a meaning-rich understanding of punishment. To explain why, we need first to recapitulate his empirical findings and the associated theoretical matrix. To briefly summarize, Michel Foucault's argument is that modes of punishment have changed over the centuries. In the period between about 1750 and 1850 a new set of practices emerged. At the start of this period, he claims, punishment was public and was directed at the body using pain as its method. Torture, execution, the pillory, mutilation, these would take place in the town square or other common space in front of a general audience. Such activity was intermittent and had a semiotic component. Often allegorical it was intended to dramatize the power of the sovereign of the absolutist era. By the mid-nineteenth century something very different was in place. Punishment was no longer communicative, as it had become sequestered behind the walls of the prison. Brutality was gone, to be replaced by routinized activities directed towards reforming, or as Foucault puts it to curiously sinister effect, "normalizing" the deviant. The process made use of scientifically calibrated techniques thought up by experts, cleverly devised to operate automatically and continuously. They involved monitoring, surveillance, classification, measurement, and discipline operating upon a "docile body."

The great novelty of Foucault's perspective lies not in the flesh of these empirical generalities—which had been noted countless times before by historians of punishment—but in the theoretical carapace within which he enclosed them. What appears to be the result of a purely juridical or technological evolution taking place within the broader landscape of enlightenment humanism can be decoded as emblematic of something at once deeper and more widespread. These transformations of punishment are homologous with, express, or embody a new and pervasive modality of social power. The movement to modernity entailed a new productive logic of administrative ordering whose imperative was to classify so as to regulate, to monitor, to discipline, to normalize. This replaced a negative modality whose functioning served to dramatize, to display, and to chastise or even destroy. In Foucault's own terms a "disciplinary power" superseded "sovereign power." Importantly, he claims the prison was only one locus of this new principle of social order. The very same techniques of body management, categorization, and regimentation could also be found in the proliferation of social control institutions under the condition of modernity: schools, barracks, reformatories, factories, hospitals. The result was a "carceral continuum" or "carceral city," a network-style modernity in which robotic bodies and manufactured souls were moved through spaces and organizations of control over the life course, normalized and made productive within an acephalous matrix of circulating and productive power.

Such a vision has not been without its critics. Yet although critique has often been accurate on points of detail it has never been fully compelling. The reason is simple but rarely noted. The tessitura of criticism and that of Foucault do not exactly coincide because intellectual products investing in "facts" and those investing in "theories" tend to make divergent truth claims. This is most clearly visible in the debate on *Discipline and Punish* that took place in France in the 1970s involving Foucault and a panoply of historians.[18] Critics charged that he had neglected the nonprison forms of punishment that persisted; that he failed to specify concrete historical agents; that he squeezed three or four centuries of penal evolution into a short time frame, or that he overlooked the premodern monastic prototypes of disciplinary social organization.[19] Perhaps too Foucault had overplayed the stability and pervasiveness of the disciplinary revolution and so was unable to explain the persistence of political disorder and contestation in nineteenth-century France.[20] Foucault's response to all this was to indicate a disparity in register, to argue that the critique was not relevant because he was slicing the cake differently from conventional historians. His interest was less in what happened than in uncovering the logic of function and operation, the set of principles or ideas that underpinned efforts towards a new form of power, the templates of knowledge that made it thinkable. "When I speak of a 'disciplinary society,' one should not hear 'disciplined society,'" he writes, "When I speak of the diffusion of methods of discipline, this is not to claim that 'the French obeyed.'"[21] This response is more than a little curious notwithstanding accuracy on a technical point of order, for his book repeatedly treads the boundary between claims about the intellectual logic of a system and the extent of its institutionalization in earthly practices. The point can be pressed by indicating how his own writings indicate the back-and-forth movement between concept and experiment, the ways that experience provided information for the refinement of disciplinary models, that the emergence of disciplinary society was an empirical project grounded in institutions as much as a theoretical one emanating from the pen. As Foucault himself forcefully shows, the disciplinary dream was not thought up in a vacuum, but in a practical laboratory where ideas were tested and refined on subject populations of soldiers and malcontents, pupils and lunatics.

All this said, it seems to me to be less useful to indicate the incomplete institutionalization of disciplinary power or to contemplate the futility of existing critique than to spotlight the hermeneutically thin and circumscribed attributes with which Foucault invests punishment. One reason for this neglect was his "genealogical method," derived from Nietzsche, which insisted on looking to activity not motivation, to the "how" of power and not the "why." The injunction here is to sidestep the thorny and allegedly misleading question of meaning and to measure process and effects, to go "beyond structuralism and hermeneutics," as a noted book on Foucault claimed in its subtitle.[22] A second reason why meaning drops out is his vision of history. One of Foucault's core stories in *Discipline and Punish*, as in his earlier books on psychiatry and medicine, is of a domain where expert knowledge becomes triumphant as the centuries tick by. First there are manifestos oriented around the quest for rationality, efficiency, and outcomes; next there are real buildings and organizations that to a large extent carry these out. This is a world without continuing civil or folkloric inputs where technocrats and experts call the tune, and where the relevant context of meaning for understanding what is going on can be reduced to the circulation of arrows on a flowchart or the tedious protocols in a drill instructor's handbook. For Foucault punishment might be "meaningful" but only in this desiccated, instrumentally rational sense. There remains no affect or passion, no symbolism and no culturally specified imperatives other than those relating to domination. This is an oil and vinegar vision of penal culture with the new and old, disciplinary and symbolic, scientific and religious radically separated by the disjoint march of time.

There is a very clear parallel here with Weber's picture of societal disenchantment.[23] Weber's iron cage has become Foucault's model prison. Just as religion was replaced by the iron grid of modernity, so have the rich, thick, spectacular and ornamental qualities of premodern punishment been replaced over the centuries by ever more efficient, rational modes of regulating human bodies. Foucault was a more careful student of Nietzsche than one might imagine. *The Birth of Tragedy* has experienced its own eternal return in *Discipline and Punish*. Adaptive upgrading under the condition of modernity has seen a calculated and diminished economy of meaning replace those prior Apollonian and Dionysian expressions of emotion or symbolism. The methodological corollary of Foucault' position is clear. Analysts need now to demystify and map rather than imaginatively reconstruct the enchanted modes of thinking whereby our recent ancestors might have invested punishment practices with other than technocratic significance. Further, one need only look to the pronouncements of experts, those authorized to speak reason, the architects of disciplinary control. Whereas the semipublic qualities of punishment under sovereign power gave space for diffuse public inputs through crowd behavior, pamphleteering, campaigning, and coffeehouse talk, the emergence of the prison and the growth of the carceral city led to a logic of function in which power operates largely without civic debate. There is no real space for critique or input into penal policy from outside of the carceral system once this becomes a closed-off realm of expertise, built form, and routine activity. Foucault's modernity is a society of professionals and functionaries, of drones and bodies not citizens. It is a world where the truth about punishment can be found in reports and manifestos, laws and architectural diagrams rather than newspapers, memoirs, or novels directed towards a wider public sphere.[24] Here then is a vision that can seduce with its clarity and daring. It is also a temptation that must be avoided. For the argument that punishment has become closed, driven overwhelmingly by norms and techniques of rationality and hermeneutically thin institutional cultures, and cut off from wider spheres of meaning and judgment is quite simply wrong.

Reconstructing Durkheim's Legacy

From the perspective of a truly cultural sociology of punishment, Foucault's major work on the subject is flirtatious. Most notably in those opening chapters on the spectacle of the scaffold it promises much. Here symbolic operations are part of the apparatus of power. There are metaphors of theater and drama, references to emotional mood and some understanding of punishment as a meaningful atonement or expiation. Alas, these promissory gestures fall by the wayside as the pages that follow relentlessly document the pragmatic and demythologized operations of disciplinary power. It is instead Émile Durkheim who can provide a more steadfast and unwavering guide when it comes to developing a culture-rich account of punishment.[25] Advocating Durkheim is not without its risks, and perhaps for this reason his legacy for thinking about punishment remains underacknowledged. Although broadly recognized as a foundational figure for criminology, he is often referenced in perfunctory ways. For many criminologists Durkheim is one of the busts on the mantle of the formerly important. Like the nineteenth-century biological determinist Cesare Lombroso or the enlightenment humanist Cesare Beccaria, Durkheim is commonly understood as a person pivotal for the development or history of criminological theory. He is a presence to be included in survey lecture courses but not to be taken seriously as a source for current inspiration. The French master is most often associated with the simplistic, problematic, tautological legacy of his functionalism, with psychologistic explanations of the tie between structure and sentiment and with the positivistic advocacy of the social fact. When thought of in a good light by criminologists, it is most likely that the reference is to *Suicide,* a book in which Durkheim pioneered the use of social statistics and made complex arguments about the link between deviance, anomie, and social disorganization.[26] Whatever we might think of him, Durkheim is not generally understood as providing detailed resources for a more complex semiotic or hermeneutic decoding of penal activity. To discover another, more cultural Durkheim worthy of our intellectual investment we must engage in some creative reading and theoretical reconstruction. I will draw upon the explicit legacy of his earlier writings and fuse these to the implicit bequests of his later work, as well as look to diverse studies by his students as I formulate a set of tools for the understanding of punitive activity as a cultural expression. In the remainder of this chapter and in the case studies that follow I will map out and deploy what can be thought of as this Durkheimian "cultural logic" of punishment.[27]

At this point it is useful to break with protocol and offer a capsule summary of the argument of this book. We should understand the tie between punishment and the social not as primarily political or administrative but rather as revolving around signifiers of order and disorder, purity and pollution, the sacred and evil as well as ritualized and regulatory efforts to influence these. Efforts at social control are a semiotic process and pay homage to cultural imperatives. Concerned with the regulation of unruly offenders, the judicial mandate to punish is underpinned by cultural codes requiring practical solutions to the peculiarly cultural and moral problem of disorder.

The legitimacy of any given activity or policy depends upon a perceived ability to classify, regulate, and purify—to produce and maintain a surplus of order over disorder. Historically this has proven to be a difficult task for several reasons. Disorder is a perpetually moving target. When one form of the unruly, evil, or disgusting is eliminated others are found. Previously minor disorders, for example, might start to loom larger. Ordering is an obsession that must repeatedly generate new demons and witches, sometimes within the criminal justice process itself. As Durkheim pointed out long ago, in a society of saints even trivial acts become elevated to the status of major crimes.[28] Further disorder can take many forms. Its names are legion. It might be detected in the wild behavior of the condemned or imprisoned, the prurient and primitive activity of crowds and publics, the leaky boundaries of the human body, the penal excess of the state, or inconsistent and genre-bending narrations of punishment itself that do not allow some neat closure. Dealing effectively with one form of disorder might entail in some ironic or unintended way the production of another form, especially given the contagious, unpredictable qualities of the sacred. Creating cultural order is rather like trying to solve the Rubik's Cube. As you get one facet uniformly blocked out, things start to go awry where you are not looking.

Ordering discourses and practices operate in complex semiotic fields. Because multiple cultural resources are available for the perception and evaluation of penal practice it can be difficult to attain authoritative closure over interpretation. There are triggers and trip wires everywhere once punishments are narrated and interpolated by diverse discursive and figural regimes. Expert knowledge can collide with humanist sentiments, unconscious or unfortunate resonances, political tropes, or the scatological and unauthorized narratives and images in popular culture that might detect or invent forms of disorder and so destabilize legitimate penal practices. Harsh punishment, for example, can be argued to insult and fragment the self or presage the moral chaos of absolutism. It can be subverted by comedic or tragic metanarrations as a form of cruelty or as a farce, unleashing the lawless demons of sadism and mirth. To add yet more contingency to the mix, efforts at generating order can crash head on with the unruly powers of the sacred. Whether intended or not, punishment is likely to be perceived as a ritual intervention attempting the purification of the soul and the mortification of the body. Death, pain, and transfiguration are its stock-in-trade and with these the unpredictable and malevolent forms of sacred energy are likely to come on stage.

Contra Foucault, I shall argue that such concerns and constellations of proliferating meaning have become *more* not *less* important in the administration of justice over recent centuries. There has been a net growth in broader societal reflexivity over criminal justice process. The expansion has been fuelled by the structural emergence of the public sphere and mass popular culture, and at the microlevel by intensified and reworked sensibilities, sensitivities, and subjectivities. Policy is now severely constrained, with reforms oriented around meaning control as much as the regulation of deviance itself. In this way the collective conscience speaks.

To make this argument is to elaborate a late-Durkheimian model of criminal justice, albeit in a rather complex way that reflects multiple currents in his intellectual legacy. The task of the next few pages is to justify the position. The aim is not so much to recapitulate what he "truly" said about crime and punishment, as it is to critique, rework, and reconstruct— in short, to extract the nub of Durkheim that reflects the spirit of this intellectual age and our project as much as his. This is an exercise that gears up Durkheim's writings with the mechanical advantage of a subsequent hundred years of cultural theory.

To start somewhere near the beginning: Writing in his doctoral thesis *The Division of Labour in Society* of 1893, Durkheim argued that "in the first place, punishment constitutes an emotional reaction."[29] In this understanding the urge to punish was driven by nonrational collective desire: "What we are avenging, and what the criminal is expiating, is the outrage of morality."[30] So criminal acts for Durkheim can be understood as violations of the collective conscience and sanctions as expressing and rebuilding this shared normative life of the community. Contra Foucault, Durkheim insists that even in the modern world punishment could never be a fully rational response to disorder. To be sure, it is more codified, institutionally regulated, and detraditionalized. Still, the operation of criminal justice has simply "adapted to the new conditions of existence created for it without thus undergoing any essential changes,"[31] and so "punishment has remained an act of vengeance, at least in part."[32] A second contribution of *The Division of Labour* for our purposes lies in Durkheim's argument that the emotional reactions that drove punishment were themselves underpinned by defined cultural systems. This was more than a theory of collective psychology. Such cultural inputs into social control had a specifically religious character. Spiritual taboos and interdictions had played a major role, for "penal law was essentially religious in origin,"[33] and "offences against the gods are offences against society."[34] Over subsequent centuries the evolution and codification of law had simply layered complexity onto this underlying nexus. Institutional differentiation and societal diversity have tempered the impulse to punish. Yet they have not eliminated the substratum of the sacred that still envelopes the collective conscience and its derivative legal codes. Hence Durkheim insists that even today "penal law . . . continues to bear a certain stamp of religiosity."[35] Sanctions against offenders express societal disapproval not only at material breaches of the law but also at "attacks upon something which is transcendent" or "something sacred."[36] Behind the surface logic of mundane redress we can find a "quasi-religious characteristic of expiation . . . [which is] an integrating element in punishment. Certainly it only expresses its nature metaphorically, but the metaphor is not without truth."[37]

In this early work Durkheim is pointing to punishment as being about cultural reason more than power. Hence he is able to make the famous and rather brilliant claim that the act of punishing is not really about the criminal offender at all. It is an act of imaginative reordering or expiation that offers a way of thinking and reinforcing moral boundaries, thereby rebuilding solidarity. The malefactor's suffering is neither a utilitarian means of reform into productive labor or citizenship nor a calibrated method of discouraging future offending. Rather it is "a sign indicating that the sentiments of the collectivity are still unchanged" and so serves to "heal the wounds inflicted upon the collective sentiments."[38] Crucially, then, in the first few chapters of *The Division of Labour* Durkheim begins to understand punishment as a kind of speech act in which society talks to itself about its own moral identity, for the "real function is to maintain inviolate the cohesion of society by sustaining the common consciousness in all its vigour."[39] The criminal body and the apparatus of control are not so much nodes in the circuits of power as Foucault would have it but tools for thinking. They are first and foremost symbols and ciphers in a reordering exercise, only secondarily efforts towards administrative reason.

This approach from the 1890s contains much that is of use for our project. Durkheim shows that punishment is about meaning and its communication; he points to the religious origins of the law and insists that moral community inputs remain from the "collective conscience." He further is explicit that rationalization under the condition of modernity has not eliminated these protean forces, it has merely diffused, rerouted, and blunted them. Here we find the rudiments for a radically anti-Foucaultian position.[40] There are, however some problems diverting attention from these virtues. Most famously, Durkheim's functionalist logic dominated interpretations of his writings through to the 1980s, giving the impression that he could not live up to contemporary demands for social theory to account for power and agency, specify causality, or indeed give autonomy to culture.[41] So the active, creative, and spontaneous qualities of the protosemiotic model of punishment buried in the *Division of Labour* have not been widely perceived. In the functionalist reading of Durkheim, deviance is primarily a threat to stability that automatically triggers a series of defense mechanisms. This is a rather robotic model in which systems logics are determinate and where homage is paid to the god of societal equilibrium. Neither the identification of deviance nor the invention of suitable punishment is taken to be a practical problem for situated actors. Further, levels of tolerance for deviance and consequent patterns of sanctioning as variously retributive or restitutive were tied in a seemingly mechanistic way to emergent social complexity and the structural logics of subsystem integration, as a more flexible and reflexive "organic solidarity" comes to replace a more repressive and impulsive "mechanical solidarity" in course of the transition to modernity. This perception was furthered by the slightly later extended essay *Two Laws of Penal Evolution* in which Durkheim suggested that the intersection of two structural dimensions (societal differentiation and the concentration of political power) determined the severity and form of penal practice.[42] This pushed meaning out of the analytic frame and allocated near-complete explanatory primacy to the morphology of the social system. In sum Durkheim's two major texts on punishment raise significant problems for thinking about the more proximate processual contestation and shaping of criminal justice activity, for theorizing what goes on at the level of the local, contingent, and empirical, and for analyzing everyday struggles over concrete technologies, activities, and priorities.

More seriously for the task of this book, Durkheim offers few pointers in these two works for identifying the content of cultural codes on punishment. Durkheim's utility here is compromised by the problematic language game of a "collective conscience" with its "nervous currents" and "vibrations." This unhelpfully moves us away from a more contemporary understanding of culture as a shared, contested, and circulating "code" or "narrative" (such as will inform this book) and towards hazy theories of crowd psychology, group mind, collective trauma, and therapy. For all its cultural promise Durkheim's early functionalism leaves us with a model looking rather expressively or hermeneutically unsophisticated. It is "society" that determines the meanings of the punishment, and the range of these meanings appears rather limited—to obtain vengeance, to effect repair, to express outrage. There is no real space here for a dialogic

understanding of punishment activity as a communicative process involving the sending and receiving of messages, ambiguity, or the analysis of
multiple and intersecting, complex and layered systems of meaning. In
sum, *The Division of Labour in Society* sets in place a frame for the cultural imagination of punishment, but it is an imperfect one. We can see
these imperfections playing out in perhaps the most celebrated application of the early-Durkheimian schema, Kai Erikson's *Wayward Puritans.*[43]
In this text from the 1960s we find an explanation of religious persecutions
and witch trials in seventeenth-century Massachusetts with reference to
the problem of community boundary maintenance. Erikson argues the
evil Other is identified and sought out by criminal justice activity in response to societal needs, especially anxieties within the utopian colony,
for self-definition. This is a cultural explanation of punishment, but only in
the weak sense of culture responding to system stress and strain through
the ritualized identification and amplification of minor deviance. There is
no explicit model of an underlying, enduring, and robust cultural system
that might specify the codes that mark out friends from enemies, witches
from saints, the virtuous from the corrupted or legitimate from illegitimate forms of social control activity. The result is an analysis vulnerable to
reworking by critical theory. And indeed critics have often suggested Erikson has little engagement with political realism, insisting that he might do
better to look at the land politics behind religious factionalism, or gender
regimes that would have made particular groups vulnerable or that could
have facilitated labeling. We might do better ourselves, however, if we realize that Erikson was not cultural enough and return to Durkheim's later
works in the search for clues on where to look for meaning.

To generate a more tractable cultural model from Durkheim's promising start in *The Division of Labour* we need first to consider more closely
his statements on the nature of morality under the condition of modernity.
Most important, Durkheim notes that the loosening and generalization
of the collective conscience has generated a new kind of moral awareness. This is organized not only around sentiments of tolerance but also
around a new grounding for the sacred in what he terms the "cult of the
individual." Pivotal here is the social obligation to treat others with dignity
and respect:

> The human person, by reference to the definition of which good must be distin-
> guished from evil, is considered as sacred, in what can be called the ritual sense
> of the word. It has something of that transcendental majesty which the churches

of all times have accorded their gods. It is conceived as being invested with that mysterious property which creates a vacuum about holy objects, which keeps them away from profane contacts and which separates them from ordinary life.... Such a morality is therefore not simply a hygienic discipline or a wise principle of economy. It is a religion of which man is, at the same time, both believer and god.[44]

Subsequently elaborated by the symbolic interactionist Erving Goffman,[45] this insight provides the basis for understanding social life as a series of ritualized face-to-face encounters wherein the sacred status of the self is continually reaffirmed. Breaches of this normative order, acts that disrespect the body or the mind, the character or autonomy of the person, generate a "feeling of revulsion"[46] and are subject themselves to sanction. As we will see throughout this book, such ideas are directly applicable to the ways that we think through the acceptability of punishment technologies and practices. This provides a useful counter to the Foucaultian idea that growing individuation in criminal justice is all about micromanagement and control. Further, it allows us to theorize an important set of cultural brakes on unrestrained disciplinary interventions. Discipline can be legitimately applied only when it is not seen as violating sovereignty of the individual and their body. If Foucault's master narrative of criminal justice is the growth of disciplinary control over the centuries, Durkheim's might very well be the rise to moral authority of this "cult of the individual."

We can also turn to a wider set of Durkheimian resources for rethinking his legacy, starting with writings that might seem on initial inspection to have no relevance to issues of crime and justice. The lectures that were collected under the title *Moral Education* were given by Durkheim in 1902 and 1903. These contain several fascinating chapters dedicated to the exploration of the purpose of punishment in schools or what he calls "*la pénalité scolaire.*" Constructed in the spirit of civic republicanism, we can detect here a stronger emphasis on the communicative functions of punishment than in *The Division of Labour,* which had preceded it by just a handful of years. This is indicated by some subtle shifts in vocabulary. As the italicized words below suggest, punishment in this later work becomes envisaged as more performative, more demonstrative, and as involving the more contingent encoding and decoding of information with possibilities for failure anticipated. It seems even more closely aligned with the defense not only of civic virtue but also that which is most sacred and which involves the imaginative faculties. The teacher needs to be resolute in punishing every infraction, for "hesitation, doubts and weak convictions" would be "necessarily *communicated* to the children" and lead to a "weakening of the moral *faith* of the class." Faced with a disciplinary infraction the teacher needs "*to show* in an unequivocal manner" that "the rule is still *sacred* in his eyes."[47] In this more strongly communicative and semiotic understanding, "punishment is nothing more than a *material sign* through which an internal state is translated; *it is a notation, a language* by means of which the public conscience of society and the conscience of the teacher *express* the feelings *inspired* in them by the act they reproach."[48] *Moral Education,* then, starts to open up the path to a dramaturgic, semiotic, and more strongly religious theory of punishment. From the promising start of the *Division of Labour* it takes us closer to a viable and developed cultural approach.

The reason for this increased promise lies in Durkheim's broader intellectual biography. From the mid-1890s onwards his thought came to focus on the centrality of religion for social life, drawing upon themes that had been present but subservient in his earlier work. Alongside this interest came a shift in theoretical logic. Moving away from the social structural or morphological determinism of his prior tracts he came to believe increasingly in the constructive role of cultural codes and ritual activities. These allowed Durkheim to develop a more dynamic and voluntaristic, but also more semiotic model of social life, one that gave priority to what he called "collective representations" in patterning human motivation and solidarity.[49] These collective representations are the images, symbols, totems, myths, and stories through which a society could come to understand itself and its environment and then imaginatively bootstrap itself into existence as a "society" rather than as merely a collection of individuals. This new interest found its first clear expression in the collaboration with his nephew Marcel Mauss for the slim volume *Primitive Classification* and lasted until Durkheim's final masterpiece, *The Elementary Forms of Religious Life.*[50] It can also be located in the works of students such as Henri Hubert and Robert Hertz. Durkheim's argument from around 1903 onwards was increasingly that determinative cultural codes marked the world out into the sacred and profane (mundane). For Durkheim's school the ideal was just as "real" as the material and could and should therefore be recovered through the scientific analysis of beliefs, practices, and material culture. In the words of his students, such "religious ideas, because they are believed, exist; they exist objectively, as social facts."[51] These imaginative templates enable societies to make sense of the world by organizing their environments and experiences using broader, extra-contextual symbolic patterns. Such cultural systems live symbiotically with the collective rituals that reproduce them, these being oriented around that deep gulf separating the sacred from the profane, the pure from the polluted. Pivotal are rites of purification, sacrifice, and expiation that prevent symbolic contagion arising from the illicit or accidental mixing of sacred and profane categories. In short, the argument of *The Elementary Forms* is that much human activity is not directly utilitarian but rather is organized around the dramatic manipulation of symbolic forms, and is subject to regulation by collective representations and classifications. Of particular interest to the current project was Durkheim's observation that the sacred is both ambivalent and dangerous; not simply a force for good aligned with the maintenance of the social order, it can all too easily take a malevolent form. What Durkheim's student Robert Hertz called the "left sacred"[52] is a manifestation of divine evil rather than divine grace. Unpredictable, threatening, contagious, and yet compelling, the left sacred is unruly, inspiring awe and dread. In all societies it has required deft handling through ritual activity and spatial exclusion. There are rites, for example, in which evil is removed from the community—such as the expulsion of Azael's goat by the ancient Hebrews—and taboos and injunctions through which the spiritual contagion of death is carefully managed.[53]

For a truly cultural approach to punishment to take shape we need to meld the ritual and symbolic sensitivities of this later Durkheim with the earlier Durkheim's insistence that punishment was meaningful and communicative. Manifestly about religion, the *Elementary Forms* and its satellites provide us with a set of key resources for thinking about punishment and culture, for Durkheim understood the entirety of social life as underpinned by quasi-religious codes. The sacred, the profane, ritual, purity, pollution, atonement, evil, sin, taboo, classification, sacrifice, the cult of the individual—our vocabulary for thinking about the intent, activity, and reception of punishment must change radically if these concepts are to be taken seriously. Just as Durkheim had earlier argued in *The Division of Labour* that the primitive desire for vengeance in the popular will persisted as a substratum driving punishment even in our time, we can understand these basic, protean cultural categories running through and under what appear to be more rational, modern, scientific, instrumental, or bureaucratic tendencies in punishment activity.

Omens for this task of theoretical reconstruction and renewal towards a late-Durkheimian approach to punishment can be found in diverse

and unlikely places. Some of the most influential work at the interface of
sociology and criminology during the twentieth century has repeatedly
touched upon such themes en passant although for the most part without direct reference to the Durkheimian legacy. The result is a body of
literature that comes tantalizingly close to the position developed here
but somehow fails to make the necessary intellectual connections back
to the French master or to produce a truly global and synthetic vision
in his name. Goffman drew upon Arnold van Gennep—a rival figure
who had famously critiqued the *Elementary Forms*—in pointing to the
strongly ritualized efforts at transforming the self that were involved in
the dehumanizing process of the total institution such as a prison or mental hospital.[54] Martha Grace Duncan chose to invoke Freud when suggesting that images of pollution, slime, and excrement have been central
to our thinking about the convict.[55] Stanley Cohen made use of Howard
Becker's symbolic interactionist labelling theory when he spoke of the
delinquent youth as an evil "folk devil," bypassing Durkheim's thinking
on the invention of deviance.[56] Harold Garfinkel talked of the court as a
"degradation ceremony" but again without conspicuous reference to the
elaborated tradition of Durkheimian thinking on ritual.[57] Jack Katz refers
to crime as activity involving the seductions of evil for the perpetrator
but tips his hat to phenomenology. Notwithstanding a vocabulary replete
with concepts such as divine wrath, magic, and sacrifice there is no sustained citation in his work to Durkheim, nor to Durkheim's followers who
wrote so extensively about the subversive and spontaneous, alluring and
dangerous "left sacred" such as Robert Hertz or Georges Bataille.[58] In a
majestic cross-national historical study, James Q. Whitman points explicitly to the role of meaning, showing that status degradation has been central to punishment in the United States and the avoidance of degradation
pivotal in France and Germany.[59] Although he admires Durkheim as the
"greatest of theoretical sociologists," Whitman does not see his study confirming the master's deepest intuitions. Rather, he takes it as broadly falsi-
fying Durkheim's claims that the growth of contract or organic solidarity would necessarily lead to the demise of "harsh justice." When various
scholars have explored the cultural and emotional dynamics of punishment, using ideas about ritual, cultural contamination, signifying activity,
moral sensibility, and tolerance, they have often drawn inspiration from
the seemingly more historically sensitive work of Norbert Elias[60] rather
than putting these into a Durkheimian frame and speaking of the cult of
the individual, the fear of pollution, or the moral implications of organic
solidarity.

The reasons for this quarantine of Durkheim are multifarious. They reflect the anxiety of influence, a desire of authors to distance themselves from the polluted "functionalist" and "positivist" Durkheim as already discussed, and a misunderstanding of the depth of his legacy for cultural theory that we now realize extended through various backchannels to inform both structuralism and poststructuralism.[61] There is also the problem that Durkheimian thinking on crime has been corralled by *The Division of Labour*. With its tight coupling of structure, evolution, and process this offers a rather deterministic, inflexible, and mechanistic theory that seems to be out of step with the theoretical march of our times. Put simply there has been too little effort to creatively rethink Durkheim. To be fair the lack of citation also reflects the powerful, developed, and attractive qualities of other intellectual traditions and agendas—symbolic interactionism, poststructuralism, and psychoanalytic literary criticism have all earned their stripes. The whys and wherefores, the push and pull factors behind Durkheim's apparent neglect need not concern us here. We must only recognize that diverse studies such as those mentioned above establish the prima facie viability of a late-Durkheimian approach wherein cultural codes define evil, pressures come from a collective conscience that call for its elimination, and the criminal justice process functions as ritualized effort towards the containment and elimination of pollution. We should also recognize the pressing claim I made earlier for Durkheim to become the intellectual center of gravity for all this diffuse activity. What is required here is density, not volume.

Aside from the work of unwitting fellow travelers, the task of moving Durkheim to center stage in the explanation of criminal justice can gain credibility and energy from movements endogenous to the explicitly Durkheimian tradition.[62] First, there have been efforts to transcend the debilitating legacy of functionalism. This has involved bringing agency, power, and contingency into the analytic fold and moving away from abstract levels of social explanation towards more proximate and concrete planes. So we now have the tools for thinking on how ritual and social exclusion might be linked or how classifications with religious origins might be strategically mobilized to replicate and reinforce more secular hierarchies. In short, Durkheimian sociology has undergone a retooling that has successfully enabled a shift from the analysis of system to the analysis of event. Second, we have a good set of ideas on how the kind of communicative and semiotic cultural process Durkheim identified in so-called primitive settings involving face-to-face ritual interaction might play out in complex and differentiated societies. These include, for example, reflections upon mass communications as a realm of myth-making activity; understandings of the public sphere as a realm of contending speech acts involving centers and peripheries; theories of social dramas and social performance; a conception of public life as ritualized and stylized communication; the idea that institutions are themselves coded as sacred and profane.[63] We might further indicate refinements to the Durkheimian legacy that have drawn upon a century of interpretative theory to develop more systematic and elaborated models of cultural systems. Structuralism and poststructuralism, most obviously, offer conceptual repertoires such as "code," "narrative," and "discourse" that can be mobilized synergistically with Durkheim's own somewhat stunted intellectual lexicon from *Moral Education* and *The Elementary Forms*. Finally, we can simply cite the extensive body of empirical research by neo-Durkheimians showing time and time again that the Durkheimian legacy has enduring traction. Much gritty social process in the modern world—scandals, strikes, revolutions, democratic transitions, wars, truth and reconciliation activity, to name but some—has been demonstrated to be at least in part about solidarity and ritual, classification, the sacred and the profane.[64]

Writing back in 1991, David Garland pointed to Durkheim as a worthy intellectual counter to Foucault in the study of criminal justice. If his work has been deeply influential and widely cited, the plea for some kind of synthesis involving mutual appreciation fell on deaf ears. In part this arose from his approach, which pointed to an abstract and distant possibility rather than offering a more concrete model and following it through with empirical demonstration. Garland's famous even-handedness probably also played a role. He measured out strengths and weaknesses of Durkheim and Foucault at a point in intellectual history where it was arguably necessary to weight the scales.[65] Today the signs are more propitious for a vigorous Durkheimian renaissance in cultural criminology. The requisite intellectual structures are now in place in Durkheim interpretation, deployment, and elaboration. To complete our suit, however, we need to briefly review three other scholars who will figure in the pages to follow: Roland Barthes, Mikhail Bakhtin, and Mary Douglas. In combination they offer resources not only for shoring up some weak planks in the Durkheimian frame but also for understanding why punishment is a domain of partly ordered and predictable but also frequently unruly and ungovernable meanings.

As just mentioned, Durkheim's model of punishment usefully pointed to a signifying content, and in particular to the way that a society might signal to itself through ritualized communicative activities. Bringing in culture and the collective conscience in this way is all very well and good as a corrective to the neo-Foucaultian reductionism that sees meaning stripped from an enclosed and bureaucratic domain. Yet unfortunately Durkheim provides neither a developed model of the communicative process nor a sufficiently structural model of the collective conscience. The result tends too easily towards abstraction and a consensus model of the social order, along with a depiction of the communication of collective representations through the collective conscience as uncontested, noncontingent, and unproblematic. To generate a more plausible model we need to bring in extra-Durkheimian influences to think through the ways in which punishment might work as a communicative process that encodes information that has to be subsequently decoded by situated actors. The work of the Russian linguist and formalist Mikhail Bakhtin provides our guide here.[66] Writing in the early decades of the twentieth century in Soviet Russia, Bakhtin had little to say about the content of culture but a lot to say about form and process. He brilliantly proposed that in each society there is a tension between the center and the periphery, these being understood in terms of both political and communicative power. The center, which is broadly equivalent to the state or to sources of legitimate authority, makes utterances that have certain formal or generic properties. Such recognized conventional qualities enable them to transmit a meaning. These encoded statements are received on the "periphery." Drawing on Jürgen Habermas, Raymond Williams, and others we can roughly equate this periphery to civil society and popular culture.[67] Here, Bakhtin argues, the communicative actions of the center collide with the folk models and the native, popular genres of interpretation through which they are decoded. There is no perfect or necessary match between what is "written" and what is "read." The result is the to-and-fro movement of statement and counter-statement in which messages from the center generate readings that are often distorted, unintended, or unexpected. Sometimes explicit struggles can ensue over frames of interpretation, at others "sleeper" critiques slowly chip away at dominant discourses as messages are persistently misunderstood or resisted on the societal periphery.

Translating all this to the context of criminal justice we can interpret judicially sanctioned punishments as in part messages from core to periphery, and shifts in punishments as attempts to say something new, to stay on message, or to shut down contending, problematic, or embarrassing interpretative possibilities. Punishments are supposed to symbolize many things, some manifest and others latent—justice most obviously, but also reason, order, and civilization. These are touchstones for legitimacy that need to be signaled. Injustice, unreason, disorder, and barbarism are their shadow. They are the dangers of potential unauthorized readings on the periphery that need to be contained. Indifference is also a possibility, though rarely a dangerous one for the state. Viewed as a semiotic process through a Bakhtinian lens, criminal justice is a didactic exercise that produces dialogical effects. Through activity, policy, and technology stories come to be told not only about the criminal and the values of society—as Durkheim proposed—but also about the relationship of the state to its citizens. Sometimes a preferred reading is well entrenched but at others it might be tenuous. History has shown, for example, how gibbets and chain gangs take on new, unsavory meanings and then fade into oblivion. Often this process is accelerated by genre disjunctions. When the periphery operates with a divergent interpretative frame from the center, this is a recipe for communicative failure. When popular culture reads the execution as a carnival, for example, then the official message is not only lost in translation but also humiliated. Time and time again in this book we shall see this process in which unruly meanings escape closed intentions and reform eventuates. Bakhtin, to sum up, allows us to understand the dynamics and implications of information exchange in a public semiotic process.

Our second extraneous influence for thinking about unruly meanings is the French semiotician Roland Barthes. When Durkheim constructed for social science the vision of a collective conscience with the collective representation at its core, this was the moment when the idea of a semiotic society was conceived. Yet it was Barthes who was the midwife, the person who first really understood the process and complexity necessarily entailed by such an intellectual premonition. Generally appropriated by the New Left as a thinker on ideology, Barthes is perhaps better understood through a different genealogy. Writing in France from the 1950s, Barthes was also the intellectual heir to Ferdinand de Saussure, himself it is now believed a student of Durkheim's lectures.[68] According to Barthes we live in a society whose culture works relentlessly and incessantly to generate and circulate what he calls "mythologies."[69] Neither necessarily true nor false, these are aggregated clusters of meaning built up from the intertwining of symbolizing chains of association. Pivotal icons and images operate as condensers for complexity and uncertainty, jamming common sense into particular ruts or triggering networks of proliferating metaphor and figuration. Objects and practices are never simply things and activities, never just utilitarian because they must always carry with them a surplus of meanings, sometimes intended but often accidental, furtive, surprising. For Barthes the new Citroën car is a cathedral of modernity, the child's artisanal toy encodes the virtue of care, Einstein's brain in its pickling jar is the holy relic of a man who unlocked the secrets of the universe, and wrestling is a kind of proletarian theater. As advertisers well know, such subtle and implicit connotations are more powerful than explicit, programmatic denotations. From Barthes then we can learn the importance of decoding cultural systems, tracing twists of meaning, realizing that the material and practical is simultaneously the symbolic, figurative, and mythological. This is a story very much consistent with Bakhtin's image of meaning taking flight and escaping control, only here the focus is placed on the complexity internal to the system of collective representation, not accidents of the communication process. As we will see below, the material, practical, and institutional fabric of punishment is simultaneously the domain of mythology. The prison, the electric chair, the guillotine, the chain gang, the panopticon—these are all emblems as much as technologies and the history of their institutionalization, both successful and failed, is one where these mythologies appear to have become more, not less, important over time in determining outcomes.

Our last theorist that needs introduction is the British anthropologist Mary Douglas. As just discussed, from the time of his collaboration with Mauss on *Primitive Classification* Durkheim understood the division of the world into the sacred and profane as the structure at the heart of culture. Further, he pointed to the control of evil and the identification, regulation, and prevention of symbolic dangers—for example, through the taboo—as fundamental problems for all cultural systems. Yet interpreters of Durkheim have relentlessly given over their attention to the positive forms of the "sacred," to the ways that rites and beliefs define and mobilize the good, pure, benign, and desirable. The result has been an understanding of the sacred as a stabilizing force tied to the reproduction of social conformity, most notably in official civic rituals. In this book I will be stressing the opposite—namely, the possibility for an evil, unruly sacred to disrupt official penal activity and signaling. This is what Robert Hertz referred to as the "left sacred," in contrast to the prosocial and beneficial "right sacred." This form of the sacred was to later inspire Georges Bataille and his colleagues in the collège de Sociologie to explore the cultural universe surrounding eroticism, death, excess, and decay. Yet of all the Durkheimians it is Mary Douglas who has done the most to theorize how cosmologies and classification inevitably generate the spiritually contagious, malevolent, and disgusting and to suggest that the control of these dangers is a universal human project that underpins many seemingly utilitarian or routine, quotidian cultural activities.[70] Douglas usefully points out that evils often take the form of cultural *pollution,* and modes of pollution are also forms of disorder. As she famously puts it, dirt is matter out of place. Such violations of a symbolic classification generate sentiments of disgust and fear and unleash dangers in need of ritual containment. She further provides two important clues where to look for such polluting evils. First, that which is ambivalent, belonging to no category or sitting on the fence between them, has a high probability of being perceived as dangerous, magical, illegitimate, or in need of ordering. Second, she indicates that the human body is a potent source of such contamination. It is porous and produces fluids that are all too easily seen as disgusting, dirty, and dangerous. Given that punishment is about the imposition of rules on those engaged in rule-breaking and that sanctions must intervene directly or indirectly on the body, Douglas's model would seem to offer a useful set of pointers for our empirical investigations. It directs us to think of the role of arbitrary cultural codes and ritualistic prohibitions in the organization of punishment, and to understand that the legitimacy of punishment is often contingent upon its ability to control pollution through imposing order, not generating pollution by allowing disorder. The empirical chapters of this book will show that this has been no easy task. Time and time again the criminal justice system itself has been thought to manufacture avoidable disorders and with these dirt, vice, evil, disgust. We will see, for example, that the electric chair makes for unruly, leaky bodies; the prison encouraged promiscuous association among inmates; the panopticon violates rather than respects the symbolic boundary splitting the public and private sphere. Further, this book will explore how potentials for disorder are facilitated and accelerated by the kinds of cultural process described by Bakhtin and Barthes. When multiple genres of interpretation are available and when symbolic connotations can be corralled no more easily than a herd of cats, disorders will be detected in even the most regulated environments.

    In our transit towards a truly cultural theory of punishment we have come a long way from Durkheim's *Division of Labour* and even further from Foucault's volume. Yet this has not been a passage without landmarks. There have been the writings of Durkheim himself and the other waypoints we have recruited to our cause. We learned from the futility of the attempt to rebut Foucault on purely empirical grounds. We also saw there exists a developed criminological corpus, a vigorous Durkheimian tradition, and a whole movement in semiotic theory that together hold out a promissory note for the claims this book is about to make. As a small payment of interest hints have been dropped throughout this chapter of what is to come below. The remainder of this book redeems the note in full. It interrogates concrete sites of penal practice both past and present, offering new interpretations and developing original conceptual resources for understanding criminal justice process. We will see that punishment can never be simply rational or just about power. Criminal justice system interventions are taken to have ritualized properties and to involve symbolic manipulations invoking, separating, and transforming the sacred and profane, quarantining the polluted, and exorcising evils. The case studies will also uncover the complexity of such cultural determinations. At their worst, uses of Durkheim become abuses characterized by overly neat and systematized decodings of cultural systems and schematic representations of a consensual social process. Rest assured that here there will be plenty of encounters with contestation, ambiguity, and paradox as well as dynamism, innovation, and hybridity. The Durkheimian model will be shown to work, but in rather messy and incomplete ways. This friction at the boundary between postulate and data is as it should be when the rubber hits the road. The alternative would be a theory without traction.

A Note on Methods

Put simply, this is a book of the kind often found in comparative historical sociology where a theoretical orientation is proposed in opposition to other current ways of seeing. The model is then applied and illustrated through a series of case studies. Some might call this theory testing. Such an approach carries with it serious dangers and vulnerabilities no matter which position is being argued. The selected sites of inquiry can appear arbitrary. Worse, it can seem as if the die has been loaded in favor of a positive result, in this case by choosing to investigate only punishments where the odds of locating a highly charged symbolic component are favorable. Much the same point can be made with respect to data sources. The exhibit at a wax museum will give a different picture of the meaning of a prison than will an architectural drawing. It is telling that Foucault himself has been accused of these kinds of selection biases. Historians have sug-

gested that the torture and death of Damiens presented at the beginning
of *Discipline and Punish* was atypical and enabled Foucault to heighten
contrasts in modes of power, that the prison timetable gives no direct insight into real daily life in prison, and that institutions like Pentonville
Prison in London were at the end of the curve. In truth most executions
were less cruel and more routinized, prison life remained chaotic well into
the nineteenth century, and the solitary system of discipline found in Pentonville was unusual. Foucault, however, knew what he was doing. Where
research needs to identify a pure cultural logic or illustrate an ideal type
it makes sense to investigate the outliers as he did. Yet there is still something deeply unsatisfying about an approach that speaks to itself rather
than to others or which illustrates its own universe of ideas on the most
favorable terms without really talking to contenders. This is a form of
monological rather than dialogical inquiry, and moreover one that will
always look a little flawed or lacking in due respect for alternatives. It
seems not to take rival claims seriously enough to wish to challenge them
head on or to care particularly about scope conditions for generalizability.
Although the Popperian logic of inquiry is problematic in the context of
the humanities, a few gestures towards a falsification can be useful—and
curiously enough, in the spirit of intellectual generosity and solidarity.[71]
Fights over the same scraps of "the real," challenging opponents on their
strongest material, offering new interpretations of familiar sites, all these
can stimulate interchange as we tread common ground and encourage the
creative ironies that emerge from the mutual interplay of perspective. The
alternative is a "he says, she says" social science.

Over the course of a season professional sports teams often do better
at home than on the road. There is the support of the fans, the comfort of
routine, the familiarity with the vagaries of stadium and turf, the night of
uninterrupted sleep. This is known as home-field advantage. I have just
suggested that, intended or otherwise, a similar logic underpins the selection of case study sites and data sources in most qualitative inquiry in sociology and history, and further, that there are costs to the cheap victory.
What is to be done? The answer is to take a lesson from the major leagues
and play our game both at home and away. When the territory is of our
own choosing we can illustrate our theory in its purest or most compelling form, showing just how much intellectual leverage it can generate in
favorable circumstances. Visiting the opponent's turf is likely to result in
more meager pickings. We might be looking for a draw or simply to score
a few points. Yet if we can show that here too our approach has some

merit then we have achieved something important, if only by introducing complexity and dialogue into the intellectual debate.

In this book, therefore, we tour a number of sites and data sources of my choosing—my home field. They are likely to deemphasize instrumental action and the routine application of discipline and power and instead highlight the symbolic and sacred dimensions of punishment. Here we are looking at the public execution and the contemporary death penalty, at artistic and literary representations of punishment, at aspects that are more spectacular, ostentatious, or bizarre, at prison tourism and wax museum fantasy, and at heated debates within civil society and the media on how to punish that we might expect to contain a stronger normative or imaginative element. Yet a good proportion of this book will be played out on turf selected by opponents, and in particular by Foucault himself in his *Discipline and Punish*. We revisit Jeremy Bentham's panopticon and the birth of the prison, we explore what Foucault hailed as the institutional apotheosis of discipline in the penal colony in Mettray, France; there is a glance at Pentonville and a trip to its contemporary incarnation in the super-maximum-security or "supermax" prisons, and we look to bureaucratic reports and plans and dry legal rulings for some of our discourse. If it can be shown that even in these places the late-Durkheimian approach offers some insight then this book will have done its job. Further I give particular attention throughout to the themes of body and technology. One of Foucault's more original moves was to suggest that by exploring their intersection we could shift from the *why* to the *how* of power, in effect sidestepping the problem of meaning. Here I try to challenge this thesis and show that *techne* cannot be explained without reference to *mythos*. Bodies and technologies are deeply meaningful, and possibilities for power to be deployed hinge upon this universe of significance.

Chapter 2 begins the inquiry where Foucault starts his, with the fall of the public execution. I suggest the switch has little to do with the discovery of a new and more efficient logic of power or the control of dangerous urban mobs and more to do with proximate local factors relating to meanings and moral boundaries. Reform was initiated when it was perceived that the public execution generated more pollution than it eliminated. It had become an unruly hybrid that dangerously transgressed the boundary between civic ritual and carnival. It produced petty moral disorders, vice, and licentiousness. It was also a failed ritual performance subject to genre-bending interpretation. Social control failed because of a crisis of meaning. In chapter 3 we turn our attention to the so-called "birth of the prison,"

tracing the movement from the disorderly jails of the eighteenth century
to the high-water mark of Victorian-era social control, from London's
Newgate through to Pentonville and Mettray. This is a journey marked by
the cultural code of order and disgust as much as by any new intellectual
logic. Further we can see that even in the most seemingly austere, closed,
and rule-driven locations there is evidence of the collective conscience at
work with its antidisciplinary counter-discourses, religious imagery, and
ritualistic urge towards the identification of evil. The chapter continues
with a variety of more contemporary settings that are closer to neutral territory. These open up a wider domain of inquiry than is usual in the prison
history literature, which often has the feel of a cruise around the flagship
sites of the nineteenth century. Investigations of widely contrasting cases
such as the supermax and the country club prisons, the prison chain gang,
and prison tourism suggest that discourses about good and evil, order and
disorder, even the beautiful and ugly, continue to play a role in regulating
penal activity and the possible extent, form and meaning of disciplinary
power.

I believe that Michel Foucault had a grudging admiration for Jeremy
Bentham and his panopticon. The deep-thinking Bentham looked to be
his intellectual equal and the panopticon a crystalline and elegant expression of a new form of power. In chapter 4 I offer a reinterpretation of
this late eighteenth-century proposal for an ingenious system of detention through surveillance. A close reading of Bentham's panopticon papers shows a hybrid rather than a pure model, and one moreover that
had its origins in the diverse moral discourses and pragmatic ideologies
circulating in the civil society of its time. This was not simply a spying machine born of implacable logic. Ideas about propriety, theatricality, spectacle, industry, and eligibility were folded into Bentham's architectural
and administrative design. The chapter continues with the investigation of
a field where Foucault is notably silent thanks to his insistence that discipline has triumphed over civil society. This concerns the tension between
panopticism and liberalism. Throughout their history, panoptic innovations have been subject to critique as polluting intrusions upon decency
and civil liberties. Such counter-narrations have pointedly limited the
extent to which the surveillance society has been developed. With chapter 5 we move closer to home territory via an investigation of a penal
technology associated with death, the guillotine. Here we see that febrile
myth can exist within, alongside, and in opposition to scientific principle
and that a rational machine designed for the efficient dispatch of human

bodies opens up rather than closes down avenues for popular mythology. In what follows we extend and cross-validate these insights with reference to the electric chair, a device never fully legitimate, never quite routinized in its hundred-year history. Chapter 6 shows that for all its scientific gloss, the electric chair came to take on mystical associations with the sacred. It was an icon surrounded by awe. Associated with the ambivalent powers of electricity it created peculiar, leaky, liminal bodies situated between life and death whose natural signs could only generate disgust. These final two case studies indicate in their most extreme form the general theoretical points I have mapped out in this introductory chapter. In the last chapter I concatenate and reflect upon these findings, pulling the various case studies together and marshalling evidence for a series of core insights. My conclusion will be that punishment is not just about power, control, and reason. Nor is it just about the law, justice, deterrence, or even "punishment" narrowly conceived. It is also about the sacred, about purity and pollution, about evil, and about ritual. Its history is one of circulating and proliferating myth as much as one of bricks and mortar, discipline and routine, protocols and laws. For punishment is a meaningful institution whose evolution and legitimacy hinges upon the tortuous history of somewhat unruly collective representations. Tracing these images and figures, narratives and symbols and placing them more squarely on the criminological agenda is the task of this book.

CHAPTER TWO

The Public Execution

The public execution seems an appropriate place to begin our empir- ical investigations. Although not the most common punishment in early modern society, it was the most ideologically important, providing the lens through which perceptions of criminal justice as a whole were filtered. For this reason the decline and fall of the public execution has been a major theme in social theory and historical sociology, as well as in social history. All this activity gives us the advantage of an established lit- erature. Foucault starts his own book with this field, but at the same time the clearly ritualistic qualities of such events make them a soft target for our Durkheimian model building. In short, the public execution looks like a propitious location, a well-chewed-over middle pasture for our task of rethinking culture and punishment.

The more precise question that detains us here is the retreat of the public execution, a process that has many dimensions. These include the movement from day to dawn; the removal of fanfare, publicity, and didac- ticism; the spatial shift to the prison gate and then the hidden execution room; the dwindling audience. For the most part, the theoretical choices and presuppositions of sociologists have consistently switched the inter- pretation and explanation of the disappearing public execution back to macrohistorical processes of a broad and somewhat deterministic cast. As a result, social theory has been insensitive to agency, strategy, and the role of situated interpretations and meanings. Historians have done somewhat better, and I will draw upon them at various points in the exposition that follows. I should begin, however, with the work of the leading social theo- rists. Anthony Giddens has accounted for the transformation of modes of punishment as simply the consequence of "an expansion of administra- tive power."[1] In this neo-Weberian understanding, which is broadly consistent with Foucault's own narrative, theatrical executions demonstrating the force of the state were replaced by a deracinated carceral procedure that was a "final sanction in the hierarchy of the removal of liberties."[2] The emphasis here is on the primacy of social-structural evolution and most conspicuously the centralization and intensification of axial power through bureaucratic and logistical armatures. For Giddens the movement of executions both indoors and behind doors fully reflects the ineluctable growth of the Weberian iron cage, with its figurative imprisonment of the individual in this case made material.

From the perspective of cultural theory, elaborations of the work of Norbert Elias by scholars like Pieter Spierenburg and John Pratt mark a significant step forward because more attention is given to meaning.[3] The focus here is on a "civilizing process" that sees violence-averse norms filtering through society. These lead in turn to the hiding of judicial violence and to the rise of sentiments of squeemishness and disgust at its operations. Where once there were gibbets with their rotting crow-pecked corpses, public floggings, and branding, now we have apparently more sanitary and wholesome penal activities.[4] We will see considerable merit in such an approach not only in this chapter but also throughout this book, where perceptions of defilement and disgust are shown to be potent in discrediting modes of penal practice, rendering them outmoded and illegitimate. Still this paradigm has a problematic causal logic, ultimately locating the shift in sensibility as a dependent variable of state formation; a position that is curiously similar to that of Giddens. Elias argued that as a medieval warrior society becomes pacified by a strong state, violence becomes less common. The control of passions and the restraint of impulse became the passport to status. Such emotion rules slowly drift down the class structure from the court society to the mob, remaking subjectivities in their wake. Structure determines sentiment, and this sentiment influences perceptions through low key and diffuse channels. I should also add that such a perspective has a rather attenuated emotional and semiotic palette. As we shall see, public executions did more than simply generate disgust at violence: they had a range of meanings that were tied in scattered and unpredictable ways to local practices of meaning and interpretation. The discourses and emotions identified by the Eliasian scholars are really just a subset of the broader and more diverse problem field of disorders and pollutions thrown up by the judicial death.

The early chapters of *Discipline and Punish* are those that are least distant from the theory advanced in this book. Here we have a Foucault who has not yet given up on meaning. Nevertheless there is confusion and ambivalence. Foucault's big picture vision parallels that of Giddens in suggesting that a dynamic involving the maximization, refinement, and coordination of power drives the transformation of practice. This marches through history, brushing aside the symbolic aspects of punishment and replacing them with instrumental procedure. As historian V. A. C. Gatrell notes, this sweeping perspective has an "easy way with agency and chronology" and has "downplayed the roles of feeling and culture."[5] Yet for all this we can still find discussion in the first pages of *Discipline and Punish* that is remarkably sensitive to the flexibility of meanings and the contingent ways in which executions could come to symbolize many things.[6] Foucault fully understands the dramaturgical qualities of the public execution and its attempted invocation of the sacred nature of the sovereign's power as well as the possibility for things to go awry thanks to the behavior of the condemned and the crowd. He even hints that such irregularities might have contributed to the demise of a long-standing institution. Yet at the same time he is unable to see the humiliations of *cultural* failure as sufficient reason for a signifying practice to be rejected in and of itself. For Foucault it is the ability of the execution to generate *political* dangers in the form of riots and class-conscious mobilization that seems to be the major problem for authority.[7] Such an analysis must discount the fact that riots had already been declining for centuries before public capital punishment was abolished and that only a very small percentage of such events led to disturbances of any magnitude. As we shall see shortly, the major problem faced by the public execution was a purely cultural one of vice and genre ambivalence. This was related only very obliquely to questions of urban insurrection. To be evenhanded we should also briefly mention here Durkheim's account in the 1900 essay "Two Laws of Penal Evolution" itself building upon his remarks in the *Division of Labour*.[8] Here Durkheim traces the end of violent punishments directed against the body to the process of societal differentiation and the decline of centralized absolutist power. This transformation weakened and buffered the appetite for vengeance and led to a more secular, less religious vision of crime where cooler passions can prevail and incarceration becomes the norm. Such an approach shares some of the problems we have outlined with other theorists. It allocates causal primacy to the social structure, ignores questions of interpretation and agency, and narrows the spectrum of relevant meaning to wrath and vengeance. Nobody, it seems, is taking local and embedded meanings seriously. The result has been a deterministic kind of social theory that accounts for the demise of the public execution in terms of a deep background of historical and structural change rather than a foreground of ongoing activity and interpretation.

I have hinted a little at what is to come, suggesting that we need a stronger and more proximate cultural explanation of the end of the public execution. Those who have read the first chapter of this book might have accurately guessed the path we are going to take. Now I map this out explicitly. All punishments, I suggest, have a signifying or expressive dimension, albeit with varying degrees of centrality and reflexivity. They are intended to say something about the nature of society, the qualities of the criminal, the features of a good society, the evils of crime, or the properties of the criminal justice system itself. The public execution is useful because it displays this ambition in its clearest and most intuitively available form. It can be easily read as a meaningful gesture of a particularly stylized or ritualized kind. Whereas rituals were traditionally taken by cultural theory to be the unproblematic carriers of dominant ideologies and value systems, social theory today recognizes the contested and performative qualities of such events and the contingencies that follow their production, transmission, and reception.[9] Actions in ritual contexts can be understood in dramaturgic terms as invoking and manipulating cultural structures, orienting bodily action and material artifacts relative to what anthropologist Victor Turner evocatively called the "forest of symbols."[10] They are efforts to construct a narrative for an onlooking audience, to tell a story, to offer a commentary on events and statuses, to channel meanings in one direction or another, to open up worlds of significance, or to close off unwanted interpretative possibilities. They confer identities, offer moral and political status, and prompt emotional and cognitive shifts in those involved as participants and observers. And they do all this *contingently,* for outcomes are never guaranteed. Strategic and expressive actions might be organized by ritual specialists and sponsors towards the production of particular narrative ends but they can still fall short. There are possibilities for contested action and failed performance, for faulty or obstinate counter-readings, for the deliberate or unintentional production of unwanted signs. In short, all rituals are potentially vulnerable to cultural failure. In what follows I trace just such a misfiring that shows how a Durkheimian analysis of ritual, emotion, collective representation, and the sacred provides traction for coming to terms with the cultural process through which an effort at didactic communication came unstuck.

Prior studies of public executions well document the ritualistic nature of proceedings.[11] There were large crowds as the onlooking audience, and there were visible protagonists in the hangmen and the condemned. Strong expectations guided action by detailing the conventional sequence of events, roles, and appropriate behaviors. Pamphlets retelling the crimes, trials, confessions, and executions of notorious criminals were sold in great numbers. These helped generate interest and emotional energy prior to the big day. Following David Garland we can understand such formally structured and anticipated public punishments as communicative acts that "outrun the immediacies of crime and punishment and 'speak of' broader and more extended issues"—such as politics, morality, and the nature of the social order.[12] What then were the intended meanings of such events? These can be retraced from the works of those who supported capital punishment in the past, from legislative debates, and from the writings of present advocates as well as from the event protocols. Least interestingly we can state that executions embody jurisprudential ambitions to do justice, to punish, and to deter—or minimally that they need to appear consistent with these ritual objectives and philosophical justifications.[13] At the deeper cultural level and following our Durkheimian perspective I suggest that they sought to destroy and cleanse that which is evil, restore order from chaos, and celebrate the moral and sacred authority of the law. Without contradicting this position we can also tip our hat to critical theory and suggest that executions dramatized the power of the state over the disobedient individual by coercing and controlling their body. In short, executions were expected to carry the heavy burden of diverse narrative objectives. Although the grim mise en scène of the gallows could bear some of this weight of representation it was hoped that the criminal would play their part too. They could look humbled, admonish the spectators to learn from their plight, confess their guilt, and express faith in God's mercy. Here there is solemnity and contrition as the victim accepts a degraded social identity. The ideal execution performance then took the form of the last act in some morality play of justice. It was a didactic operation directed at onlookers and pamphlet readers as much as at the body of the condemned and sought to show that order and right in the end would prevail.[14] Importantly this narrative agenda could enlist the dread power of sacred terror as an ally in bringing off its dramaturgical task. Like the Commendatore at the end of Mozart's *Don Giovanni*, or Mephistopheles in the concluding moments of *Faust*, the execution ceremony was intended to balance out not only the scales of justice but also

the metaphysical imperatives of good and evil through a divine intervention at once terrible, inexorable and non-negotiable—a retribution that
restored order.[15]

If such was the intent, what emerged by the late eighteenth century
was a rather different set of ritual outcomes and—if the distinction is a
relevant one—perceptions of what these were. To get an initial grasp on
this we need to start by exploring the behavior of the condemned. Some
of them made their exit in ways desired by authorities, others did not. But
in both cases possibilities were opened for alternative readings as those
about to die redefined, destroyed, or challenged the preferred or "dominant" meanings of the execution as text. In Bakhtin's sense they generated "heteroglossia"—multiple meanings that prevented a ritual fusion
and generated complexity, irony, ambivalence, and cultural dangers.

Where the condemned looked to have been wronged, to be weak, frail,
or deeply repentant, the punishment of death could all too easily appear
to be barbaric and repressive rather than just, righteous, or moral. Public sentiment could take the side of the victim, refuse the official narrative and allocate moral culpability to the state rather than to the criminal.
Such inversions became all the more potent where the conviction was supported by weak or circumstantial evidence and when the condemned was
a woman. Perhaps the most famous case fitting this pattern in nineteenth-
century Britain was that of the household cook Eliza Fenning, who was
executed on 26 July 1815 for feeding her master's family dumplings poisoned with arsenic. The evidence in the case was sketchy, and Fenning had
even eaten some of the dumplings herself. She devoted her time in prison
to writing devout and touching letters to her betrothed and to her family,
which became widely circulated. According to a contemporary she appeared for her execution the figure of propriety "neatly dressed in a white
muslin gown, a handsome worked cap, and laced boots." She declared,
"Before the just and Almighty God, and by the faith of the Holy Sacra-
ment I have taken, I am innocent of the offence with which I am charged."
She ascended the platform and expressed her innocence, her "perfect res-
ignation, and her confidence of entering the kingdom of heaven."[16] Her
performance seems to have been effective in translating popular interpretations of her death from that of a necessary to a mistaken act. One source
tells us that "the most heart-rending sensations pervaded the minds of
the thousands who witnessed the dreadful spectacle" and that "during
the remainder of the day numerous groups of people assembled in the
Old Bailey, and also in the evening opposite the house of Mr. Turner (the

prosecutor), in Chancery-lane, conversing on the subject, with whom, pity for her sufferings, and a firm belief of her innocence, seemed to be the prevailing sentiment. At the last-mentioned place the tumult became so great, it was found necessary to disperse the multitude and preserve the peace." Her funeral, held shortly afterward, was attended by thousands, and "many burst into tears at the sight of her distressed parents." One man, who, in "violation of all decency" was not wearing a hat, ventured to "make use of an expression which excited the indignation of the crowd." This comment was greeted by cries of "Shame! Shame!" Women spat in the offender's face, men shook him and pulled him by the ears, and he had to be rescued by the constables.[17]

Women like Eliza Fenning were advantaged in the projection of such a pious, reformed, or wronged self by popular stereotypes and tropes relating variously to female irrationality, to mothering, and to innocence. However, the devout self could also be produced by men—even violent men. A case in point is the highwayman Nicholas Mooney, who was executed in Bristol on 24 May 1752. Mooney performed very much in the way desired by the authorities of the time, even confessing his crimes. Yet he screws the chords of repentance to such an extreme pitch that he unsettles the harmonics and modulations of the official narrative. Mooney came to incarnate the good, deflecting attention from his guilt to his repentance, and allowing him to become reintegrated into the imagined moral community even as the legal system concluded its process of formal excommunication. Mooney, we are told, was "no less notorious for his sincere penitence and happy death than for his repeated acts of criminality and violence."[18] While in prison he wrote a confessional account of his life in which he spoke of his terrible deeds and of the just nature of his punishment. "I deserve not only death but hell," he wrote.[19] At the place of execution he joined the minister in singing and prayer and exhorted the crowd to learn from his mistaken life. Then:

> As the executioner was preparing to tie up Jones, he cried out, "Tie me up first, for I am the greatest offender," desiring that no one would pull his legs, for that he was willing to suffer all the pains of death—The rope being fixed, he cried out, "My soul is so full of love of God, that it is ready to start out of my body, and in a few moments I shall be at my father's house." The cart being drawn away, he was launched into eternity. It is remarkable, that he never stirred hand or foot, after he was turned off; but his soul seemed to have willingly taken its flight, before it was forced from his body.[20]

Mooney's funeral was also attended by several thousand people. Although Fenning maintained her innocence and Mooney fulsomely repented his guilt both died exhibiting piety and good character. They had become martyrlike holy figures rehabilitated in the collective conscience. In becoming sacred themselves they realigned the meaning of their own executions from valid punishment to injustice. Further, the death itself is renarrated into a desired end. This is an opportunity for spiritual fulfillment and the gateway to a better afterlife. It is not to be shunned but to be welcomed as a biographical terminus for the vagrant soul. Mooney's contrition and enthusiasm for a posthumous encounter with the sacred renders problematic the coercive efforts of the state and neutralizes the terrible awe of judicial death. This is death rescripted and retuned—and not to the advantage of authority.

Whereas Mooney, Fenning, and others who died like them excited sentiments of pity by means of a strong orientation towards a set of religious codes, alternative secular resources could also offer a way for actors to deny the sting of death. The execution of Lord Balmerino on 18 August 1746 provides a remarkable example of a performance in accord with urbane, debonair, cavalier, almost foppish but nevertheless aristocratic principles. Convicted of treason by virtue of his role in the ill-fated Jacobite uprising of 1745, Balmerino went to his death in unrepentant and virtuoso fashion, behaving "with the greatest intrepidity."[21] While Lord Kilmarnock preceded him at the chopping block, Balmerino enjoyed a glass of wine with his friends. When the under-sheriff came to fetch him, Balmerino asked him how well the executioner had performed his task and then turning to his friends, remarked, "Gentlemen, I shall detain you no longer."[22] Dressed in the same regimental uniform he had worn at the Battle of Culloden, he "hastened to the scaffold, which he mounted with so easy an air, as astonished the spectators." Once there he walked about "seemingly under very little concern."[23] He read the inscription on his coffin and nodded his approval. He talked to the hearse driver. He read a speech to the crowd in which he praised the king for magnanimity and mercy, but faulted him for erroneous political principles. He gave the executioner three guineas, tested the execution block and adjusted it to his liking, felt the edge of the axe, "clapped the executioner on the shoulder to encourage him," and, tucking down the collar of his shirt showed him where to strike. Impressed by Balmerino's superior demeanor during the course of the execution, the immense crowd "behaved with uncommon decency and evenness of temper," and "very little mischief was done."[24]

Balmerino's death created a genre shift and subverted the intended meaning of his ritual in a different way from that of Fenning and Mooney. He evokes not pity but admiration. He does not appropriate the sacred to his own ends but rather moves it out of the frame. He is a secular hero and political martyr. The awe and terror of death are denied, with his end being managed by him as a trifling social engagement. Death is no longer a punishment. The axe-man is Balmerino's accomplice, the axe itself his ally, the gathered crowd his sympathetic audience. By aligning his action with positive norms of civility and the performative repertoire of the "public man"[25] of the Enlightenment, Balmerino manages to rework his death so as to provide a good account of himself. Yet actions of his kind, those that displayed the self in a positive light, were not the most ideologically important for generating anxieties and the sense that something was seriously wrong with the public execution as a communicative gesture. In the cultural climate of the eighteenth century, extreme deviance provided a far more potent resource for subverting the dominant narratives and aesthetic codes of the judicial death and, as an unintended consequence, gaining the attention of state ideologists concerned with systems of criminal justice administration.

In the eighteenth century highwaymen were particularly adept at reworking and taking dramatic control of their own executions through piety not to God but rather to the outrageous, profane, and devil-may-care behavior that popular myth held had characterized their finest moments. These figures of legend saw their end as a state-subsidized opportunity to take center stage one last time, writing a final glorious chapter into their own life narrative. Dick Turpin spent his last days "joking, drinking and telling stories."[26] He went to his execution wearing a new suit of clothes, joked with the hangman and threw himself off the gallows. Jack Rann, also known as "Sixteen String Jack," lived in Newgate in reprobate style. On the evening before his execution he held a rowdy dinner party and caroused with no less than seven young women. Jeremiah Abershaw drew cartoon pictures of his escapades on his cell wall. He met his death with a swaggering bravado—dressed in an open-necked shirt and with a flower in his mouth he joked and chatted with friends walking beside the cart on its procession from Newgate to Tyburn. On the gallows he asked the hangman to wait while he took his boots off. When the executioner asked him why he wanted to do so, Abershaw shouted to the crowd: "My mother always said I'd die with my boots on, and I'm going to prove her wrong."[27] Yet another highwayman, Benjamin Neale, executed in 1749, "paid no attention to the devotions" and laughed and joked at the expense of the crowd. Just before his end he cursed them, "I shall very soon see my Lord Balmerino ... damn you all together."[28]

Not only highwaymen continued in their profligate and unrepentant ways. Renwick Williams, the "Monster of London," was a sexual deviant who had attacked and attempted to stab several women. A lover of the finer things in life, on the eve of his demise he gave a party at Newgate known as the Monster's Ball, which was reported without disapproval, surprise, or irony: "In the Merry Dance, the cuts and the *entrechats* of the Monster were much to be admired ... at eight o'clock, the company partook of a cold supper, and a variety of wine, such as would not discredit the most sumptuous gala."[29] John Price, himself a former hangman, was executed in May 1718 for the drunken murder of an old woman. During his spell in Newgate prison "he would daily go up to chapel intoxicated with cursed Geneva [gin]." On his way to the gallows he likewise "several times pulled a bottle of Geneva out of his pocket to drink," and when he arrived he was "found so ignorant of religion that he troubled himself not much about it."[30]

The highwaymen, the Monster, John Price, all behave with fidelity to the cultural template of "the rake" that was much in vogue in their era. The literary and theatrical genre of the picaresque had popularized this role, which flagged the cheapness and unpredictability of life and encouraged any urge to seize hold of carnal and base pleasures. For those who embraced this self-identity there was no need to exhibit fear or humility in the face of judicial death. To the contrary the whole execution process offered a platform to display and augment their braggadocio credentials, to cement their own myth. The presentation of a self that is at once autonomous and reckless, fearless and antisocial, shifts the narrative current of the public ceremony into a new channel. The punitive and deterrent value of the execution is questioned. The morality play is degraded to farce, and this genre switch eliminates the sacred. Events are no longer dreadful, serious, and exemplary but trivial and comical. The state was looking at a failure to communicate.

The fact that executions did not go as planned has often been noted by historians if not by historical sociologists who have glossed such details in their rush to theorize the prison. Yet historians have rarely touched upon the resources of social theory to understand what is going on, preferring to see meanings and their consequences as somehow historically grounded and self-evident. Let's probe a little further to figure out in ab-

stract terms what might be at work. We can begin by understanding the
act of dying in public as existentially challenging. When it is known that
a life is to end at a predetermined point before an audience, those who
are to die have to decide who they truly are and how they would like to
be remembered by others. This is the last chance they will have to assert
an identity. Curiously the existence of an officially sanctioned norm for
judicial death—the "morality play"—offers a resource for this action by
permitting agents to signal deviance or heightened conformity as wished.

That most careful observer of human behavior Erving Goffman noted
long ago that dying was a "fateful moment" where the self is on the line.[31]
Drawing upon Durkheim's understanding of the cult of the individual,
he further proposed that "the self is in part a ceremonial thing, a sacred
object which must be treated with proper ritual care and in turn must be
presented in a proper light to others."[32] In dying many people try to live
up to this insistent cultural obligation, even if their understandings of that
"proper light" might be diverse or other than authority might wish. The
execution was intended, in Harold Garfinkel's terms, to be a degradation
ceremony in which an abject identity is imposed on the subject.[33] Yet the
condemned try to indicate the freedom of the soul. With the onset of early
modernity and the rising cult of the individual, pressures were increasing
to demonstrate that this soul, as Durkheim remarked in *The Elementary
Forms of Religious Life,* "far from being dependent upon the body . . .
dominates it from the higher dignity which is in it."[34] The actions of the
execution victim were a desperate effort to embody this emergent principle, to show that the soul can triumph over the body, the will over the
material fate of the carapace, the individual over adversity, and so to find
a moment of freedom in a situation of constraint. Further the rhetorical
requirements of the morality play required the state to offer considerable
latitude of action in the hope that deferential contrition could be exhibited in the form of laments and prayers, homilies and psalms, solemnity
of demeanor. In combination with the existential challenge to defend the
sacred self, the largesse of the mise en scène made possible the undermin-
ing of the public execution as a semiotic system.

So the failure of the public execution was in part due to the internalized pressures and sacred obligations of preserving the self operating
alongside inflated state expectations and agendas. But to understand the
process of collapse and reform more completely we need to recognize the
part played by two other sets of social actors: the execution audience, and
the elites and intellectuals who observed them. Figure 1 is an engraving

FIGURE I. William Hogarth, *The Idle 'Prentice Executed at Tyburn,* 1747. The condemned (*a*); state officials (*b*), the mob (*c*), and higher-status spectators (*d*).

from 1747 by William Hogarth entitled "The idle 'prentice executed at Tyburn." I have marked out here four sets of agents. There are the condemned in the cart (A), the authorities charged with executing them and maintaining public order (B), the unruly crowd around them (C), and a more privileged group (D) who can afford to pay for seats in a grandstand. They are looking down upon both the condemned and the mob. In being *public,* the execution provided soon-to-die individuals with an important resource for maintaining the self. Responses from the onlooking, physically proximate audience (C, D) could encourage and reinforce an ongoing ritualized celebration of the sacred self as manifest in character, offering positive feedback and the emotional energy required to sustain and amplify a performance. As we have seen in our empirical examples, audience responses could run the gamut from respectful behavior, silence, and prayer through to laughter and insults. For the purposes of this analysis the most important component of the audience was the bawdy, drunken, and volatile "mob" (C), which was itself generally hostile or indifferent to authority.[35] Responding with laughter and badinage to the rake or with sympathy and respect for the saint, the mob's responses made the failure of executions as morality plays visible and humiliating. Like the audience at a stand-up comedy club they provided a real-time indicator of how a performance was going, an explicit and publicly available source of evidence from which other interested onlookers (B, D) could judge the reception of the conflicting and contradictory, heteroglossic messages produced in an execution and figure out which ones were winning. As we will see below, these state functionaries and elites looked at the mob, figured they were wasting their time, and thought about reform.

This peculiar state of affairs was sustained and magnified by some local and contingent factors. As already noted, a historically specific conception of the "public man" probably created a reflexive and theatrical understanding of execution ritual among participants and audiences.[36] This would have made all parties hypersensitive to displays of identity. Profit motivations and the differentiation of the emerging mass media possibly led to sensationalism and consequently distorted perceptions of penal efficacy.[37] Certainly pamphlets and news reports would have encouraged large attendances at executions and created the climate of expectation that bred disorders by drawing in a bad crowd and anticipating trouble. They might have also encouraged flamboyant behavior through the offer of free publicity. During the eighteenth and nineteenth centuries urbanization, rural-urban migration, and industrialization created new forms of inequality that could manifest at street level in a rootless, anonymous and unaccountable mob that was less embedded in community than its medieval antecedents. Aside from responding to the actions of the condemned, the urban mob could simply continue automatically within its own immodest and carnivalesque ways. Petty crime, bawdy irregularities, drunken debauch—all these were an unintended performance observed by those of higher social standing and suggesting to them the failure of the execution play as a *communicative judicial exercise in cultural and social ordering*.

Reform as Repair Work

We have no way of knowing exactly how many people died and in which ways or exactly how often the audience sided with the victim. Historians and other commentators seem to believe ritual failures were common.[38] This issue need not greatly concern us for the explanation given here looks not to a mechanical or statistical mode of causality but rather to perceptions. Failed public executions were not only "events" but more importantly potent collective representations. Endlessly circulated and recapitulated in the diverse *Newgate Calendars* and broadsheets alongside details of crime, these produced a discourse of disorder. Interpretations based upon such collective representations are the intervening variable between performative actions oriented around justice and the self and their wider impacts. Under this rubric, the onus is neither to produce evidence that deviant narrative strategies were common nor even that they were effective in influencing mob opinion. Rather, we must simply show that the public execution was perceived as problematic by those advocating reform, that there was an awareness of failure and a sense of crisis.

Evidence that such beliefs were indeed prevalent among elites can be found throughout the most influential pamphlets and in debates on punishment that took place from the early eighteenth century onward. These dwell neither on the need to reduce public cruelty as an ultimate end in itself (as Elias/Spierenburg might predict), nor the need to survey and control the criminal so as to effect normalization (Foucault), nor even on the need for more effective centralization of state power (Giddens), but rather on the semiotic needs of an ideological system and on the imperative to remove cultural disorders and restore moral boundaries. Bernard Mandeville's pamphlet from 1725 *An Enquiry into the Causes of the Frequent Executions at Tyburn* is one of the earliest and most compelling of these publications.[39] Along with a pamphlet by Henry Fielding, this is considered by historians the most significant document of its era on execution policy. Both pamphlets were widely circulated, discussed, and reprinted. Around half of Mandeville's pamphlet is spent in a furious tirade against the behavior of the condemned and of the mob at the gallows and on the parade to the scaffold. For Mandeville the whole ritual has gone badly wrong. It generates offensive minor disorders and encourages more serious evils. What should have been a solemn and sacramental event has become a genre-bending carnival of public disrespect that emits social pollution. He notes that those about to die failed to perform their allotted roles and profaned the ceremonial: "[W]hat is most shocking to a thinking Man is the Behavior of the Condemn'd whom (for the greatest Part) you'll find, either drinking madly, or uttering the vilest Ribaldry, and jeering others that are less penitent."[40] Mandeville further argues that it was a lot to ask that a hardened criminal engage in morality play behaviors.

> It is possible that a Man of extraordinary Holiness, by anticipating the Joys of Heaven, might embrace a violent Death in such Raptures, as would dispose him to the singing of Psalms: But to require this Exercise, or expect it promiscuously

of every Wretch that comes to be Hang'd, is as wild and extravagant as the Performance of it is commonly frightful and Impertinent.[41]

He indicates that interactions between the crowd and the criminal facilitate the emergence of a criminal subculture.

> Compliments, as well as Reproaches, when ill applied, are often the Causes
> of great Mischief, and I am persuaded, that the Perverseness of Opinion now
> reigning amongst us, both in applauding and discommending the Conduct of
> Criminals in their last Hours, is an accessary Evil, that very much contributes to
> what is the Subject of our grand Complaint, the Frequency of Executions.[42]

Most importantly Mandeville looked to disorderly crowd behavior as evidence of a decivilizing effect.

> All the way from Newgate to Tyburn is one continued Fair, for Whores and
> Rogues of the meaner sort . . . . There are none so lewd, so vile, or so indigent,
> of either Sex, but at the Time and Place aforesaid . . . No modern Rabble can
> long subsist without their darling cordial, the grand Preservative of Sloth, Jen-
> eva . . . these undisciplined Armies have no particular Enemies to encounter but
> Cleanliness and good Manners, so nothing is more entertaining to them that the
> dead Carcasses of Dogs and Cats . . . flug as high and as far as a strong Arm can
> carry them, and commonly directed where the Throng is the thickest.[43]

Mandeville summarizes and concludes his litany of communicative failure
in a famous last paragraph.

> If no Remedy can be found for these Evils, it would be better that Malefac-
> tors should be put to Death in private; for our publick Executions are become
> Decoys, that draw in the Necessitous, and, in effect, as cruel as frequent Par-
> dons; instead of giving Warning, they are exemplary the wrong Way, and en-
> courage where they should deter. The small Concern, and seeming Indolence
> of the Condemn'd, harden the Profligates that behold them, and confirm to
> them, by ocular Demonstration, what they encourage one another with in viler
> Language, (low, as it is, permit me to mention it). That there is nothing in being
> hang'd but awry Neck, and a wet pair of Breeches.[44]

The public execution had become a dangerous farce that made antiheroes
of those criminals who made light of death. They "encouraged where they

should deter." They were a horribly secular ritual that had been deserted by sacred awe, the vacuum being filled with base and disorderly popular pleasures—the profane. Mandeville offered suggestions for a more successful public lesson, one that could head off the ill effects of genre creep and category violation. These included Spartan solitary confinement, a monotonous diet, and no access to alcohol. In consequence the condemned would have little to do but brood on their sins and their impending fate. The results, Mandeville fantasized, would be a spectacular and terrible theater that would rekindle a sense of sacred terror through the raw emotions bubbling up from a troubled conscience.

> When a Man thus wean'd from the World, and all the Hopes of Life, should be drawn forth from his dark and solitary Dungeon ... when the Paleness of his Countenance and the Shaking of every Limb, should, without Disguise, reveal the Motions of his Heart, and his spirits neither confounded, nor bouy'd up by inebriating Liquors, should discover their real Condition and Incapacity to uphold their trembling Tenement; the Spectacle would be awful, and strike the Hearts of the Beholders . . . . .Few Profligates would be able to stand the Shock of Sounds and Actions so really tragical: Many would run away for fear of rousing the Lion kept chain'd within, and waking a guilty Conscience from the Lethargy they have thrown it in with so much Labour.[45]

Mandeville's argument is superficially in alignment with Foucault's thinking on the "birth of the prison." On closer inspection the argument contradicts Foucault's case. To be sure Mandeville believed that solitary confinement and a disciplinary regime could produce a normalized and docile individual. Yet for Mandeville this obedient and deflated criminal has value only as a signifier for a wider public. The normalization of the mental world and body of the inmate is tied to the communicative functions of punishment, and not to the rehabilitation of the self as productive labor or as a component in the circuits of power. Moreover the intent is to bring the sacred back in as a form of terror, to unleash the beast rather than exclude it from penal administration. In short, Mandeville's *Inquiry* suggests public executions were a peculiarly cultural problem in need of a reordering cultural solution.

We see much the same concern with signaling bodies in the work of Henry Fielding, novelist and quondam London magistrate, who treated criminal justice reform at length in the other landmark essay of the eighteenth century, *An Enquiry into the Causes of the Late Increase of Rob-*

bers.[46] This title, like Mandeville's, suggests the criminal justice system was not working as desired. Fielding likewise attributes the blame for this failure to the behavior of the condemned and the response of the crowd, these operating to effect a genre shift in interpretative register.

> The Day appointed by Law for the Thief's Shame is the Day of Glory in his own Opinion. His procession to Tyburn, and his last Moments there, are all triumphant; attended with the Compassion of the meek and tender-hearted, and with the Applause, Admiration and Envy of all the bold and hardened. His Behavior in his present Condition, not the Crimes, how atrocious soever, which brought him to it, are the Subject of Contemplation. And if he hath Sense enough to temper his Boldness with any Degree of Decency, his Death is spoke of by many with Honor, by most with Pity, and by all with Approbation.[47]

We have already seen these two patterns of behavior and outcome, Boldness and Decency, in our case study material. Fielding's analysis is one of criminal justice as a problem of practical narratology. It is about telling a story through ritual and getting the right genre across to the "readers." He saw a need to transform the narrative of the public execution from one of comedy or tragedy to one of horror or stereotyped melodrama. If the "left sacred" of dread that follows the violation of taboo has disappeared, our ambition should be to get it back. Thus he says we must "raise an Object of Terror, and, at the same time, as much as possible, to strip it of all Pity and all Admiration." In *The Symbolism of Evil* French philosopher Paul Ricoeur follows Aristotle and notes that the essence of tragedy is the coalescence of sentiments of "Pity" for the victim of misfortune and "Terror" at the manifestation of a fateful divine retribution.[48] This analysis of the emotional dynamics of tragedy is consistent with James Joyce's observation that "Pity is the feeling which arrests the mind in the presence of whatever is grave and constant in human suffering and unites it with the human sufferer. Terror is the feeling which arrests the mind in the presence of whatever is grave and constant in human suffering and unites it with the secret cause."[49] Fielding understands that innovations are needed to effect a separation of these two emotional currents. Although the turbulence of their congress is useful for poets, he notes, it can be hurtful to the politician. The mind of the execution spectator needed to be connected with the terrible, hidden, and sacred powers behind retributive justice without interference from the pitying, empathic self.[50] Fielding offers three ordering suggestions to this end. First, the criminal should be condemned with celerity after being sentenced so that a negative typification would continue—"the Resentment of Mankind being warm, would pursue the Criminal to his last End, and all Pity for the offender would be lost in Detestation of the Offence."[51] Second, Fielding suggests that executions take place behind closed doors for "the Mind of Man is so much more capable of magnifying than his Eye."[52] This private execution would encourage an imaginative amplification of terrors. It would further punish offenders "who would thus die in the Presence only of their Enemies; and where the boldest of them would find no Cordial to keep up his spirits, not any Breath to flatter his Ambition."[53] His third suggestion is to increase the solemnity of proceedings and enforce rules for dour dress and comportment. In short, Fielding sought, like Mandeville, to rationalize the process so as to screw down the emotional and semiotic register, to restore and channel the powers of the sacred as a communicative and deterrent tool.

We can find confirmation of our theory that execution reform was driven by dramaturgical and communicative concerns in the works of those who advocated toughening them up. These suggest that worries over meaning as expressed by intellectuals like Mandeville and Fielding can be analytically separated out from humanitarian and civilizing norms as a cause of reform. They are no cloaked idiographic expression of some extended process of normative civilization, but rather efforts to deal with the practical problems of failed signaling, genre creep, the absent sacred, and proliferating witnessable disorders. Some saw the hiding of punishment as allowing for the intensification of levels of pain and suffering. Such was the opinion of William Paley, part-time philosopher and archdeacon of Carlisle:

> Barbarous spectacles of human agony are justly found fault with, as tending to harden and deprave the public feelings, and to destroy that sympathy with which our fellow-creatures ought always to be seen; or, if no effect of this kind follow from them, they counteract in some measure their own design, by sinking men's abhorrence of the crime in their commiseration of the criminal. But if a mode of execution could be devised, which would augment the horror of punishment without offending or impairing the public sensibility by cruel or unseemly exhibitions of death, it might add something to the efficacy of example . . . Somewhat of the sort we have been describing, was the proposal, not long since suggested, of casting murderers into a den of wild beasts, where they would perish in a manner dreadful to the imagination, yet concealed from view.[54]

Similarly the anonymous author of *Hanging Not Punishment Enough* from 1701 did not advocate privatization but rather a return more painful modes of execution such as starvation and flogging to death as a solution to the problem of generating horror. Mandeville himself suggested criminals could be exchanged for the slaves captured by the Barbary corsairs. The fact that these more violent alternatives were mooted suggests that there was no inevitability to the hiding of the execution. It was one among many candidate strategies for getting the ritual back on message.[55]

Toward the Present

It might be thought that the material presented here has only curiosity value or is of purely historical interest, that it has nothing to tell us about the form and nature of contemporary executions. Not so. We could begin by noting that the eventual transformation of the execution into private activity was indeed propelled and sustained by ongoing anxieties about popular disorder. Writings and analyses by reformers like Fielding and John Howard played a major role in the removal of the procession to Tyburn. From 1783, London's principal executions were conducted outside Newgate and with progressively less fanfare. Victorian arguments over the public execution continued to be marked by worries about commoner responses. In the Parliamentary debate on capital punishments from 1840 we find talk of "contamination and the brutalizing and demoralizing effect" of the public execution and an outcome that saw the "multitude became hardened, and literally acquire a taste for blood."[56] Such fears of a Jekyll and Hyde transformation in the lower classes were amplified by widely published accounts of executions undertaken by sensitive observers. Dickens, for example, had little sympathy for those strung up when he reported on judicial deaths but was horrified by the "atrocious bearing, looks, and language of the assembled spectators" and famously wrote of this in the *Times*.[57] In 1868 an act was passed shifting British executions behind the closed doors of the prison. France saw its last public guillotining with the much-attended and unruly death of the mass murderer Eugene Weidmann in June 1939. After this event the authorities finally came to believe that "far from serving as a deterrent and having a salutary effect on the crowds" the public execution "promoted baser instincts of human nature and encouraged general rowdiness and bad behavior."[58]

Privatizing operations all but eliminated the humiliations of visibly failed communication to the public. They had the collateral advantage of allowing death row procedures to be systematically reworked and reformed so as to minimize possibilities for disordering counter-narrations. The dying prisoner today is watched only by officials, journalists, priests, and relatives. Opportunities for showmanship are reduced by death-row procedures that isolate and pacify the victim. Prisoners wear standard garb and their last days and moments follow a close-written timetable. Robert Johnson reports that most U.S. prisoners go to their deaths in a passive, resigned state. Their personality and will have been eroded by the years spent waiting for death and through the subtle control of the situation exerted by death row teams.[59] This evolution can be understood as a retreat from the high-stakes game of public execution, which allowed the victim considerable freedom of action in the hope of attaining a large ideological or moral payoff.

If the state has battened down the hatches and is now guided by a precautionary strategy rather than risky and extravagant gambits, this does not mean its approach has become purely "defensive" to the point of having no communicative purpose.[60] Justice must still be seen to be done and increasingly in ways that do not violate the sacred status of the self. This is why witnesses and journalists are allowed to be present. Fully effective, publicly exhibited, and accountable status degradation requires not only the coercion of the body but also the voluntary abasement of the spirit. This compliance of mind is demonstrable only through action, and for action to be meaningful it must partly be nonconstrained. "If an individual is to act with proper demeanor and show proper deference," wrote Goffman in a different context, "then it will be necessary for him to have areas of self-determination."[61] In other words windows of opportunity designed for the display of deference are built into the fabric of the degradation ceremony, making these vulnerable to appropriation by the condemned. It would be instrumentally rational to drug the criminal unconscious days before their death, or to bind them hand and foot, or to kill them with a quick bullet to the back of the head when they were not expecting to die. Yet this kind of judicial procedure would be a semiotic failure. What is required is a person who talks to the press, sleeps well, chooses their last meal with care, and then walks of their own accord to the death chamber to die quietly. Such a person accords legitimacy to the death penalty simply by doing routine. It is hoped that they die in an orderly way and as a sovereign individual.

So it is that even after the relocation of the execution behind closed doors we can find structural opportunities for the condemned to deny the sting of death and to express a commitment to deviant identity, to celebrate their own cult and rescript the execution towards ambivalence. Consider the following examples. Carl Panzram, a sociopath and the self-declared slayer of twenty-two, was executed in September 1930 at Leavenworth Prison, Kansas. Panzram jeered at onlookers as he walked to the gallows and demanded that the chaplains leave the scene. "Hurry up, you bastard" he shouted at the executioner.[62] Gary Gilmore, executed on 17 January 1977, refused to appeal his death sentence, openly despised the civil rights groups and lawyers who did this on his behalf, and showed no signs of nervousness on the day of his execution. Killed by firing squad after a hearty breakfast of eggs, hamburger, coffee, and toast, Gilmore's celebrated last words were "Let's do it!"[63] Jesse Bishop was gassed for murder on 22 October 1979. He refused to make appeals for mercy or a stay of execution, which he considered undignified. A hardened career criminal, he told prison officials "[t]his is one more step down the road I've been heading all my life." He looked all the witnesses in the eye as he sat in the chair, gave a "defiant shake of his head . . . and made a thumbs up motion." He smiled before the cyanide was dispersed and then deliberately took several deep breaths.[64] The "blonde bombshell" Ruth Ellis was the last woman to be hanged in Britain. As she was being tied up she "pursed her lips . . . almost posing in the same manner as she did for the gentleman folk at the camera club," a gesture that startled even the hangman himself.[65] Faithful to the deviant traditions of the eighteenth-century death, such performances suggest that the moments when the criminal justice system end a life remain a fateful opportunity, a point at which actions can trigger narrative shifts and where these will be noticed by onlookers. The death penalty remains meaningful and contestable not only in the abstractions of debate ("Is it right or wrong?"), but also in the concrete details of each life's end, the play of gestures and signs at the moments in which the sacred self is extinguished.

One final example suggests a historical reversal has taken place and that such assertions of a deviant identity are no longer the most potent force for reshaping the collective representation of the death penalty. Edith Thompson was executed in London in 1923, her conviction appearing with hindsight to be a terrible miscarriage of justice. At the time she was perceived by many as a black widow who had cynically manipulated a younger man into murdering her husband. Protestations of innocence

got her nowhere. A petition raised over a million signatures for the com-
mutation of the sentence of her lover, but only a few thousand for herself.
Yet the circumstances of her death led to a rehabilitation of her public
character and a renewed campaign against the death penalty. Thompson "disintegrated as a human being on her way to the gallows," her hair
turned grey and she was hanged unconscious. Following her execution she
became a totemic symbol, a cause célébre in the effort to end capital punishment in Britain. Subsequent to her death the executioner James Ellis,
who had hung scores of people, attempted suicide, claiming that he was
haunted by Mrs. Thompson's ghost. The officiating chaplain fell seriously
ill, and one prison wardress went permanently insane. Every official of the
prison associated with the execution resigned.[66] Thompson, it seems, had
unwittingly unleashed a counter-discourse of the execution not only as
cruel and undignified but also as the domain of sacred terrors.

What are we to make of this? Today ways of dying that generate pity
or respect are more audience-resonant than those that are comic, mock-
ing, or defiant. This inversion of the eighteenth-century pattern is loosely
coupled to the waning of deterrence theory in underpinning support for
the death penalty.[67] Capital punishment is now more than ever intended as
an expressive and not a utilitarian act. It embodies the desires of the collective conscience for revenge upon evil and reminds us, as Walter Burns
put it, of "the moral order by which alone we can live as human beings."[68]
Last moments that play to nonviolent norms, that emphasize coercion and
pain or problematize "evil criminal" status, exert the most leverage against
such structures of legitimacy and feeling. Further, the spirit of terror has
now switched sides. In Henry Fielding's time it was precisely an injection
of the fateful, mysterious left-sacred with its avenging awe and tremendum that was needed for a communicatively effective execution to take
place. Yet today execution procedures seem designed to keep this at bay,
to present a resolutely secular activity and to do so by signifying exactly
what Bernard Mandeville did not want signaled: "That there is nothing in
being hang'd but awry Neck and a wet pair of Breeches." If victim actions
denying horror through narrative deflation towards comedy and a low
mimetic realism had major implications in the past, today it is by enlisting
horror and engaging in narrative inflation that the state's narrative can be
most ardently challenged. This is the lesson of Mrs. Thompson's death.

So ends our first chapter. Before moving on it is useful to flag some
core lessons that will crop up in the rest of this book. The execution has
proven handy for this task because it presents in an intuitively accessible

form many themes that are sometimes present only in a more subdued way in other modes of criminal justice. First, we have seen that punishments are not just events and techniques but also activities with meanings. Consequently as analysts we need to engage in some interpretative activity, to figure out those meanings whether intended or read, produced or received, manifest or latent. Second, we can trace how these meanings are influenced by historically embedded cultural codes, interests, hierarchies, and social actions. These are the proximate contexts for signaling and sense-making activity. Third, the analysis has shown that not only the activity but also the reform of punishment can be explained in terms of communication and semiotics. Changes over time can be thought of as an effort at spin control by the state, minimizing humiliations for authority or putting the narrative force of punishment back on track. Fourth, civil discourse and wider collective representations are as important in this Bakhtinian dialogue as the work of criminal justice professionals. The meanings of punishment on the nonbureaucratic, nonstate periphery are not restricted to dry and dusty institutional readings but involve complex intersections with the myths of popular culture, with literature and symbolism, and involve the mobilization of emotions. We need cultural theory to understand this, not just criminological or institutional theory. Fifth, Durkheim's perspective provides a way into this universe. Time and time again we find ideas about the collective conscience, the sacred, ritual, the collective representation and totem, the cult of the individual, pollution, and evil giving us traction in figuring out what is going on. In this chapter we have seen that punishment is about managing the unruly left sacred, making accommodations to the sacred dignity of the self, minimizing collateral pollutions, shaping collective representations, proposing ritual innovations, and amplifying or turning down myth.

Foucault, of course, would have been halfway with us in this chapter. His work on the public execution fully acknowledged its signifying role and the residual influence of the sacred, even if he did not fully recognize that the demise of the public execution was driven by a crisis of meaning and not simply the evolution of new and improved forms of power. In the next chapter we move to his home turf, where I will suggest that the emergence and form of the prison can be explained through a cultural logic not so very different from the one used here.

CHAPTER THREE

The Prison

As *The Birth of the Prison,* Michel Foucault's subtitle to *Discipline and Punish* attests, the prison stands out as the dominant armature of penal modernity. It is the instrument of social control that cannot be ignored. For the Durkheimian model to be taken seriously it must be able to account for this institutional form. There is another reason too why we must turn to the prison here and in chapter 4. While fines may be the most common sanction and technologies of death generate a greater emotional charge, it is the prison that is at the center of not only penal administrative activity but also the wider penal imaginary. The iconography of "punishment" has at its heart a coherent set of visual representations circulating around the prison archetype, something we all know from popular culture. In the background there are watchtowers, searchlights, walls, and razor wire and those big gates that slam shut. Nearer are the cells, bars, walls, gangways, visiting rooms with orange plastic seats, black telephones, and the thick scratchy Plexiglass where palms are pressed. There are guards with batons looking arrogant and inmates looking insolent and both groups in uniform. If we permit events to unfold we can expect exercise yard fights and shower room rapes, queues for grim canteen food that will be eaten with infantile plastic utensils and a book trolley eternally trundling down some endless gantry pushed by a superannuated lifer. The prison, we might say, has all the qualities of a myth that represents itself to us in a surfeit of icons. The success of Foucault's book, measured in terms of popular interest and sales, itself attests to this remarkable status in the *conscience collective*—as does the ubiquitous prison movie and the enduring prison memoir as profitable genres of artistic production.

Notwithstanding this rich vein of symbolism, systematic efforts to mine the prison as a publicly meaningful institution have been few and far

between. The broad objective of the academic literature has been rather
different. This can be summarized as follows: For much of the twentieth century, scholarship was dominated by a species of atheoretical but
well-documented Whig history. Prison reformers were seen as progres-
sives—even as heroes—doing their best to improve the living conditions
of inmates and fuelled by evangelical fervor and humanist sensibility in
various proportions. In the 1970s and 1980s this approach was decisively
replaced by a more cynical sociological understanding that drank from
the fount of the hermeneutics of suspicion. Spearheaded by Michel Foucault's *Discipline and Punish* and backed up by scholars such as Michael
Ignatieff and David Rothman, this move contextualized the prison as a
brutal system of punishment and social control of ever-growing, insidious power.[1] The motivations of reformers could be redescribed as false
consciousness or sidestepped altogether through a shift from the study of
meanings to the study of practices. For all their goodwill those humanitar-
ians and rule governed bureaucrats were the bearers of new and more
intensive forms of cruel regulation. The prison was not about retribution
or deterrence or the imposition of legal sanction. Its latent function was to
destroy the autonomous self; to control dangerous classes; and to permit
the ideological masking of more subtle and pervasive modes of regulation
in schools, factories, hospitals, and administrative systems. In the wake of
this paradigm shift the refinement and reform of the prison system over
the past two centuries could be understood as a series of sometimes more
and sometimes less well-intentioned efforts leading to these sinister, coun-
ter-democratic, and exclusionary ends.

As I mentioned in chapter 1, this literature achieved a great deal by
deploying the sociological imagination. It moved our understanding of
the prison's purpose away from juridical individualism with its bookish
fictions of the legal subject who must be punished, beyond the collection
and adumbration of facts by empiricist archive miners, and it usefully tran-
scended the intentionalist fallacies of more conventional histories. The resulting collectivistic, structuralist approach was profoundly informed by a
social theory that inscribed the prison as one among many carriers of modernity's aspirations for order. Yet the nature of this inscription is flawed.
Although there is some treatment of the isomorphisms between criminal
justice institutions and those of the broader society, this is still a largely
internal history. It explores ideas about prisons and other social control
institutions—"welfare," for example—as these are bounced around by
experts and authority, but does not show how these might relate dialogi-

cally to the activity of a wider civil sphere with its own distinctive and autonomous moral culture and codes. Consequently the impulse towards order is attributed to the workings of power, not some diffuse sensibility, ethos, or more precise cultural system. Although meanings have not been entirely neglected, those that gain analytic attention have been the cool bureaucratic cultures and institutional logics of policy makers and administrators. Documentation from such sources provides a convenient resource from which a sinister, Kafkaesque, instrumental logic can all too readily be read off. Timetables can be decoded to reveal an intellectual template for controlling the body, prisoner classifications interpreted as a new form of regulatory knowledge, prison designs as a methodical appropriation of lived space. Such data rather easily suggest a surfeit of order and the triumph of instrumental reason, just as the analysis of dreams will inevitably confirm the triumph of the unconscious.

A subtly alternative approach is to treat the prison more hermeneutically and less hermetically. This does not mean reconstructing the thoughts in reformers' heads but rather retrieving the cultural categories and codes underpinning how society thinks about or imagines the prison. We need to see the prison as a text and signifier perpetually redrafted in response to extramural cultural pressures and meaningful imperatives that are only loosely coupled to administrative or judicial ambitions.[2] The iconic popular culture properties of the prison touched upon above provide a prima facie warrant for such a turn, suggesting that the prison exists as both mythology and materiality. It is a nexus of codes and images as much as a set of artifacts and procedural rules. To more fully understand its evolution and survival we need to explore the interplay of these two dimensions. The story to be told has three interlocked claims, which are a specification of those set out in chapter 1.

(1) True enough, the evolution of the prison within modernity has been all about order, disorder and ordering efforts. However, the process should be understood not only in the Foucaultian sense of circulating power but also in the way outlined by the anthropologist Mary Douglas, who contends that the urge to classify and regulate is inherent in all societies. That which threatens such classifications by transgressing or confounding moral or cognitive boundaries can be deemed dangerous. Douglas points in particular to dirt, disease, and bodily activities as core sources of abomination. Consistent with this hypothesis we will see evidence that petty licentiousness and depravity, infections, and squalor within prisons are key concerns in public discourse. Recommendations for increased

separation, regulation, and administrative classification of inmates of the kind described as insidious by Foucault are also efforts to limit forms of disgusting disorderly contamination that have great cultural but little political importance. Reformers might be better described as moral entrepreneurs engaging in housecleaning. They are neat freaks rather than control freaks.

(2) Just as important as the effort to regulate cultural disorders internal to the institution, civil discourse regulates the prison by detecting, describing, and censuring those moments when penal activities and institutions threaten the boundaries of their own classification under the sign of "prison." Administrators do not have a free hand, for sometimes what they think is a "prison" is not seen as a "prison" by others but rather as a freak or monster. A given prison or regime of administration might fail this test of typification if it appears to be too hard or too soft, as somehow uncivilized or as mimicking wider civil life too closely such that it no longer represents some form of "Other" place.[3] Sometimes the prison becomes recoded as a repressive and barbaric anachronism, in others as insufficiently distinct from everyday life or even as a house of fun. In both cases scandal can eventuate that seeks semiotic redress and the return of any wandering prison to its appropriate place in the constellation of properly prisonlike institutions. Importantly these civil discourse constraints operate to limit the range and penetration of the disciplinary techniques available to experts working within institutions. The world of the carceral continuum described by Foucault is one where power and knowledge have a free run. This claim is false. Cultural expectations and external readings make every disciplinary intensification or relaxation vulnerable to renarration. Discourses of excess can easily set in referring variously to torture, squalor, or pleasure as markers of a failed "prison."

(3) Notwithstanding the fact that the prison is bureaucratically administered and routinized, authorities have been forever unable to fix its wider meanings in the rather clinical terms that agree with their interests. The quest for buttoned-down legitimacy and a quiet life out of the public gaze has been continually subverted by the association of crime, criminals, and the prison with evil, with the extraordinary and with the charisma of transgression. These high-powered semiotic resources unleash unruly or unauthorized discourses that repeatedly contradict and problematize the antiseptic image of the prison. They further create legitimacy problems by magnifying the association of the prison with disordering powers. If a prison generates and concentrates rather than controls evil, then its worth

is questionable. Perhaps for this reason much of the organization of the prison can be described as efforts to counter spiritual and moral pollution.

In sum we can use our Durkheimian perspective to explain why the prison has had a troubled reputation over the past two hundred years. It is a signifier caught in the crossfire of intersecting discourses on crime, morals, civilization, and the state. Deeply institutionalized in one sense as a legitimate and familiar way of dealing with felons, the prison system can simultaneously be understood as profoundly vulnerable. Although its walls might close the physical circuit of the total institution, it is perpetually open to public renarration as the site of potential dangers and disorders, as a place of evil and pollution. Its meanings are both multiple and consequential. This is a story that this chapter will trace at three sites often walked through by criminological historians, Newgate, Pentonville, and Mettray, as well as some that are less familiar. Each case will emphasize a different facet of boundary transgression, meaning multiplicity, and the localized interplay of the discourses of excess squalor, discipline, and pleasure. Not a comprehensive history of the prison, the case studies in this chapter offer instead an empirical illustration for our different, Durkheimian way of accounting for the "birth of the prison."

Lessons from Newgate

The analysis begins around the time Foucault starts his, with the movement for reformed prisons towards the end of the eighteenth century. Our narrative, however, is one where cultural anxieties rather than power and knowledge are center stage. It is around this time that institutions of confinement, both great and small, came to be read as net producers of disorder and contamination rather than order, these changing perceptions no doubt reflecting late-Enlightenment sensibilities and the slow unfolding of a civilizing process.[4] Disorders could take several forms, but consistent with Mary Douglas's logic, each involved the perceived violation of symbolic boundaries—embodied, institutional, personal, moral, and social. From these transgressions, broader narratives came to be generated of the early prison as the locus of excess squalor or excess pleasure, as a reprehensible and failed institution.

To start, we can note that in the late eighteenth century there was great freedom of movement through the semipermeable membranes of the not-yet-total institution, both those interior to its boundary and those separating it from the outside world. The result of this interchange was a distribution of concerns about moral regulation. To some extent these were about the reform of "dangerous classes" in society at large and the hope that the deterrent force of the prison would help the unruly mob clean up its act. But to a far greater one it was simply a matter of spring cleaning the prison and removing the irksome and humiliating moral pollutions and dangers that festered within its walls. These, after all, were something for which the authorities themselves could be held publicly accountable.

The case of London's major prison, Newgate, can illustrate this point.[5] During the eighteenth century inmates could mix indiscriminately with family, friends, and other day visitors to the extent that it was often difficult to tell who was locked up and who was a free citizen. Violent criminals were kept cheek by jowl with debtors, whose crimes were essentially civil in nature and who often brought their wives and children into the jail with them. Good cells and furnishings could be rented out, enabling the reproduction of the broader class system within the walls. External social status and wealth were imported and dramatized through such superior living conditions, a situation resulting in oblique rather than clear lines of deference and authority once jailers became factotums for wealthier residents.[6] Within such a system the lack of formal bureaucratic control could allow abuses of power to flourish, these feeding off fears of moral degradation. For example, in 1813 the pamphleteer Daniel Eaton very visibly accused Newgate's jailer of profiteering from illegal monopolies on the sale of goods and services. Prisoners were "prevented from sending where they please for certain objects of necessary food and consumption, viz. beer and coals,"[7] a policy that violated "principles of fair competition." Respectable prisoners who refused to pay a premium for such goods or for their accommodation were threatened. Eaton found himself in a situation where he "should pay for the furniture . . . or be removed to the Common Felon's side." Such association with evil individuals he felt could only be a "painful and degrading one."[8]

Eaton's concern that a gentleman might be forced to share space with a lowly criminal was widespread rather than merely the idiosyncratic and vexatious allegation of a malcontent. This was why his pamphlet, like so many others, sold well. It was believed at the time that the mingling of categories of inmate—the dangerous with the harmless, serious with the petty, murders with debtors, men with women, the innocent with the corrupted, the untried with the guilty—placed virtue in danger. What was

known as "promiscuous association" would lead to a prison that humiliated and debauched. Here there was the atmosphere of profane urban
marketplaces like Billingsgate and Covent Garden, as well as the brothel
and the tavern. Vice would breed in such an unregulated, unhealthful
atmosphere where classifications were not enforced or respected. As the
Gentleman's Magazine reported in 1757:

> The men and women prisoners are all put together till they are locked up at
> night, and have perpetual opportunities of retiring to the dark cells as much as
> they please; the women, indeed, are generally such as do not need much solici-
> tation to this commerce.[9]

So it is hardly surprising that Newgate was described in the early eighteenth century as "[a] confused Chaos without any distinction, a bottomless pit of violence, and a tower of Babel where all are speakers and none
are hearers."[10] Here was the disgusting antithesis of a civil society. It is no
accident that Mrs. Elizabeth Fry, the noted philanthropic campaigner for
women's prisons, was forcibly struck by this embodied disorder around
a century later nor that her most famous and influential, most-cited passages document the horrors arising out of weak regulation. Giving evidence to the Parliamentary committee of 1818 on prison conditions she
famously conjures her experience on entering Newgate, speaking of the
"dreadful proceedings that went forward on the female side of the prison;
the begging, swearing, gaming, fighting, singing, dancing, dressing up in
men's clothes; the scenes are too bad to be described."[11] This was an unruly
scene that subverted conventional gender roles and in which the cross-
class contamination of the virtuous was a perpetual risk, for "the lowest
of women" could be found alongside "respectable married women and
maid-servants."[12] Fry's position was typical of the other Quaker reformers, including J. J. Gurney and Samuel Hoare, who detested the noise and
dissipation of unreformed prisons, seeing this as a profanity that would
generate insensitivity and depravity rather than the contemplative inner
reform that would create a spiritually purified self.

If prisons at the turn of the eighteenth century were disordered institutions of slippery boundaries and confounded identities, this was to have
further implications for their signaling functions. In addition to producing
pollution internally they were failing to become a public signifier of shame
and hardship. They were semiotic disasters because they didn't look like
prisons should. We find latent possibilities for this reading traced in the

novels of the eighteenth century where the imprisonment of a major character is seen as a temporary and only slightly unpleasant interlude in their wider life narrative. As Sarah Anderson points out, in novels from Daniel Defoe's *Moll Flanders* (1722) to Samuel Richardson's *Pamela, or Virtue Rewarded* (1740), Henry Fielding's *Tom Jones* (1749), and Tobias Smollett's *The Adventures of Peregrine Pickle* (1751), prison is but a "mild interruption in an individual's ongoing path toward financial, spiritual or domestic fulfilment."[13] Harshness, many argued, was needed so that disorderly places like Newgate could properly serve as a deterrent to the true criminal. For this reason the Reverend Sydney Smith would later approve of the treadmill, invented by Cubitt in 1818. This would be "a perpetual example before the eyes of those who want it, affecting the imagination only with horror and disgust."[14] Smith was dismayed that pre-Victorian prisons were sending out a very different kind of message. If the Bastille was the sacred site of dramatic struggles against tyranny, Newgate and other sites like it were widely encoded as the locus of bacchanalian popular pleasures rather than punishments. Newgate was not simply unsanitary, it was also debauched. There was a tap open to those who could pay. Inmates could play cards and gamble. Whoring was known to be common.[15]

Although geographically localized within the prison walls, such mundane activities were amplified in their reputation and effects through the emergence of a profitable literary genre. Besides recounting the crimes and misdemeanors of felons, the celebrated *Newgate Calendars* offered a carnivalesque panorama of bawdy fun and debauch. Much like the tabloid *News of the World* today these managed to celebrate the life of excess even as they decried it in reproducing and circulating images of depravity. Based upon the Session Papers, which offered a somewhat dry and official account of proceedings at London's premier court, the Old Bailey, the *Newgate Calendars* became embellished with details and illustrations not only of crimes and trials, but also the wild goings-on in prison and at execution. We find such representations aesthetically refracted in *The Beggar's Opera* (1728). Responding to Swift's alleged remark that "[a] Newgate Pastoral might make an odd, pretty sort of thing," John Gay produced a work where crime and punishment, vice and whim are conjoined in a spectacle of popular pleasures. Whereas Gay, like Defoe and Richardson, was able to laugh away such licentiousness by narrating it in a comedic genre that made light of boundary transgressions, one hundred years later concerns about moral order were being viewed most seriously. There had been a genre shift. As Anderson shows, the confinement that had been represented as an inconvenient episode in a picaresque life journey was increasingly written in gothic terms as producing mental turmoil, even terror. By contrast with the blithe spirit of the prison scenes in the mid-eighteenth-century novel, in later stories such as William Godwin's *Caleb Williams* (1794), confinement is a dark and traumatic experience signaling the presence of despotism and corruption.[16] This arose, however, not from a surfeit of regulation but rather from its absence.

Whereas the moral dangers of unruly prisons were only belatedly recognized, disease was a form of pollution taken seriously right from the start. Prison conditions were highly unsanitary, but then so were those of many other places in the seventeenth century. The prison, however, was singled out as a den of disease and decay scattered with miserable and pestilent bodies. Hence the *Gentleman's Magazine* of July 1767 wrote of a visit that had revealed "a most wretched class of human being, almost naked, with only a few filthy rags almost alive and in motion with vermin, their bodies rotting with bad distemper, covered with itch, and scorbutic and venereal ulcers."[17] There were widespread fears that "gaol fevers" could originate in such conditions and spread through miasmic effluvia into the surrounding areas, thereby contaminating more respectable populations. For example, in 1750 four judges at the Old Bailey were believed to have been struck down as a result of close, crowded contact in court with prisoners and "a draft poisoned with infection" that carried in their direction from the bail dock.[18] A form of typhus, this particular jail fever was estimated to kill some thirty Newgate inmates alone every year. Medical ills, then, could be added to moral ones, each adding resonance to the imagery of the early prison as a polluted and polluting institution. It was not only the case that Newgate exemplified disorder, it also multiplied and exported it. Its yards and cells bred disease, taught crime, and encouraged loose morals and debauchery.

Today at least some of these attributes of unreformed jails and debtors' prisons might be given a positive spin by liberal-minded criminologists. They embed the institution in the community, provide sources of social status other than the degraded one of "criminal," and offer rich resources for sustaining the self against the pains of imprisonment. Two centuries ago they were taken by most to be deeply offensive.[19] As the eighteenth century progressed, civilizing, boundary maintenance–obsessed norms had taken a firmer hold, and disorder, dirt, disease, and moral contamination became more and more important dimensions of concern. By the early nineteenth century the will was sufficient for purifying rituals to be adopted and enforced. These are evident, for example, in Elizabeth Fry's early nineteenth-century reforms for the Newgate women, which included establishing a school, providing religious instruction, and allocating sewing work. Her rules had a Quakerish emphasis on cleanliness. Conversation was to be polite, not forbidden, and behavior modest and orderly. It is entirely consistent with our hypothesis that for Fry this task of prison reform was linked to the wider mission of her "obsessive craving for spiritual purification, her desire to do God's work."[20] Reform was about imposing a sacred cultural order, discipline a means to this end.

That such housecleaning concerns were not limited to the more spectacular case of Newgate can be traced most clearly in the writings of the great prison reform campaigner John Howard. A country gentleman of Christian tendencies, Howard was appalled by prison conditions and began a series of arduous tours to investigate these, first in Britain, but later with benchmarking activity overseas. His landmark volume, *The State of the Prisons in England and Wales,* which first appeared in 1777, was an international bestseller. This was a somewhat unusual result for a book that is a systematic and detailed account of prison conditions in regional and marginal locations. It contains measurements of cells, descriptions of diets, the weights of chains, and so forth. Such a publishing result makes sense when we consider that Howard must have touched a nerve of cultural sensibilities, for the meticulous traveler repeatedly punctuated his dry, objective data with vivid descriptions of filth and expressions of disgust. Prisoners who went in healthy, he tells us, were soon "expiring on floors, in loathsome cells, of pestilential fevers and the confluent smallpox." The "air which has been breathed is made poisonous to a more intense degree by the effluvia of the sick and what else in prisons is offensive . . . the leaves of my memorandum book were often so tainted that I could not use it till after spreading it an hour or two before the fire: and even my antidote, a vial of vinegar, has after using it in a few prisons, become intolerably disagreeable."[21]

On initial inspection the confluence in Howard's writings of medical and penological discourses seemingly confirms Foucault's speculations on the synergies between diverse articulations of expert knowledge. Yet a close reading shows a motor of change that is subtly different, for the impulse for reform is an emotional response of disgust, and its partner is pity. It is this dramatic quality, of course, that explains Howard's wider public reputation and influence. This is not an abstract and clinical gaze related to health and dominion but one that is tied up in a passionate tableau of purity, pollution, and moral empathy. As Randall McGowen correctly puts it, Howard was "offended" by "disorder and inattention" and "characterized such disorder as oppressive for prisoners."[22] We see this most clearly when Howard talks of promiscuous association across the sexes and argued that standards of decency and personal safety were violated. When such fundamental classificatory boundaries were crossed and "numbers of both sexes are shut up together for many days and nights in one room. This occasions much confusion and distress."[23] In the case of a debtors' prison there was "danger of infection and corrupting the morals of children . . . The number of men in the same room, and of lewd women admitted under the name of wives, prove that this affair needs some regulation."[24] The profane imagery of the tavern and bordello formed the analogical foundation for this vision of cultural pollution, of "midnight revels so that most of our goals are riotous alehouses and brothels."[25] Once again it seems, the prison was not a prison. Howard's proposed solutions involving classification and separation were intended primarily to remove these contaminating evils. They denote the triumph of a new cultural sensibility as much as any merely technical disciplinary innovation. Solitary confinement was tied to inner repentance rather than robotic reform. As in America's Pennsylvania system the implementation of segregation was underpinned by themes of order, morality, and salvation rather than those of efficiency and output.

By the end of the eighteenth century then we find discourses of the prison as depraved, cruel, dirty, and unhealthy falling into place as the prevalent set of collective representations. Disorders that had once been below the horizon of concern were now busily blipping away on the radar screen of mortal dangers. These troubling echoes and pings endured well into the era of Foucault's so-called disciplinary society and fostered a genre of profitable early nineteenth-century pamphleteering that continued Howard's legacy. Part jeremiad, part travelogue, part exposé, in such works authors with good intentions found a ready market in audiences thrilled by the detail of scandal and ambivalently attracted to accounts of evil and swarming disorder. Sir Thomas Buxton's severally reprinted work of 1818 should suffice as illustration. The result of visits to prisons at Tothill Fields, St. Albans, Ghent, Bristol, Guildford, and elsewhere it is marked by a pervasive imagery of the creeping evils of category permeability.[26] On page 10 we read that Buxton's visit to one prison had revealed a "promiscuous assemblage of hardened and convicted criminals"; "air fowl and putrid"; "contagious and loathsome disease" and "noxious effluvia of dirt and corruption." By page 14 the tone has hardly changed: the new prisoner who has been remanded but not yet legally convicted might "find himself in bed, and in bodily contact, between a robber and a murderer, or between a man with a foul disease on one side, and one with an infectious disorder on the other." In such a zone of "filth and contagion . . . purity itself could not remain pure." On page 18 we find the turnkey telling Buxton that "the smell on first opening the door" in the morning, "was enough to turn the stomach of a horse."

As late as 1836 the official prison inspector's report into Newgate revealed much the same set of concerns.[27] At this point in time we are just a few moons away from Mettray and Pentonville and the alleged apogee of a refined disciplinary logic in the 1840s. Yet familiar worries are still being voiced. There was the promiscuous association of the convicted, untried, and insane. There was the free movement of people in and out of the jail. There was evidence of vice such as prostitution, gambling, pornography, and drinking. "We discovered a pack of cards, apparently much used, a cribbage-board and pegs, and two draught-boards and men"; "We also found several books: amongst them Guthries' Grammar, a song book, the Keepsake Annual for 1836, and the [name omitted] by [ditto], 18 plates, published by Stockdale, 1827. This last is a book of a most disgusting nature, and the plates are obscene and indecent in the extreme"; "no provision is made for washing the linen of the prisoners in the prison: and as scarcely sufficient soap is allowed to wash even a shirt, a prisoner who has no friends is in a manner constrained to use his foul linen"; "persons of notoriously bad character, prostitutes and thieves, find admission. Many of the prostitutes are very young girls, sometimes not more than twelve or thirteen years of age: others have visited different men, yet are admitted under the name of wives and sisters"; "almost any quantity of beer which the prisoners can afford to purchase may be brought into the wards." It is hard to imagine a less Foucaultian passage, and this from representatives of the center and not the periphery of the disciplinary society. The prison inspector's obsession here is with petty vice, bad taste, and the sins of the flesh, the worldly fruit of the fertile soils of cultural pollution. This is a deeply meaningful, not technocratic, language game.

Prison reform has been understood variously: as the imposition of a new form of power, as a humanitarian or religious attempt to redeem souls and replace Bastilles with accountable institutions, and as a manifestation of the growth of expert knowledge. Another way to see this process is in semiotic terms. The case of Newgate and others of its time suggests that the birth of the prison was an attempt to purify a problematic institution, just as the reform of public capital punishment was an effort to repackage a failing ritual. The Victorian penitentiary's obsession with order arose not from some transcendental will to power but from growing disgust at disorder.

Before we leave Newgate and its ilk behind to look at the new, re-formed prisons that replaced them as showpieces of penal modernity, we must briefly note that repeated efforts at reform of old jails failed to provide a much-needed narrative facelift. Newgate was closed down at the start of the twentieth century having never cleansed its reputation, being called even at this time by the *Sphere* "unsavoury."[28] The earlier association with moral depravity was compounded during the Victorian era by Newgate's role as the London center for judicial executions, and thereby it came to be consecrated and infected with the contaminating powers evil. On 7 February 1903 it took its curtain call in a sale of relics within its "gloomy precincts" that was "attended by crowds of the curious and the speculative." Prices reflected the repute of the institution. The toll bell went for 100 pounds, the pole where the black flag fluttered after executions for eleven and a half guineas. Items from the condemned cells, we are told, were particularly sought after.[29] Unruly, diseased, dangerous, evil—Newgate represented all these, but it was never a symbol of order. Rather, it was a negative icon, a condensation of fears and anxieties, a shaming symbol of pollution that had to go.

Pentonville

A prominent exhibit in critical theory's history of the prison is Pentonville. The alleged *capolavoro* of instrumental punitive reason, London's show-piece prison built in 1842 is viewed by Michel Foucault, Michael Ignatieff, and others as the high water mark of Victorian regimented brutality and as an institution that "quickly became a model for prison architecture and discipline" around Europe.[30] One might easily object to all this theoretical attention and claim that Pentonville was an outlier. In 1850 Hepworth Dixon was still able to report in Howardian terms on the prisons of the city of London as dens of "idleness, illicit gaming, filthiness, moral and material disorder, unnatural crowding together, unlimited license . . . and universal corruption of each other."[31] Yet instead of treading this route and arguing that the institutionalization of disciplinary logic was less complete than critical theory might imagine, it is more worthwhile for our purposes to indicate the ways in which Pentonville itself expresses a cultural reason and generated its own set of mythologies. From a late-Durkheimian perspective Pentonville is a temple of purification. It was the flagship response to the pollution and disorder that we have seen were busily discrediting Newgate and various provincial houses of detention over the prior half-century or so. Pentonville's timetables, drudge work, and design can, of course, be decoded to show the stone-hearted will to power of abstract social forces. But they can just as easily be taken to indicate a pathological, ritualized mania with order and ordering, an obsession with removing dirt to the point of objective dysfunctionality. As Martha Grace Duncan reports, solitary confinement, silence, and discipline generated mental illness. Rates of insanity in Pentonville were known at the time to be well above the norm for prisons, and yet still the regime continued. This was fundamentalism, not science.[32]

We can start with the exterior. It is less accurate to think of Pentonville's architecture as austere by consequence of its functionality than to think of the built form as encoding both austerity and functionality. It was the visible symbol of a commitment to ordering logic. Here was a signifying edifice that could be favorably contrasted with disorder and decay. "Devoid of pseudo-Gothic ornament, it has aesthetic qualities which are visible even today," wrote one set of commentators some fifty years ago. In its time it was "a startling contrast to the rotting hulks at Chatham and Sheerness" that still held convicts.[33] The "deliberate austerity of its architecture" detected by John Pratt was a marker of an orderly as well as forbidding institution.[34] The theme of pollution and its control can also be traced in the dreams of Pentonville's creators, seeping and creeping through the cracks in even the driest official document. The surveyor general of prisons, Major Joshua Jebb, insisted that "the site of a prison should be dry and airy, and removed beyond the influence of noxious exhalations, or prevalent fogs."[35] Designs and policies were underpinned by the belief that the separate system could control spiritual pollution. "An effort has been made," wrote Jebb, "both by law and in the regulation and discipline of many prisoners, to obviate the *evils* arising from the association of Prisoners."[36] Hence the monastic separation, a system of work intended to confer moral purification, and relentless religious instruction. Discipline was born not so much of the desire to obtain functional conformity but from the imperative to eliminate spiritual corruption as time, stone, and thought did their tasks.

For the Victorian mind, earthly crime, mortal sin, and moral depravity were caught up in an imaginative matrix alongside disease and dirt.[37] Each could multiply and refract the other. For this reason Joshua Jebb's explication of his design reveals an obsession with sanitation, air circulation and the cleansing of bodies—more so perhaps than to the issue of security. For example, there was a receiving room where new inmates could be "examined, cleansed and dressed" and an adjacent "closet for fumigating and purifying clothes."[38] In Jebb's publication extolling the virtues of Pentonville some nine out of the thirty-eight pages are given over to a discussion of a ventilation system that makes a firm and telling binary separation of fresh and foul air. There was an assurance of the "withdrawal of a stated quantity of foul air from each cell."[39] We find an innovative and expensive heating system that was "the means of warming the fresh air when necessary, without injuring its qualities or affecting its hygrometrical condition."[40] Within each cell there was state-of-the-art technology for the purification of the body, each being "fitted-up with a soil pan and trap, and a copper basin for washing, with waste pipe."[41] It is hardly accidental that special attention was given to maintaining the sanctity of the Chapel. "The extraction of foul air from the Chapel should be effected," insisted Jebb. "At Pentonville prison the foul air passes into the roof of the chapel, thence through the clock tower," and at the same time "fresh air should be introduced at a low level into each stall."[42] Like a trip to a sanitarium or the seaside, Pentonville was a place where health-giving airs would cleanse body and soul.

With the removal of pollution would come institutional respectability. Towards the end of Jebb's report is a plate with a caption that reads, "Perspective View of the Interior of One Corridor, from the Central Hall."[43] A detail from this is reproduced here as figure 2. After pages of grim technical illustrations showing locks, cells, and those notable ventilation shafts this picture is something of a surprise. Like many such representations provided by architects, Jebb's image offers a vision of the building in use, one not unlike those concept drawings we find today for airports and shopping malls. This is a telling aspiration or fantasy, remarkable in its audacity for it depicts bourgeois visitors strolling and conversing in the halls of the model prison. Contra Foucault, Pentonville was not imagined as a closed institution devoid of civil input, but rather as a space cleansed of taint suitable for genteel public recreation and instruction. As the image makes clear, Jebb even envisaged women and children coming to this arcade-like location for pleasure and without fear that their sensibilities would be offended or their respectability threatened. Pentonville, it seems, was conceived as a purified space, an arcade for virtuous exercise and social intercourse as much as a machine for the production of disciplined bodies.

FIGURE 2. Interior perspective view of Pentonville (detail). From J. Jebb, *Report of the Surveyor-General of Prisons on the Construction, Ventilation and Details of Pentonville Prison* (London: HMSO, 1844).

If visitors to Pentonville were in truth few and far between, remarks by the curious suggest it was modestly successful in its hunt for bourgeois approval as a locus demonstrating "advanced social development."[44] In contrast to Howardesque stories of squalor and depravity arising from boundary transgression, in 1850 we find Hepworth Dixon writing enthusiastically and with utopian hints of "perfect order, perfect silence . . . a new and different world."[45] On his inspection, the Archduke of Austria was favorably impressed by the regularity and modernity of the building before heading on to visit Madame Tussaud's wax museum.[46] Henry Mayhew and John Binny's report of 1862 on their trip also suggests Jebb's design was on target as a symbol of purity and order. They remarked on the "bright, and cheerful, and airy quality of building; so that, with its long light corridors, it strikes the mind, on first entering it, as a bit of a Crystal Palace, stripped of all its contents. There is none of the gloom, nor dungeon like character of a jail appertaining to it."[47] They noted the "Dutch-like cleanliness pervading the place" and spoke with astonishment of "convicts . . . sweeping the black asphalte pavement till it glistened again as if polished with black-lead," others "on their knees washing the flags of slate" and the "cloud of dust rising from the sweepers' brooms."[48] In a society where it was said that cleanliness was next to godliness, such activity was progress indeed.

If Pentonville could be narrated by contemporaries as a purified and respectable space, this was not the only possible reading. Once ejected into circulation as a signifier, Pentonville came to generate meanings that were remarkably unstable and contested in the wider civil discourse. Authority could not batten down the allusions and metaphors that proliferated and multiplied in public life. For example, it might be surprising to those raised on a diet of Ignatieff and Foucault that Pentonville could be seen as a place of excessive privilege. While the Chartists argued it was an inhumane English Bastille and connected penal process to the pollution of political oppression, others suggested Pentonville was not prison enough. By virtue of its effort to signal distance from squalor, Pentonville had rendered itself vulnerable to counter-narration. Offering centrally heated accommodation, free food, and shelter, it could be likened to a palace by Thomas Carlyle.[49] At the time of the opening, newspapers delighted in reporting ultramodern features.[50] Hepworth Dixon was also astonished by the amenities.

> Let us now enter the cell ... It is admirably ventilated, on the newest scientific principle, and by means of warm air is kept at an even and agreeable temperature. It even has the luxuries of a water closet, and of an unlimited supply of warm and cold water. The bedding is good and clean ... There is a bell handle too, which needs only to be pulled to command the instant attention of a paid servitor. Light work is to be had also for amusement and to vary the routine. Very pleasant! At regular intervals the prisoner goes to chapel to hear gospel; and to school, where competent masters are waiting to offer their services to instruct him. But what is there penal in all this? Someone asks. For our life we cannot find out.[51]

Other visitors reported back on the high-quality diet. Famously Mayhew and Binny remarked that "the most genuine cocoa we ever sipped was at this same Model Prison." It was freshly roasted, ground and brewed on the premises from the finest imported beans and was made with water "not of the slushy Thames, but ... raised from an artesian well several hundred feet below the surface, expressly for the use of these same convicts."[52] Critics contrasted this lifestyle to the squalid conditions of the British worker. Here, then, was another boundary confusion critique. Pentonville was not a prison. It was a freak, a luxury hotel that mocked the honest toil of the deserving poor and violated the less eligibility principle. Exit the cocoa.

"Privilege" was not the only counter-discourse that could displace the hegemony of "order" as a way of reading Pentonville. This most austere of prisons, this high temple of reason could become keyed to the gothic sensibility that had shadowed the aspirations of science for nearly a century. Even the silence was meaningful. In a telling choice of words, Hepworth Dixon noted "the stillness of the grave reigns in every part."[53] We might also consider the technique of hooding and masking prisoners outside their cells to prevent communication and to efface identity. A prisoner in such utilitarian garb is shown in figure 3. Henry Mayhew and John Binny were struck by this practice, and in a particular way. They speak of "eyes

FIGURE 3. Male convict of Pentonville. From Henry Mayhew and John Binny, *The Criminal Prisons of London and Scenes of Prison Life* (1862; London: Frank Cass, 1971).

seeming almost like phosphoric lights shining through the sockets of the skull. This gives the prisoners a half-spectral look ... the costume of the men seems like the outward vestment of some wandering soul rather than that of a human being; for the eyes, glistening through the apertures in the mask, give one the notion of a spirit peeping out behind it."[54] These revealing comments show the association of the prison with evil and mystery could be found even here at the apogee of the disciplinary ambition. A draconian policy intending to dehumanize and administer could be easily renarrated as simply spooky. We find echoes of this discursive layering even in criminological writing today. In the recent and authoritative *Oxford History of the Prison* Randall McGowen tells us that "the prison in the mid-nineteenth century was quiet and orderly, drab and functional," before mentioning in the very next sentence that "the eeriness of the building was exaggerated by the ghostly forms of convicts in uniforms and masks."[55] However rationalized it might have been as an institution, however austere its intended semiotic, Pentonville has always been a problematic and mysterious signifier.

Mettray

Singled out by Foucault as the "completion of the carceral system" and as the "disciplinary form at its most extreme, the model in which are concentrated all the coercive technologies of behavior," the boy's reformatory of Mettray has a pivotal role in his thinking. For Foucault, Mettray in the 1840s was a "training college in pure discipline" and an exemplar that assisted in the wider "normalization of the power of normalization, in the arrangement of a power-knowledge over individuals."[56] Was this *Colonie agricole* systematic and ordered? Yes. Foucault is right about this. Visitors in the 1840s reported movement "to the sound of trumpets and marching in military order."[57] They further noted the routines of morning schooling and afternoon farm work, learning trades, a host of petty rules and regulations whose inevitable infringement would bring punishment, minute record keeping, and medical and psychological examination. But the surface details of discipline and regulation do not exhaust Mettray nor come close to capturing its inner logic. A closer look shows it to be a charismatic institution with complex and hybrid cultural origins. This was deeply meaningful place, one that must be decoded if we are to interpret rather than simply describe its disciplinary regime.

One might begin by pointing to the welfarist motivations behind the project rather than its oppressive disciplinary ambitions. Charter documents show that Mettray's founders were well aware of the complex social origins of deviance. They noted "the unfortunate condition of the poor classes, and the state of moral inferiority to which they are condemned by the absence of a good system of education."[58] But taking this line does not get us too far. Foucault's system can encompass welfare as well as punitive discourses by redescribing these as two component dimensions of a more general circulation of power. Welfare, in his account, is yet another aspect of control. It is more useful for our purposes to note that Foucault's trump card of discipline masks the reality that Mettray—like the panopticon that we will explore in a later chapter—was a mongrel institution, a mishmash of conflicting codes and imperatives and not a pure and distilled essence of the disciplinary imagination. Even contemporaries could see this. Looking to the manifesto of the colony's founder, one critic wrote this was "a truly bizarre assembly of heterogeneous words and ideas, which seems to prove that there exists in the spirit of its directors some strongly regrettable confusion, indecision, and contradiction."[59] Here is a clue we can follow, for by decoding this ideological jumble we can come closer to the heart of Mettray and to understanding why the impulse toward disciplinary control took particular forms. The *why* of power can help us explain the *how*.

The first theme to be noted is a republican ethos. Mettray must be interpreted as a curiously French institution and not simply the carrier of some cookie cutter Euro-discipline. Training for the boys was designed not to make them docile, but virile, upstanding, and incorruptible. They were to be transformed from the scum of the earth into the salt of the earth, to become useful citizens of the republic schooled in military discipline, firefighting, farming, and even lifesaving swimming. So Mettray was not unlike the Foreign Legion. It was a place where the application of particular disciplines was driven by a code of honor oriented around the service of *la patrie* and the esteem of peers. Visitors from London's Philanthropic Society noticed this nationally specific ethos immediately. Sydney Turner, the resident chaplain of the society and Thomas Paynter, a committee member and police magistrate, were sent on a fact-finding mission to see if the Mettray experiment could be replicated in England. Their report makes for fascinating reading for they insist (contra Foucault's picture of transposable institutional schemas) that "there can be no mere transplanting of it [Mettray] to this country."[60] From their perspective Mettray's system of rewards and punishments had been organized around the pursuit of visible and secular status rewards, such as a place on the colony's honor roll. "The desire for reputation and approbation, by which their country-men are so strongly marked," was "among the most powerful of the im-pulses which are brought to bear on the 'colonists.'"[61] This public and civic dimension to conformity contrasted with the English system, where more emphasis must be given to the "power of thinking, and the habit of think-ing rightly" and more attention paid to the "great rule—overcome Evil with Good."[62] Likewise, Félix Cantagrel noted the presence of a patri-otic republican imperative. "Thanks to our institution," he wrote "these children, lost by their country, can pay off their debt and become equally suited to defend the soil of their nation and make it fertile."[63]

Cantagrel's comment points us towards our second hermeneutic key. Earth, *terroir,* this was the almost alchemical locus where the nation met na-ture. In Mettray the mission of producing honorable citizens engaged syn-ergistically with an Arcadian vision. Mettray's founder, Frédéric-Auguste Demetz (1796–1873), was profoundly influenced by Rousseau's utopian romanticism in proposing a farming colony without walls where "the boy would be improved by the land." "The house," he stated in his proposal for the colony, "will be built on the most favorable, picturesque site. The view of this beautiful countryside will vividly impress itself on the imagi-nation of the children, they will come to love the soil, which they will make fecund through cultivation, and it will leave in their hearts some happy memories."[64] As for the agricultural work, this would expose the boys to the beauty of nature and so "make the best sober workers and robust soldiers."[65] His dream was of a bucolic sanctuary as much as a prison, a place that allowed boys to be separated from more deeply pol-luted hardened criminals in tough adult institutions, and then inspired to-wards moral progress through contact with the purifying forces of nature. These youth should be considered as "innocents,"[66] whose violation of the law was not made under the condition of full criminal responsibility. As article 66 of the *Code pénal* stated, the boys were "sans discernement." They needed to be separated from the more intensely contagious evils of adult crime (most invariably described as a form of "corruption") and from real criminals or "corrupted men."[67] Children "find in prison," wrote one advocate, "the corruption of bad advice and bad example." This was simply a distasteful "revolting disorder" from which they needed to be rescued.[68] However, it was not only the adult criminal and the prison that were contaminated. Pivotal to this binary discourse that separated innocence from experience, the youth from the true criminal, was a dualistic opposition between the purity of the countryside and the pollution of the city. In the eyes of its sponsoring organization, Mettray was encoded less as a prison than as a reserve for children, a "guaranteed refuge, which will have all the advantages of distancing them from the hearths of corruption maintained in our grand centers of industry."[69] This explains the intensive and productive training in agriculture and trades rather than factory work. These would permit a small town life on release, lest "the unhappy child will be abandoned to all the hazards and all the perils . . . of the city."[70]

Once again, visitors were quick to perceive the hidden code, in this case the Arcadian dimension buried within the everyday life of the colony. Paul Huot, for example, went on a picnic with the boys. "Lit by the soft rays of the September sun," he wrote, the scene "made us all feel a certain emotion." It is telling that Huot likened the simple event to the great festivals of the Revolution or to those of ancient Greece. Here, he tells us, was an episode "symbolic of the childhood of the earth."[71] So in spirit Mettray was not really modern as Foucault claims but antimodern. It was a bucolic retreat, a ritualized and enchanted sanctuary from the disorders and dangers thrown out by modernity itself.

With a healthy, life-giving institution such as this Demetz had no difficulty recruiting distinguished individuals such as Alexis de Tocqueville and French royalty to the Société paternelle pour l'education morale et professionnelle des jeunes détenus. Nor was it a problem to encourage notables such as Matthew Davenport-Hill, the Reverend Sydney Turner of the Philanthropic Society, or Willem Hendrik Suringar, the founder of the "Dutch Mettray" to visit. Indeed such was the volume of these humanistic tourists that Demetz set up a *hôtel de la colonie,* and a minor genre of literary production, the Mettray traveler's tale (from which I have been quoting), emerged. In contrast to profane and liminal places such as Newgate or La Force, which were to be avoided, Mettray was a sacred place for reformers all over Europe. "No Mahommedan believes more devoutly in the efficacy of a pilgrimage to Mecca, than I do in one to Mettray," wrote the British humanist Davenport-Hill after his visit.[72] For Davenport-Hill Mettray's crowning glory was its pedagogical rather than disciplinary orientation. It was a "must see for philanthropic tourists."[73]

Davenport-Hill's curious choice of religious analogy alerts us to the third component in Mettray's cultural genome: it was a sect, not a bureaucracy. Demetz, and the project's major benefactor, the Vicomte Bretignères de Courteilles, were seen by contemporaries as visionary charismatics, "powerful and magnetic,"[74] engaged in what was deemed at the time as the "holy work"[75] of rehabilitation. Every sect requires a myth of origin, and so we find the journey of the initial, experimental group of inmates to Mettray related as a foundational moment, a progress of disciples to some promised land. Commentators repeatedly told of the boys' astonishment at being allowed to eat at the same table as the honest gentleman in a ritual of commensality when en route, and of how these deprived souls were enchanted by the sight of the moonlight on the river as they journey through the night. The trip was described as a "pious caravan" or "charitable pilgrimage"[76] towards a place of redemption.

In the reports of visitors, Mettray is depicted not only as progressive and humanitarian but more importantly as a place of spiritual purification. The Philanthropic Society's men, for example, speak of it as the home of a charismatic cult. In their eyes Demetz was not just an administrator but also an ascetic who "lays it down as a principle that self-denial in yourself is the essential condition of usefulness to others; and he teaches this in his own example, living himself in all respects as he requires the officers and boys to do."[77] He had made a "disinterested sacrifice" of his own ambitions.[78] Mettray as a sacred place required its staff in turn to "renounce the world"[79] following the pattern established by their Gandhi-like leader. This important observation allows us to confront the idea that Mettray was simply an impersonal organization of rules, roles, and buildings. Rather, it was noted that "the self-devotion and benevolence of M. Demetz's character have had much to do with the rapid and gratifying success that has attended his efforts." Consequently it could be reported that at Mettray "nothing is merely routine, merely mechanism; all is pervaded and animated with the earnest real character of the resident Director."[80]

Max Weber showed that charismatic authority in contrast to bureaucracy always brings problems of replication and succession. It is consistent with my theory but troubling for Foucault's that visitors to Mettray were concerned about these matters. Untutored though they may have been in classical social theory, contemporary commentators fully understood that Mettray could not simply be cloned because it was much more than an assemblage of off-the-shelf disciplinary techniques. It was a meaningful institution born from a ritualized, ascetic solidarity. Hence export to England was always going to be problematic regardless of the problem of national republicanism. If "taken up as a piece of government or corporate machinery, to be carried on by a mere code of discipline . . . it will probably and perhaps justly fail," Turner and Paynter write.[81] Institutions

like Mettray, they pointed out, needed to be "engaged in as a work of religion"[82] such that the boys come to "act rightly spontaneously and not me-
chanically, or by force."[83] A visitor from a few years earlier, Félix Cantagrel,
is in agreement with this anti-Foucaultian assessment: "[T]he success of
the colony rests not on its system of functioning . . . but on the capacity, the
intelligence of those who lead and maintain its activities."[84] Related to the
matter of propagation was the question of succession. "The question natu-
rally and continually suggests itself," remarked Turner and Paynter "How
will this go on? How can the work be made to prosper when he [Demetz]
is removed from it?" Likewise Cantagrel was concerned who might step
into the shoes of Demetz and the Vicomte Bretignères de Courteilles: "An
institution is a lot less solid, which depends on the coming together of a
pair of personalities."[85]

So in the case of Mettray, disciplinary techniques with their associated
instruction and work were underwritten by a republican ethos, Arcadian
mythologies, and charismatic asceticism. This was the cultural frame that
shaped its pattern of control and provided a wider public legitimacy. Yet
as the institution became routinized following the passing of its founders,
its methods themselves became suspect. They were recoded as brutalities
that were inherently polluting rather than purifying. By the early decades
of the twentieth century Mettray found itself often represented as a scandal, and so became a key signifier in a wider campaign against the very
children's penal colonies it had once inspired. In the 1930s this discourse
intensified, in part as response to the crushing of a revolt on the Belle Isle
in 1934 and the ensuing unseemly child hunt. A report by the journalists
Louis Roubaud and Alexis Danan assisted in seeing Mettray off, which
was closed in 1939 just before its centenary.[86]

Today we find Mettray taking on meanings very different from those
with which it was encoded by Demetz and early visitors or recoded by
later critics and Michel Foucault. If no longer an Arcadian retreat, it is
equally more than a reliquary of collective memories about functions and
intensities. As a signifier in a wider public sphere it has become a site of
literary pilgrimage thanks to its place in the biography and writings of
Jean Genet. In the semiautobiographical *Miracle de la rose,* Genet drew
upon his juvenile experiences in Mettray.[87] For this inmate Mettray and its
disciplinary regime provided a resource for the sexualized fantasy involving hierarchy, domination, and submission that was to be a leitmotif in his
work. Here the institution is triumphantly reinscribed in terms of the discourse of pleasure and creative self-actualization. It is both a prison and

not a prison, a source of identity, a place where the cult of the individual can be celebrated today by writer and bookish tourist alike. Importantly for Genet and for my argument, Mettray was sacred in his eyes. He famously described it as a "paradise" even as he outlined its harsh regime.[88] Using Proustian techniques, the narrator of *Miracle de la rose* recaptures the past with a nostalgia that is also reverential. Then, as the literary critic Richard N. Coe puts it, Genet goes about "eliminating the profane dimension of time by superimposing different fragments of experience in time one on top of the other" and then "super-imposing a third plane of experience . . . this is the plane of the sacred, of existence which is still technically in life, but in fact outside life, space and time alike."[89] Foucault interviewed Genet about Mettray but never seems to have come to terms with the reality that the institution had a symbolic or imaginative dimension lurking just behind the disciplinary facade. To have done so would have been to admit that discipline and meaning can indeed go hand in hand.

Newgate, Pentonville, Mettray: these were sites of deeply meaningful practices. Newgate was an institution tainted by debauchery and squalor, marked by feeble boundaries and diverse miscegenation. Pentonville was a utopian solution to this disorder. It was a disciplinary shrine to purity. Mettray was a sectlike refuge where austerity and nature would purify wayward innocents. In time this too became rescripted as a chaotic den of vice. Each of these sites can be understood as an ambiguous and contested object at the heart of the eternal struggle between purity and pollution. It might be thought that such diverse and colorful readings belong to another time, that the prison today has become banal or that meanings have been routinized. No so. The remainder to this chapter documents continuity in cultural process. Again we find a civil discourse reflecting upon institutions, practices, and innovations, sniffing out disorders, locating evil, engaging in critique. We begin with the spiritual heir to Pentonville, the "supermax" prison.

The Supermax Prison

The supermax prison is conventionally interpreted as a strongly punitive, high-security technology for holding dangerous individuals such as terrorists, psychopaths, and mass murderers. Its birth is usually attributed to an act of prison-generated disorder. On 23 October 1983 two guards were murdered by members of the Aryan Brotherhood prison gang in the federal penitentiary at Marion, Illinois. The prison was deemed ungovernable. A twenty-three-hour lockdown resulted that lasted for years.[90] From this inauspicious start the idea slowly consolidated that the most dangerous inmates should be held apart from routine felons. As *Corrections Today* reported, these were the people who "continue to wage war on the correctional system and society from inside existing state facilities," usually through the use of violence on other inmates or through gang activities.[91]

From the late-Durkheimian perspective the innovation can read as a defensive, boundary-maintaining maneuver designed to control radical evil and petty pollution, to cut out incivil disorders like riots, rapes, and murders. Like Pentonville before it, the supermax prison offers a sterile environment of less than splendid isolation. The predatory offenders are held in solitary confinement, their movements monitored, and their cells minimalist. The inmates are cut off from each other, with most services delivered to their seventy-square-foot den, where they remain on average twenty-three hours per day. Even exercise is a solitary affair in a cage, for "when we let them rec together they were killing each other."[92] Guards rarely interact with the inmates, but maintain contact through intercoms and surveillance cameras. The doors are operated automatically and consist of a perforated metal sheet, whose dime-sized air holes can be closed off should the prisoner start making trouble.

For all its ingenuity and ability to regulate interpersonal embodied disorders, like so many harsh institutions before it the supermax prison has become vulnerable to attack in civil discourse. Its very austerity has been renarrated as a marker of excess. The supermax prison violates the boundaries of the sign of the prison. It is read as a freakish torture chamber. Media reports on supermax prisons endlessly, repetitiously, voyeuristically recount the detail of deprivation—the meals that come in through a slot in the door, the day's food ground into a loaf for the recalcitrant, the exercise cage with its rubber ball, the thirteen-inch, notably black-and-white TV beaming religious and educational programs.[93] An accurate account? Perhaps. Yet it is also one that freely circulates the signifiers of clinical sadism and petty control freakery. This is a purgatory, a spooky nonplace "with almost no human contact, akin to a living death."[94]

Attempts by prisoners' advocates to introduce the Eighth Amendment feed off this wider discourse in which new forms of harm and disorder are located at the core of the antiseptic operation of the clean machine. If the supermax prison was able to clamp down on interpersonal violence, this came at the price of mental health problems and the consequent disrespect and disorganization of the self. We find this theme maintained, for example, in the 1991 *Madrid v. Gomez* class action suit against the "neo-Orwellian hell" of Pelican Bay State Prison in California.[95] Or put another way, the supermax prison could be described as the "high tech equivalent of the nineteenth-century snake pit."[96] Critics warned that supermax-generated disordering behaviors could be projected outside the institution upon release. Peaceful communities were threatened because supermaxed convicts were no longer human. There was the case of Robert Scully, a small-time crook who became a brutal murderer on his release from Pelican Bay in 1995. "Kept in a sensory deprivation box for years on end," he had become evil, "a creature of brutal and obsessive impulse," and "a violent animal capable only of acting on instinct."[97] Obsessive order was now said to create chaotic disorder. Solitary confinement in the supermax prison was driving prisoners "stark raving mad . . . just as it did to prisoners in the Pennsylvania System of confinement 170 years ago."[98]

Such parallels are worth exploring, for debates over the supermax indeed mimic those of another period. During the nineteenth century in the United States and England alike there was contestation between two models of penal administration. The Pennsylvania or "separate system" had Quakerish origins and involved prolonged periods of isolation. In Durkheimian terms this can be understood as an enforcement of the ascetic path towards ritual purification. Silence and solitude were thought to bring reflection on past actions, awareness of wickedness, and penitence. The Auburn system, developed in New York State, involved collective work activities and meals within the daily round. During the ideological struggle between these two patterns, critics of the separate system zeroed in on the question of mental disturbance, suggesting that this was a mode of prison organization that produced rather than reduced disorder. Pentonville was called a "maniac making prison" in the *Times* as it told of an inmate carted off to the asylum.[99] Dickens shared this perspective. During an early tour to America he visited the Philadelphia prison and later famously spoke of an inhumane process that involved "tampering with the mysteries of the brain."[100] Two generations later, the writer John Galsworthy was to publish an open letter denouncing closed-cell confinement, speak of an inhumane "machine of justice" and dramatize the mental agonies of solitude in a notably confronting scene in his play *Justice*.[101] So the innovations of disciplinary knowledge in its purest form were vulnerable to a humanistic critique. They were read as the robotic and cruel application of bureaucratic logics to human problems, as generating the evils of abuse, as intrusions into the deepest pockets of the sacred self. It is a twist that Foucault truly never foresaw, that heavy discipline itself could be narrated as polluted and evil and that such retelling could have real impacts. As the nineteenth century wound on separate systems were gradually wound back, partly for reasons of cost but also because of the growing credibility of such counter-narration. They just looked bad.

History has repeated itself. In recent commentaries we find the supermax prison overwhelmingly described as a profanity. It is a place that, like Pentonville, can generate its own mystique and disorderly gothic horrors. A feature in *Newsweek*, for example, referred to the U.S. Penitentiary Administrative Maximum Facility (ADX) in Florence, Colorado, as a "new Alcatraz" and as the "Hellhole of the Rockies." "The cells look like they were designed for Hannibal Lecter," it continued, referring to the spooky fictional psychopath usually portrayed by actor Anthony Hopkins. "The triangular main building is like something out of M. C. Escher—full of angles and obstructions that aren't quite what they seem . . . that makes it hard for inmates or visitors to tell precisely where they are within the prison building, which complicates planning rescues or escapes."[102] The Estelle Unit at Hunstville, Texas, could be described in the *Atlantic Monthly* as a "computer-controlled hidden hell at the heart of America's burgeoning incarceration establishment," a place where "a prisoner self-mutilated, slashing at the veins in his hands until his blood spurted over the walls, the floor, and the steel seat of the cell he was in, like a peculiarly vivid Jackson Pollock painting." Here the air filled with the "howls and screams of the close-to-naked inmates. It was a hideous sound that would have been familiar in the lunatic asylums of bygone centuries."[103] Likewise, the *Times-Picayune* quotes a Harvard psychiatrist in its feature review on the new supermax prison at Tamms, Illinois.[104] He speaks of inmates "smearing themselves with faeces, mumbling and screaming incoherently all day and night, some even descending to the horror of eating parts of their own bodies."

As an institution dedicated to control, it is ironic that over the past twenty years the supermax prison has been unable to control its own narration. This is a place of Gothic disorders, of chaos, madness, and evil where souls are destroyed. Far from being a technology that was cleaning up prisons and preventing disorders, the supermax had simply made the state responsible for barbarisms. Ruling on a Pelican Bay inmate's class action suit, federal district judge Thelton E. Henderson spoke of "senseless suffering and sometimes wretched misery"; "grossly excessive force," and "constitutional violations." Once again a spotless, high-tech prison had become simply another Bastille.[105]

The Country Club Prison

The pollution of the supermax has not indemnified from critique more liberal interpretations of the idea of confinement. Consider the demise of the federal minimum security prison. Aside from the cost savings inherent to the low-security environment, such institutions have the merit of separating out nonviolent offenders from the violent and thereby mitigating some of the unintended pains of imprisonment. Such a rationale could not protect an apparently humane and worthy punitive option from satirical renarration. The "country club prison" or "Club Fed" was to serve as an emblem of weak deterrence and liberal failure before being phased out in the 1990s.

Narrations in this case usually took the form of farce. We can see discourse on the country club prison replicating some of the patterns of that on eighteenth-century Newgate but with a subtly different emphasis on patrician rather than proletarian pleasures. The complaint here is not on lowly disorders of the body nor carnival but rather the problematic boundary between punishment and leisure that is violated by signifiers of luxury. Commentaries relentlessly play upon the incongruities arising from the juxtaposition of the signifier "prison" with images of privilege and exclusivity. Such an ironic inversion of expectations could only lead to the conclusion that the federal minimum security prison could not be typified as a "prison." These were boundary-defying institutions that needed to be brought back into line.

Blessed with a great climate, the celebrated Lompoc facility in California held white-collar inmates such as the Watergate conspirators, as well as doctors, lawyers, and dodgy real estate developers. In the *New York Times* we read how this prison was without walls or fences, and how members could enjoy cable TV, tennis and jogging, and a salad bar.[106] Mimicking the kind of resort rankings we find in *Condé Nast Traveller,* the July 1992 issue of *Playboy* magazine ran a feature listing the county's top prisons in terms of quality of life and amenities. The jail in Fairbanks, Alaska, rated highly for serving fresh king crab. The Oahu Community Correctional Center, Hawaii, offered aerobics classes and held luaus with hula dancers and roast pig on holidays. Boulder County Jail offered a "smoke-free environment" where "several times a year local musicians perform open air, co-ed concerts." Meanwhile, at Evans County Jail in Georgia "inmates dress in robes and slippers, lounge on down pillows and watch movies"—an image which immediately conjures thoughts of publisher Hugh Hefner relaxing in his Playboy Mansion.[107]

The low-security women's prison in Danbury, Connecticut, offered 348 acres of rolling New England hills and was once the home of Watergate's G. Gordon Liddy. The problem here, we are told by the *New York Times*, was keeping people out. Prison officials were trying to stop locals using the land for bucolic recreational activities such as snowmobiling, boating, skating, flying kites or simply walking the dog.[108] A *Los Angeles Times* report on the former prison at Eglin Air Force Base in Florida conjures up the imagery of inmates arriving "in fancy cars driven by chauffeurs." "These big shots," it continues, "may try Italian lawn bowling or indulge themselves on the tennis courts, play a game of racquetball or take a turn on the foot trail that winds through the landscaped grounds and past a lake." In the evening they can watch movies and visit the commissary for a cup of cappuccino and some Häagen-Dazs Macadamia Brittle. One prisoner said "he learned a great deal from a stock options course taught by an inmate who used to be a commodities broker."[109] When the notorious inside trader Ivan Boesky was put away in the low-security wing of the Lompoc federal prison camp outside Santa Barbara, California, the London *Times* enjoyed reported whimsically that he could look forward not only to a job paying 11 cents an hour but also to tennis and softball, a golf driving range and jogging track, and the fragrance of roses and eucalyptus trees.[110] Just as the cocoa ration at Pentonville had marked out a "palace prison" to the Victorians, these country club prisons were looking like luxury resorts. Regardless of low costs and low recidivism rates they had to go.

The Chain Gang as Ambivalent Signifier

If the country club prison was to succumb to the critique that it produced excess pleasure and so was not a prison, and the supermax prison narrated as a dungeon of high-tech horrors, then perhaps efforts to innovate should be visible and traditional. We might perhaps improve on the conventional prison by making life there just a little tougher. But there is no easy channel between Scylla and Charybdis: take the case of the chain gang. As John

Pratt points out, punishments directed against the body survived longer in the deep South than in the north of the United States.[111] These reflected the relatively weak penetration of a civilizing process into an agrarian society whose culture had been decisively influenced by the experience of slavery. As is well known, although the outcome of the Civil War went some way towards effecting institutional and legal change, the cultural system lagged. This lagging was facilitated by federalism and institutional fragmentation into systems of local justice. Visible displays of humiliation and brutality were found generally acceptable even when rejected elsewhere in the United States, especially those directed against black bodies. The chain gang finally came under sustained attack in the South of the 1920s and 1930s. Memoirs of abuse, usually from white inmates, started to generate scandal. Assisted by its own Hollywood genre the chain gang became associated with brutality, corruption, and overwork and was to finally disappear in the 1960s.

Yet by the 1990s efforts underpinned by the politics of penal populism were being made to revive the chain gang. Conservative advocates were attracted to its ability to function as a visible symbol of tough justice in contrast to the closed world of the prison. Hence when Senator Charlie Crist of Florida advocated the reintroduction of public chain gangs in 1997 he made the curious suggestion that tourists driving through the state would be reassured by this display of the rule of law. Likewise, Democrat supporter George Kirkpatrick believed that they would be an effective deterrent to marginal drifters for "the best billboard for migrant criminals to see is these folk out on the road."[112]

Such cheery sentiments and empathic speculations could not eliminate a wider and embedded concern that the chain gang remained a polluted practice. Critique played along two themes. The spirit of the first was that the chain gang did not respect the cult of the individual but rather degraded and humiliated. When Alabama reintroduced chain gangs in the 1990s the media were soon circling. Newsweek spoke of a "haunting spectacle" and quoted an inmate saying, "This ain't nothing but a circus, a big old zoo. We all animals now."[113] The chain gang, it seemed, violated the boundaries of an appropriate punishment experience by subjecting the individual to prurient voyeurism. This critique was echoed when the populist sheriff Joe Arpaio introduced all-female chain gangs in his Arizona county to pick up trash and clear weeds along highways. It was noted that motorists honked as they went past. Critics such as Donna Hamm of the prisoners' rights group Middle Ground once again used the words "circus" and "zoo."[114] These are telling metaphors suggesting not only subhuman treatment but also the immorality of visibility and the gaze. The chain gang could all too easily be read as polluted because it debased even those who saw it. This was not about work or discipline but was "about humiliation, the modern-day equivalent of the ducking stool." Liberal commentators to the *New York Times* agreed with this assessment insisting that the chain gang's purpose was simply to "let motorists gorge on a visible symbol of punishment and humiliation," thus and it was "morally repugnant."[115] In fine, the chain gang eliminated the sacred right to appear with dignity before other people.

The chain gang could also be keyed to more regionally specific narratives of pollution. Consider, for example, the way a reporter described the early morning scene at Limestone Correctional Facility in Alabama. Under the headline "Link to the Past," the writer makes telling and effortless reference to a forest of old-growth collective representations.

> The inmates are not talking yet, but hugging themselves and stomping their feet in the cool air of dawn. The tracking dogs, pampered bloodhounds, are asleep in their kennels.
>
> In groups of five, the prisoners, dressed in white, approach the guards and then kneel before them. The bright metal chains come out of their wooden boxes, clinking and rattling, and then the men are strung together, ankle to ankle, five on a leash.
>
> It seems like the old days, the long-ago time. But the images are modern, a stereotyped Dixie porn of the bad old South rising from the grave, old scenes of young black men shuffling along in chains under the glare of shotgun-toting white guards wearing dark shades.[116]

Because the chain gang could so readily conjure the imagery of slavery and Jim Crow, African American groups were able to quickly and effectively condemn them as an incitement to the evils of racism. Powerless blacks would be on display to passing whites in air-conditioned automobiles. "Let there be no mistake about it," wrote a contributor to *U.S. Catholic*, "there is an unambiguous historical connection between chain gangs and slavery. At the beginning of this century chain gangs were used as a mechanism to keep African Americans in involuntary servitude even after Emancipation."[117] "The practice is riddled with racial connotations, dating to the use of chain gangs in slavery," wrote another critic hoping to stop their introduction in Kansas and suggesting that this move could sully its clean reputation as a free state at the time of the Civil War.[118] This sensibility could even be registered overseas. "Most people, and certainly all black people, instinctively associate chain gangs with slavery," wrote a critic in the London *Times,* pointing to the fact that slaves were chained when transported for sale and that African Americans are likely to be overrepresented in prison populations.[119] The semiotic connection between chain gang and racism was so entrenched that the chain gang could be only too easily paired with the electric chair as evidence of the wider "harshness and discrimination" of criminal justice.[120] Efforts were made to shed the deeply polluted racist overtones. Governor Fob James Junior of Alabama, for example, implemented scrupulously racially mixed chain gangs (three blacks, two whites). Yet he was soon to have good excuse to drop the culturally disastrous policy. When an inmate was shot, the state implemented individual shackling in place of collective chains. An effort to communicate about crime and punishment, the chain gang is a problematic disciplinary technique whose symbolic shackles generally prove too weighty for its advocates.

Consuming the Prison

Over the past few pages we have seen that the prison of modernity with its diverse policies and disciplinary modalities might be thought of as more than a simple administrative technology organized around the circulation of power or the punishment and reform of the self. It is simultaneously an imaginative innovation whose evolution responds to the deep cultural imperative for order and purity. It is a signifier tied to a wider nexus of visions and imaginings of social life and social pathology. Throughout their history prisons have attempted to cleanse *themselves* as much as to control their inmates. Reforms and attempted innovations have also been ritualistic efforts to eliminate pollutions and evils, both great and small, and to align specific institutions and practices with the legitimate sign of the prison in a wider civil discourse.

Recognizing the prison as a once and future contested signifier rather than simply as the domain of penal practices can alert us to a sensitivity in the collective conscience. This is the growing tendency to read the prison as deeply polluted, shameful, and evil. It betrays itself, for example, in the hiding of the prison over recent decades. As far back as the late-Victorian era we find prisons starting to have a negative impact on property values.

As John Pratt eloquently puts it, "for the general public, it was as if the very idea of the prison had become indelibly tainted with ugliness and morbidity, both in terms of what its design represented, and knowledge of the leperlike population hidden behind its walls."[121] An undesirable landmark, the prison, like the lunatic asylum, was damaging real estate markets more through symbolic contagion than through any rational calculus of danger. After all jail breaks were rare. Resident protests saw new prisons constructed in increasingly remote, out-of-town locations rather than in the leafy suburbs. Urban blight came to surround the older Victorian prisons in what Pratt neatly calls a "pathological symbiosis of decay."[122] In response, prison architecture changed over the twentieth century, with newer institutions hidden by plantings and mounds. Names have adjusted too. Now we have the "corrections center" and "holding facility," just as the garbage dump has become a "transfer station." Such camouflaged and neutered identities suggest a distance not only from the vivid tableau of Newgate but also from Jebb's image of a concerned public taking an informative and relaxing stroll through the arcades of Pentonville. The problem of pollution has engendered a defensive semiotic strategy of dissimulation and invisibility. It is this cultural process that has facilitated what progress there has been over the past century and a half towards bureaucratic closure. As the public turns its back on a polluted institution and its evil inmates, popular interest in prisoner welfare has drifted. But this does not mean that public interest in the prison itself or what it symbolizes has decreased. Indeed, in some ways the prison is now more attractive than ever.

For all the problems that symbolic evil and pollution pose to bureaucratic authorities and concerned residents it can have its compensations, even financial ones. We find this colorful spectrum of advantages refracted out most clearly in the unlikely prism of prison tourism and prison-themed consumption. It is in this arena that we can draw our chapter to a close, indicating in its most heightened form the diversity and commodity value of the prison as sign. In years gone by, executions, Bedlams, and Bridewells provided a recreational destination for the curious. Today visitors find something equally compelling in the temporary imaginative assumption of a transgressive identity that can arise from entering into direct personal contact with the spaces of evil. This has proven to be especially the case for those iconic prisons that have come to the fore as carriers of myths where themes of brutality, heroism, and the supernatural are intertwined. Such prison tourism can be understood as part of a wider social trend sometimes thought of as "dark tourism" that involves explorations of sites as diverse as battlefields, slave plantations, and death camps. This has been propelled by the contemporary touristic desire for encounters with the "extraordinary" and "authentic" rather than packaged and routine. It has been further accelerated by the availability of suitable venues. Every year older prisons are taken off line, rendered obsolete by innovations in prison design and management. Planning rules and heritage zoning can also play a part. If demolition is not an option, then conversion to some other use—perhaps even as a hotel—provides a way to pay the bills.[123]

There are many abandoned and historic buildings, yet few disused factories, warehouses, or schools ever become tourist attractions. Who cares? It is the mythologies surrounding the prison that marks them out as a profitable draw for visitors. These myths can involve heroic stories of triumph over adversity. For example, in Robben Island, off Cape Town, tourists are motivated primarily by the locale's role in the collective fight against the unqualified evil of apartheid.[124] At Alcatraz the major hook has been the prison's centrality to movies such as *The Birdman of Alcatraz, The Rock, Murder in the First,* and *Escape from Alcatraz,* which celebrate more individual struggles against the bureaucratic evil of a brutalizing and inhumane prison system, and inmate efforts to preserve the dignity of the self. Such touristic locations are particularly attractive if they can be associated with unusual levels of pain and suffering, if they are in some way evil or polluted beyond the norm. Alcatraz has the iconic blessings of isolation, swirling currents, allegedly shark-infested waters, and a policy of secrecy that kept the media at a distance for years. Further there is resonance with the myth of Tantalus. The inmates could gaze at the bright lights of the city just a mile or so away. A steady supply of notorious criminals such as Al Capone and Machine Gun Kelly amplified a reputation as a den of sinners. From a late-Durkheimian perspective it is no accident that it was commonly known as "Hellcatraz" or as "Uncle Sam's Devil's Island." Such terms are none too subtle in indicating the presence of profound evil, although whether this is the property of the institution or its inhabitants is moot.[125] The narrative is fixed in books and postcards as well as in virtual locations such as the Web site www.alcatrazhistory.com. A little clicking here and there shows a strong focus on notorious individuals, degrading prison conditions (such as "The Hole"), and escape attempts. The site begins by locating the web surfer in the subject position of the new inmate and conjures an image of chilling horror.

Imagine yourself cold and shivering on a damp and thickly fogged-in morning. Heavy steel shackles squeeze your wrists and ankles, and the constricting metal seems to amplify the cold. Your movements are constrained, which makes it difficult to maintain your balance as you embark on the island ferry. You catch a brief glimpse of what will soon be your new home across the foggy bay.[126]

If the cultural matrix that supports prison tourism brings both public interest and revenue, it can also be a meaning pattern that generates problems. Prison tourism is itself prone to a second-order renarration as voyeuristic and morally suspect, as the exercise of a polluted gaze. Trying to control this can present severe problems of genre management. For example, visitor efforts to uncover stories of "Hellcatraz" have continually run up against the official ideologies and heritage values of "Alcatraz." Authorities seek to design tours that are instructive about the natural history of the island, its once important lighthouse, the relationship of Native Americans to the island, and its role as a military fort. They also wish to introduce complexity into narrations and focus in Foucault-like ways on shifting visions of crime and punishment as these have played out in the administration of the prison. They narrate celebrated inmates in ways that highlight their petty character: the Birdman was a thug, Al Capone was a tax cheat, and so forth. Few are interested. Rangers report frustration that Hollywood sensationalism has cheapened this serious mission and wish they could "burn every negative of Hollywood film."[127] So at Alcatraz prison tourism has resulted in expert knowledge fighting a losing battle against popular culture, much as prisons throughout their history have seen experts besieged by unruly collective representations. Propelled by the seductions of evil, the experience of visiting a sacred space is one that celebrates myth and rejects institutionally sanctioned but rather unexciting forms of knowledge. By encouraging visitors to the island of Alcatraz, the National Parks Service has unwittingly perpetuated what it wishes to eliminate. The subversive power of evil and its ability to trump more bureaucratic, authorized cultural narratives can also be found in Huntsville, Texas. The identity of this place has been overcoded by its role as the center of the state's prison industrial complex. Notoriety and symbolic pollution have eliminated efforts to cultivate more positive meanings for the town. Huntsville wishes to bill itself as the birthplace of the patriot Samuel Houston. Yet despite the best efforts of the local visitor center, trippers seem less interested in lessons about this man who "lived and practiced law" than in undertaking a prison driving tour and seeing its eight prisons, including the Walls Unit Prison where inmates are put to death.[128]

The general problem of finding a socially acceptable way to manage the consumption of evil can be found worldwide in the vexing matter of prison hotels. These institutions mimic the classificatory problems of the country club prison and eighteenth-century Newgate. The boundary between the prison and pleasure is once again confounded and transgressed, but now the familiar problematic is uneasily inscribed in the domain traced by collective memory rather than penal administration. Controversy over the consumerist appropriation of the signifiers and spaces of punishment has been most intense when some aspect of a shameful or heroic national narrative is obliterated or trivialized by tourist developments. Hoheneck Castle was at one time East Germany's women's prison for female dissidents. Plans to convert this into a hotel experience were met with howls of protest by former political prisoners. Guests were to be offered the chance to sleep in a tiny cell and eat bad food for $122 per night.[129] A similar outcry followed efforts to convert into a three-star hotel the former prison in Prague where dissident hero and later president Vaclav Havel had been imprisoned. Once again, the feeling is that like oil and water, fun and the prison shouldn't mix. Suffering leaves a stain, a sacred mark that must be respected, not cheaply commodified.

Notwithstanding such cultural obstacles, successful prison hotels can be found in places as well-heeled and diverse as Lucerne, Boston, and Oxford. The last of these, Oxford Prison was converted into a hotel and luxury apartments after its closure in 1996. Here the faintest whiff of evil is combined with the prison's minimalism to generate product differentiation. To give the building character and attract customers, the high-end developers Malmaison (most famous for their overlarge beds) retained some prison motifs and infrastructure such as the metal catwalks and stairs, and the heavy wooden gates. The governor's office has become a wine bar. Notably, however, sensibilities surrounding the evil left sacred remain and have influenced design decisions. Areas deemed too macabre, such as the execution chambers and the treadmill room, have been converted into offices.[130] A little less upscale is the Langholmen Hotel in Stockholm. This offers Spartan, prison-style rooms and sells striped T-shirts and plastic shackles. It is said to be a popular venue for murder-mystery dinner parties.[131]

As the Oxford Prison and Langholmen show, former penitentiaries are an ambiguous and malleable but also potent signifier whose ethos can be reworked as a resource for profitable aesthetic creativity. If sinister and heroic meanings with their gothic and romantic narratives are sufficiently suppressed, prisons can even be read as a vanguard institution of modernism. The apparatus of discipline and austerity becomes itself transvalued as an expression of the sublime and chic. Prison-design washstands, toilets, and other simply and solidly engineered stainless steel fixtures have come to be seen as emblematic of distinction rather than degradation. When Amanda Freedman converted her three-bedroom Victorian house into a one-bedroom, open-plan minimalist space, she chose kitchen units, door locks, and toilets from a manufacturer who caters to the prison market.[132] The *Wall Street Journal* reports that prison-style toilets by Acorn Engineering selling for $1,000 a piece were a hot item—they could make an award winning towel rack.[133]

Perhaps we should conclude with the Acorn toilet. The tour presented here has highlighted that there is more to the history of the prison than Foucault's rather grim picture might lead us to suppose. Always more than a closed body of rationalized, routinized knowledge and techniques, the prison is a contested signifier. In its life and afterlife the carceral has never been able to escape from myths that autointerpolate within a complex system of signs. The very evolution of the prison system, the precise techniques of discipline, these are profoundly shaped by the quest for public legitimacy. They are a response to the stubborn and obstinate tellings that circulate in civil discourse and endlessly generate trouble. The prison is a collective representation at play in a semiotic minefield whose nodes are purity and pollution, order and disorder, evil and its elimination. Even after the last inmate has departed, the prison remains a potent signifier, a dangerous myth. Its meanings are legion, and so it must be handled with care.

CHAPTER FOUR

The Panopticon

Writing in 1965 the cultural critic Gertrude Himmelfarb lamented the neglect that the panopticon had suffered in scholarship. "Not only historians and biographers," she wrote, "but even legal and penal commentators seem to be unfamiliar with some of the most important features of Bentham's plan."[1] Now our grievance might take a contrary form. Historians of punishment and theorists of surveillance alike have pushed Jeremy Bentham's remarkable contraption to the center of attention. We are able to quip that time has proven the wily utilitarian right. For today's intellectuals the panopticon truly is "inescapable."

Pivotal to this thematic ascendancy, of course, was Michel Foucault's decision to treat the panopticon simultaneously as the intellectual blueprint for a new modality of power, as the theoretical emblem for his vision of surveillance society, and as an empirically significant moment in the evolution of punishment systems. This tour de force jump started a new literature that is profuse but not without problems. The historians of punishment have become caught up in a web of details but not engaged with the broader theoretical claim. For example, the fate of panopticism might be contrasted with that of alternative models for penal administration, from the Speenhamland system of parish poor relief to flagship projects like Pentonville, whether realized or simply programmatic.[2] The impetus here tends to be descriptive (what happened?) rather than analytic or evaluative. As for the social theorists, they take panopticism as a warning and Foucault as a legitimating charter for abstract and wide-ranging discussions on modernity and its discontents. For the most part they have not looked in detail at Bentham's original proposal but rather taken Foucault at his word, then engaged in theoretically informed dialogue on contemporary para-panopticisms, ranging from security cameras to information technologies to reality television shows. The focus here seems to be on

cataloging modes of panopticism and surveillance, inventing creative ne-
ologisms for the diverse panopticisms that characterize contemporary life,
and allocating responsibility between the state and private enterprise for
each of these.[3] Criminologists, meanwhile, seem concerned mostly with
applied and empiricist questions of measurement and efficacy. What, for
example, is the effectiveness of surveillance cameras for crime reduction?
Do they impact upon fear of crime?[4]

What is missing in all such hubbub is a systematic interrogation of Foucault's own account of the panopticon through an effort to theoretically
interpret Bentham's writings. To be sure, the historians have taken occasional pot shots. Yet these appear ad hoc and incidental to whatever task
of historical exposition is at hand. The general thrust of such reports is
that the panopticon was a-typical and should not have been given centrality in an account of nineteenth-century penal evolution. This, however,
is a largely empirical critique that can only engage tangentially with the
core concerns of social theory. What is attempted here is a broader and
more sustained incursion against Foucault's position that first uses the historian's concern for the empirical to revisit Jeremy Bentham's proposal
and then offers some general reflections on punishment technology and
society. The conclusion will be that Foucault's version of Bentham's panopticon is in some ways inaccurate—it was not the unadulterated spirit of
disciplinary observation. Further we will also see that it can be understood
in broadly Durkheimian ways. The panopticon was more than a simple
and efficient technology. It was intended as a communicative institution,
was open to its civil society, was informed by the cultural expectations and
moral sensibilities of its time, and was tied to sacred, utopian visions as
well as to unintended profane imaginings about social control.

The panopticon is peculiarly well suited to become the lever for broad
reflections on Foucault's sociology of punishment, the force of critique
being amplified by its analytic and symbolic function as a middle-range,
"empirical" illustration of his more abstract genealogical principles. After
all, some thirty or more years after the publication of *Surveiller et punir* it
is the panopticon—to which he devotes an extraordinary chapter—that
really stands out as the central exhibit in Michel Foucault's analysis of
the disciplinary logic of modernity. When the abstractions are forgotten,
the somewhat sinister image of the panopticon remains and reminds. For
Foucault, Bentham's "cruel, ingenious cage" fixes in a crystalline form the
essence of new modalities of social control revolving around surveillance,
classification, expert knowledge, and the restless, incessant imposition of

discipline.[5] Here, it would seem, is an architectural contraption whose origins and logic of functioning lie nowhere other than in the ruthless pursuit of technological efficiency and the cold-hearted fusion of power and knowledge in the age of reason. For in taking the panopticon as representative of a new logic of control, Foucault presents us with a device that is emptied of cultural inputs other than those of modernity's administrative aspiration. Whereas the spectacle of the scaffold had involved reference to the sacred mandate of sovereign power and had been surrounded by superstitious observances, the panopticon is presented as simply a machine for the systematic and rational reform of deviants.

For all its persuasive force and rhetorical brilliance such a treatment of the panopticon is deeply misleading and in need of challenge. The origins of Foucault's error can be found in his hyperbolic, all-or-nothing approach to the transformation of punishment with the onset of modernity. As we reviewed in chapter 1, for Foucault the years between around 1750 and 1840 saw a dramatic shift between two modalities of power. In the prior era social control was enforced through intermittent, public displays of violence against the body. These spectacles of suffering were allegorical and didactic. They were a semiotic system, theatrical displays directed to an audience of unruly onlookers and with deterrent intent. By the nineteenth century, punishment had moved out of the town square and into sequestered institutions administered by knowledgeable experts. Now power operated through a continual and relentless process using rational techniques of surveillance, classification, and discipline to enforce conformity and to normalize—or as liberals would have it "reform"—the deviant. These disciplinary institutions go on to conquer society, replacing the hierarchical feudal system with a so-called "carceral city" or "carceral archipelago" of ordered and regulated populations. In this dystopia culture persists only insofar as prisons and other reformatories are driven by norms and rules of efficiency and calculability. This is a "thin" institutional culture of instrumental reason rather than a "thick" culture where penal process can be modified or constrained by deeply held, nonrational convictions, by moral ethos, by the mythologies wherein it becomes embedded in multiple semiotic fields as a contested symbol. Foucault's representation of the panopticon is necessarily consistent with this metanarrative. It has to be so, for it is a key exhibit in his case. But like the glove in the O. J. Simpson trial, it fails to live up to closer scrutiny. When we try it on for size we find that the theory, like the glove, doesn't fit.[6] The problem is not so much that Foucault oversimplifies for purposes of intellectual effect, but

rather that in neglecting the complex and hybrid, negotiated, culturally inflected aspects of Bentham's proposal he fails to develop accurate insight
into how disciplinary ideas might be shaped, motivated, and tempered by
cultural forces "on the ground," to see that the "how" of punishment might
indeed be influenced by more than simply instrumental reason.[7]

Those who are unfamiliar with the panopticon are fortunate that the
principles behind this innovation were laid out in a typically rigorous fashion by its sponsor, the ultrasystematic utilitarian philosopher Jeremy Bentham in a series of letters of 1787 and in two lengthy postscripts.[8] Each
innovation is meticulously described, explained, and justified. It is this unusually rigorous approach that no doubt attracted Foucault, himself an
orderly thinker, as he looked to outline a new logic of control.

> The building is circular . . . the apartments of the prisoners occupy the circum-
> ference. These cells are divided from one another, and the prisoners by that
> means secluded from all communication with each other, by partitions . . . The
> apartment of the inspector occupies the centre; you may call it if you please
> the inspector's lodge. [There is] a vacant space . . . between such centre and
> such circumference . . . To the windows of the lodge there are blinds . . . The es-
> sence of it consists, then, in the centrality of the inspector's situation combined
> with the well-known and most effectual contrivances for seeing without being
> seen. . . . the persons being inspected should always feel themselves as if under
> inspection.[9]

Such one-way observation would limit possibilities for collective action
and result in self-policing conformity. Foucault enthusiastically translates
this utilitarian blueprint into his wider sociology of control. The effect of
the panopticon, he writes, is "to induce in the inmate a state of conscious
and permanent visibility that assures the automatic functioning of power"
in which the prisoner becomes "the principle of his own subjection." Bentham had provided a "diagram of a mechanism of power reduced to its
ideal form." Here was a technology that was intended to reform. It was designed to "increase the possible utility of individuals," thus "making useful
individuals." Moreover its lessons have been multiplied and exported, for
today "panopticism is the general principle of a new 'political anatomy'
whose object and end are not the relations of sovereignty but the relations
of discipline."[10]

But is this all there is to the panopticon? My suggestion is that we can
identify conflicting logics of punishment and "thick" cultural inputs when
we interrogate Bentham's writings. Recovering these does not mean re-

verting to a Whig history where humanitarian values are contrasted to disciplinary culture. Rather, the approach taken here is to read the panopticon as a locus where the will to power plays less of a role than we might expect and where multiple cultural codes intersect and are expressed. This process of cultural input and output can be detected along several dimensions:

1. The rationale and motivation behind the scheme: Contra Foucault the reform of inmates does not seem to be high on Bentham's list of priorities. My emphasis will be on the intersection of panopticism with utilitarian, utopian, and laissez-faire templates and the ways in which such ideological inputs tempered Bentham's vision of what Foucault was to term the "carceral continuum."

2. Moral influences on the panopticon in Bentham's blueprint: Here we see cultural norms and values about appropriate limits to punishment, about decency and reform working not only to shape the forms of discipline and surveillance but also to limit their reach. These motifs relate to justice, privacy, and propriety.

3. The reception of the scheme in its age: Foucault brushes off the real-world failure of Bentham's panoptical scheme and the fact that it was never built, insisting that he is investigating the new logic of power. Yet this outcome should have been deeply problematic for him. If the panopticon truly provided a "best fit" with the new juridical/penal ethos he has identified it would have been enthusiastically adopted. By investigating the reasons for the failure of the panopticon to be constructed we will come to understand that punishment technologies and professional ideologies themselves are mythologized and are subject to cultural evaluation.

4. The reception of the scheme in our age: By looking at the work of commentators on panopticism we can come to read it as an intellectual node that is immersed in a complex field of symbolic forms. The panopticon is more than a mute technology forced upon unthinking subjects, for it is an icon and set of practices that have been narrated in turn. Foucault's "carceral continuum" is itself subject to regulatory, reflexive discourses. These are moral and political and relate to our understandings of the good society.

The Cultural Logics of the Panopticon

Foucault's interpretation of the panopticon was of a device whose principal objective was the *reform* of inmates, a disciplinary technology for the automatic reorganization of the soul and the provision of a docile body.

Harsh conditions were a means to this end. Yet Bentham does not share this perspective. In his masterful second postscript to the panopticon proposal he lists the fourteen ends of an institution of punishment. The most important of these is in fact deterrence:

> Example, or the preventing others by the terror of the example from the commission of similar offences. This is the main end of punishment.[11]

In other words the panopticon was intended to stop crime. To do so Bentham realized it had to *communicate* a message to a wider public, influencing the calculus of the costs and benefits of wrongdoing. It needed to be tough, or put another way, "disciplinary," so that crime would look like a bad idea. There was also a need to show that wider public that expectations about "reasonable" punishment were being met. As John Pratt has pointed out, the "less eligibility principle" demanded of all reformatories and modes of poor relief that they offer living conditions less attractive than those available to the honest working poor.[12] To do otherwise would be to encourage crime and to perpetrate an injustice. We find this expectation reflected in Bentham's "Rule of Severity" "the ordinary condition of a convict doomed to a punishment ... ought not to be made more eligible than that of the poorest class of subjects in a state of innocence and liberty."[13] To be sure, life in the panopticon would require submission to disciplinary elements—a harsh regime of labor, a monotonous if unlimited diet, and the humiliations of inspection. Yet the intent of these was partly cultural. The panopticon had to signal the punitive to criminals and demonstrate conformity to community expectations. This semiotic ambition found its logical conclusion in the insistence that the panopticon be an open rather than closed institution. Less eligibility and punishment had not only to be done, but also had to be seen to be done. Far from being a closed-up institution oriented around changing a few miserable souls, for Bentham the panopticon was to offer up a vivid cultural performance to a witnessing civil society. Coining the motto *multum ex scenâ*[14] (literally, much from the stage) he argued that punishment needed to exercise a "repulsive influence ... on the minds of bystanders." This philosophy lay behind his insistence that—contra transportation to Australia—the panopticon should be near London. In the wake of the 1780 Gordon Riots and at the time of the magistrate Patrick Colquhoun's famous calculation that some 115,000 Londoners lived off the proceeds of crime,[15] it was clear not only that the metropolis contained "the greatest number of spectators of all descriptions"[16] but also that it had the greatest number in need of a good lesson. Hence the plan of management was to multiply "by every imaginable device the number of the visitors and spectators—a perpetual and perpetually interesting drama in which the obnoxious characters shall ... be exposed to instructive ignominy."[17] I will return shortly to this intriguing theme of theatricality and display.

Returning to Bentham's list of the ends of punishment next we find (2) "the prevention of prison offences" followed by (3) "preservation of decency." Well down the list we find the first item dedicated to reform, (9) "Provision for their future good behavior," followed by (10) "religious instruction" and (11) "intellectual instruction." Such priorities suggest that the panoptical technology—like Pentonville, discussed in chapter 3—was an innovation primarily about deterrence, secondarily about maintaining social and moral order within the prison. To the extent that the panopticon was a normalizing technology, it was one aiming primarily at the normalization of the subject for life within its walls. The technology was about getting prison rules followed, preventing unruly and unseemly behavior, stopping interpersonal pollutions. In truth Bentham himself was phlegmatic about the possibilities of permanent reform or integration into the legitimate labor market after release, suggesting a network of subsidiary panopticons of lesser severity into which inmates could be discharged.

Aside from less eligibility and the desire for publicly visible instructive deterrence there was another set of cultural drivers behind the severe disciplinary and architectural logic of the panopticon. Bentham was influenced by an eighteenth-century cultural cluster that attributed beneficial powers to laissez-faire capitalism and espoused the merits of the small state. Foucault is rather opaque on the relationship of disciplinary institutions to the capitalist mode of production but seems to pitch his argument at the level of elective affinity. Yet in Bentham such ties are immediately visible and causal. An admirer of much in Adam Smith, he envisaged the penal institution as a profitable enterprise. For decades the Poor Laws had been a thorn in the side of the dominant classes. They feared the mob and pitied the deserving indigent but resented paying for a safety net. When Bentham famously wrote that the panopticon had untied the Gordian knot of the Poor Laws[18] he was referring to the fact that such institutions could become attractive to the private sector and thus run without cost to the public. The panoptical principle would allow fewer staff to be employed, thinner walls to be built, and better work rates to be accomplished. Again, the elaborated system of surveillance activities, rewards, and punishments that was proposed that had little to do with the reform of the deviant. The aim here was simply the maximization of profit in a situation where there was a monopoly employer, a captive and no doubt unwilling labor force, and a reluctant taxpayer. If the panopticon was a "mill for grinding rogues honest and idle men industrious" as Bentham insisted in a letter to Brissot, this was largely so it could turn a profit.[19] If it could pay its way, then the cultural impediments that discouraged public investment in penal infrastructure could be bypassed. It was this economic imperative that required the prescriptive, unproductive punishments laid down in the 1799 Penitentiary Act to be abandoned. The contractor, Bentham said, should be free to select whatsoever was a remunerative way to employ his captive workforce. Rewards such as improved diet, perhaps meat and beer,[20] and even pay would be an incentive to production. Here was an institution primarily designed to make money rather than remake souls, one in which the governor would be an industrial Gradgrind, not a philosopher, and one who would not burden the unwilling taxpayer.[21]

So deterrence, less eligibility, and cultural pressures for self-sufficiency were drivers of harsh, disciplinary conditions. Yet culture also had a hand in ameliorating the intended rigors of panoptical life. Notwithstanding Bentham's utilitarian bent, we find throughout his writing evidence of a reason that is moral as much as disciplinary. His aim is not simply to have a maximally efficient institution but also one that could juggle a number of cultural imperatives. Among these was the need to punish and yet to remain humane. Punishment for Bentham was more than just a technique of control, it carried normative responsibilities. He started his earlier "Rationale of Punishment" by underlining that punishment was evil but necessary.[22] The trick then was to punish to the minimal extent required for the maintenance of good order. The quest for efficiency should involve a kind of moral/pragmatic calculus. So the "Rule of Severity" needed to be tempered with the "Rule of Lenity." This explains why in his panopticon writings Bentham admits that solitary confinement is "certain in its effect" when it comes to "subduing the contumacy of the intractable,"[23] yet he argues at the same time against it, insisting that "solitude . . . is torture in effect, without being obnoxious to the name."[24] So whereas Foucault sees the isolation of inmates as fundamental to the operation of the panopticon's mechanism of discipline and surveillance, Bentham—at least by the time of his postscripts—rejects this and even speaks sentimentally on the benefits of human solidarity in shared institutional accommodation. "Each cell is an island: —the inhabitants, shipwrecked mariners cast ashore upon it by the adverse blasts of fortune, indebted to each other for whatever share they are permitted to enjoy of society, the greatest of all comforts."[25]

Likewise, Bentham's concern for the classification and separation of inmates into classes within the panopticon has less to do with the operation of power/knowledge oriented around strategies for reform than concern for the welfare of petty criminals in a context of promiscuous association (mixing) with hardened offenders: "Like those on whom the Tower of Siloam fell," he says, drawing authority from a natural disaster in the Bible, they could be "distinguished from many of their neighbours more by suffering than by guilt."[26] In this desire to minimize sin and prevent depravity through rationalizing the internal order of the prison, Bentham has much in common with the early prison reformers we encountered in chapter 3.

Foucault's account suggests that panoptical systems will be characterized by unrestricted surveillance powers and a purely clinical mode of inspection. After all, the panopticon is all about power and so we will find "a visibility organized entirely around a dominating, overseeing gaze."[27] It comes as a surprise then to find in Bentham's advocacy passages more strongly consistent with Elias's position on modernity as a series of responses to visceral moral emotions, or Durkheim's on the sacred dignity of the individual than Foucault's of modernity as a system of infinite control. For example, one advantage of the panoptical gaze was that it could minimize the risks of polluting and degrading symbolic contamination. Bentham remarked that in places such as Newgate inspectors usually had to enter each cell one by one and so "come almost in contact with each inhabitant." The panopticon however would take a "great load of trouble and disgust . . . off the shoulders of those occasional inspectors of a higher order, such as judges and magistrates, who, called down to this irksome task from the superior ranks of life, cannot but feel a proportionable repugnance to the discharge of it."[28] Concessions were also made to the sensibilities of the prisoners. In his detailed specification of sanitary facilities Bentham proposed each cell should have an earthen pipe rather like a chimney pot so that human excrement could disappear from view. There was also to be a "slight screen, which the prisoner might occasionally interpose" that "answers the purpose of decency."[29]

In the same spirit of moral quarantine elaborate precautions were to be taken to maintain sexual proprieties not only between inmates, but also between observers and the observed. As Foucault's own medical writings make clear, surveillance does not preclude by its very nature the exer-

cise of the male gaze on the female body. Yet without apparent utilitarian justifications in terms of ultimate ends Bentham proposed a series of
rules and procedures limiting powers of inspection so as to ensure that
the "laws of virtue" were maintained. At not inconsiderable trouble and
inconvenience women were to be housed in a separate part of the institution, there were to be female inspectors, and yet more screens, blinds, and
partitions serving the cause of modesty. These elaborations were especially relevant to the moments when women were bathing or dressing and
were as much to protect the male inspector from "voluntary trespasses
against decency that might be committed by a female prisoner, through
impudence, or in the design of making an improper impression upon the
sensibility of an inspector of the other sex" as to protect the modesty and
virtue of the inmate herself.[30] And even the atheistic Bentham made culturally required concessions to religion. There was to be a chapel, whose
existence necessitated further complex and expensive alterations of the
panoptical design. Sundays were set aside for religious and secular study
rather than work, a time that Bentham describes as a period of creative re-
ward and relaxation rather than as a time of droning disciplinary instruction. The inmates, he rhapsodized, might engage in the joys of psalmody,
or perhaps amuse themselves by drawing and coloring scenes from the
Bible in an open-air amphitheater.[31]

Coming finally to the quality of surveillance itself we find a picture
somewhat different from what we might expect. Foucault, to be sure, notes
that the panopticon was to be open to public inspection, taking this as evidence that the panopticon was the sine qua non of the surveillance society.
He neglects to reflect upon the consequences of this observation for his
broader vision of a carceral archipelago of closed institutions and of intru-
sive state surveillance of individuated populations by experts. Bentham,
in contrast to Foucault, can be understood as an enlightenment product
with a stronger understanding of the possibility and need for an autonomous civil sphere that could itself hold the state to account. He was a keen
reader, for example, of Voltaire. Subscribing like many of his time to the
cultural binaries that maintained that power corrupts and darkness hides
evils, he sees the open society as a way of preventing despotism, as a means
of avoiding polluted Bastille-like institutional outcomes.[32] For Bentham
publicity was an effective check on power. "Against abuse," he wrote,
"there is but one effectual security, and that is the scrutiny of the public
eye."[33] At a time when some systems for prison administration granted inspection powers only to magistrates and other experts Bentham envisaged

a public gallery. Visitors would be able to see the inmates and even speak to them through tin tubes. The press could report on scandals and improvements. To maximize this public visibility the panopticon as already mentioned was to be built near London—the "great seat of inspection" and have its doors "thrown open to the body of the curious at large—the great open committee of the tribunal of the world."[34] This model of surveillance proposed is one very different from what we might anticipate from a casual reading of *Discipline and Punish*. It is one that seeks to encourage but not colonize, the civil sphere and thereby both guarantee humane prison standards and foster community deterrence.

Perhaps more intriguing still, the public gaze was to be something other than the obsessive, dispassionate eye of the invisible guardian. Whereas Foucault sees surveillance replacing spectacle, the real genius of Bentham's proposal was to recruit spectacle into surveillance. For example, sitting in their lodge, the family of the inspector would provide unpaid labor. Looking out on the prisoners would be a "great and constant fund of entertainment ... the scene, though confined ... not altogether an unamusing one."[35] The idea that fun and surveillance could go together was expanded into plans for river excursions and a fantastical panopticon tavern as part of a more complete experience for day trippers. The panopticon, then, would compete with the wax museum and pleasure garden as a public entertainment.[36] As Janet Semple astutely points out, the elaborated understanding of a panopticon town or civilization of gardens and reformatories developed by Bentham in his unpublished notes draws upon the utopian tradition in British thinking such as that of Thomas Moore. Foucault's surveillance society had its origins in earlier dreams of an organized earthly paradise no less than in any new microphysics of power.

Likewise the fusion of spectacle and surveillance can be found in Bentham's plans for the panopticon's chapel. He saw this as the setting for a vivid, civilizing moral drama and not as the locus for dull disciplinary homilies. Bentham praised the luminaries of the Spanish auto-da-fé for their "knowledge of stage effect"[37] and saw much "in it of the theatre" that should be praised: "Unjust as was their penal system in its application, and barbarous in its degree, the skill they displayed in making the most of it in point of impression, their solemn processions, their emblematic dresses, their terrific scenery, deserve rather to be admired and imitated than condemned."[38] Drawing on this lesson and believing that "the manager of a theatre" was essential to a "well-composed committee of penal law" he envisaged citizens joining with inmates in worship, even as they satiated their tourist gaze. "Why should they not come . . . as well as to the Asylum, the Magdalen and the Lock Hospital? The scene would be more picturesque; the occasion not less interesting and affecting."[39]

This public attendance at religious devotion would "keep up a system of gratuitous inspection, capable of itself of awing the keeper into good conduct."[40] At the same time it would be instructive for the community. Suggesting that the dramaturgical failure of trials and executions arose from the individual exhibition of the criminal, such that they would "stand forth in effect the sole hero of the melancholy drama" (we explored this process in chapter 2) Bentham argued for the collective display of prisoners in the course of religious ceremonial. This would head off such unruly interpretative possibilities, for "the attention of the spectators being divided among so many, scarcely attaches individually upon any one."[41] Moreover the use of the mask in the manner of the Spanish Inquisition might further allow guilt to be "pilloried in the abstract" and any "salutary impression" would be "heightened by such imagery."[42] Consequently the "scene of devotion could be decorated by a masquerade . . . a serious, affecting and instructive one." For Bentham, then, depersonalization and anonymity were the means to an end in a communicative process, not one of disciplinary individuation. Like a Greek chorus, the prisoners were a tool of theater. Were Bentham's ghost to return, he would no doubt feel compelled to refute Foucault's claim that "our society is not one of spectacle but surveillance . . . . We are much less Greeks than we believe. We are neither in the amphitheatre, nor on the stage, but in the panoptic machine, invested by the effects of its power."[43] To the contrary, for the great utilitarian the panopticon was not simply an observatory for the cold eye of one over the many, but rather a theater and spectacle where the multitude could look upon a few for both entertainment and edification.

Foucault speculates that the panopticon was inspired by Le Vaux's menagerie at Versailles.[44] From a central pavilion the king could look upon the cages arrayed in an octagon. This is a weak supposition. Foucault himself concedes there is no mention of this amusement in Bentham's writings and that it had gone by his day. The reference does however assist Foucault in the use of analogy; prisoners are like animals, the observer like a naturalist busily classifying and so forth. The path taken in my analysis permits an alternative and more reliable speculation, one that is consistent with Bentham's theatrical leanings. The origins of the panopticon lie in the Rotunda at Ranelagh House (see fig. 4). Lasting from 1742 until 1803, this was a circular wooden hall some 150 feet in diameter surrounded by two

FIGURE 4. Giovanni Antonio Canal (Canaletto), *Interior of the Rotunda at Ranelagh,* 1754. Image copyright The National Gallery, London.

tiers of fifty-two private boxes facing a central octagonal bandstand. Located over the Thames from Vauxhall Gardens in Chelsea, it was for a time a popular and most fashionable destination for excursionists. Here was a space for social intercourse, display, and mutual observation, for conversation, dance, concerts, and masquerade. Further, it was a venue with which Bentham himself would have been intimately familiar. "Nobody goes anywhere else; everybody goes there ... you can't set foot without treading on a Prince or Duke of Cumberland," enthused Horace Walpole in a letter of 1744.[45] Perhaps it is here in the fusion of architecture and an aesthetically charged public life that Bentham found the germ of his big idea.

The Reception of the Panopticon

Clearly then there were cultural inputs into what we might think of as the "production" of the panopticon. It reflected the common sense of its time about religion, decency, and less eligibility and was informed by the ideological systems of capitalism, liberalism, and utopianism. It was less an ordered system for the reform of souls than a complex amalgam of cross-cutting ideologies pulled together by a thinker keenly aware of the dramaturgical possibilities of a penal institution. These motivated its penal modality and shaped its disciplinary reach. We can reconfigure many of these cultural inputs in Durkheimian terms. The panopticon was intended as visible and theatrical symbol, it was connected to the life of civil society, it reflected the moral sensitivities of its time on questions of decency and just deserts, and it was oriented around the minimization of cultural pollutions attending to conventional places of confinement.

But what of the reception of this plan? In order to be legitimate, punishment institutions and policies need to make sense to diverse audiences, including politicians, experts, and civil society.[46] In looking to the reception of the panopticon as both concrete proposal and abstract idea we find again a different story from the one that Foucault's vision of a radical historical transformation predicts. Far from being acclaimed as a template for a new era, Bentham's vision of a panoptic penal institution was never realized. Foucault acknowledges this, mentioning that the panopticon "received little praise." The discourses produced by the panopticon, he suggests, did not acquire the "status of sciences" and were attached to institutions of physical constraint so leading to what he terms an "inglorious culmination."[47] What he seems to be saying here is that evaluative cultural systems were at play external to the disciplinary matrix, that a good idea was dragged down by the cultural context through which it was elaborated or imagined. Surely such a turn to multidimensionality undermines his wider argument that power/knowledge institutions became triumphant; that official, expert discourses come to dominate others and that utility alone determines the outcomes of innovation?

Looking in a more concrete way at the reception of the panopticon can reinforce this lesson. We find diverse responses that prevented a regime organized around pure surveillance being enthusiastically transposed from paper to bricks and mortar. Of crucial importance is the fact that Bentham was unable to quarantine his invention from the more widespread cultural pollution that surrounded the jails of the era (see chapter 2). Although rationalized and hygienic to the highest degree, rather like a nuclear power station the panopticon remained a tainted product that nobody wanted in their own backyard. Bentham's efforts to find a site met with repeated obstruction. The 1790s had seen growing disillusion with the general idea that institutions could solve the problem of crime.[48] Further they continued to be associated with outcomes of squalor and degradation arising from promiscuous association, unruly conduct, and the convict stain (as in the case of Newgate discussed in chapter 3). There was an intense awareness of the moral and political danger of concentrating large numbers of malefactors in spatial proximity—not only to each other but also to the capital. On top of this, scandal had surrounded the improved penitentiaries at Coldfield Baths and Gloucester following the confinement of political prisoners by Pitt.[49] Their articulate accounts associated such institutions with Bastille-like themes of repression and excessive state power.

So although Bentham emphasized the sanitary, airy, publicly accountable qualities of his invention, critics conjured up less wholesome imagery. Testifying before George Holford's Parliamentary committee on the establishment of a panopticon penitentiary was the Reverend John Becher, who spoke of "cages with 1,000 convicts, and the whole will exhibit an assemblage of human beings with the same ferocious dispositions, the same offensive exhalations, and the same degrading propensities, that characterize the brute creation."[50] Fears of homosexual activity stalked Bentham's financially and sentimentally driven preference for collective sleeping arrangements. Notwithstanding his insistence on the virtues of open public inspection, the independently contracted panoptical governor was seen as having too much power, thus opening possibilities for tyrannical abuse. The scheme was also understood as too secular and as giving insufficient attention to religion and repentance as a way of purifying the deviant. John Howard's model with its focus on solitary confinement and penitence, for example, was quite simply a better cultural fit with the expectations and fears of the decision makers.

As for the print media, here Bentham's contraption was acknowledged as an ingenious novelty but this could not save it from damning ridicule.[51] Commentators made word plays. It was a "visionary scheme" that could be "easily seen through."[52] Bentham, who proposed himself as the independently contracted governor, was likened a greedy honey collector in his glass beehive[53] or "penal panorama."[54] Bentham's elaborate plans for the defense of the building from the mob were laudable, for the prison was too soft on criminals—it was "charming and comfortable" and so needed to be fortified against attack from without. There were also hints that the ethics of nonreciprocal vision were problematic. The *Morning Chronicle* argued that the jailer should be called the "keeper and keeper . . . easily becomes peeper" and spoke ironically of the need to "banish that scoundrel secrecy out of the world."[55] Here, then, is a response of lively wit and skepticism very different from what we might expect from a reading of *Discipline and Punish*. It is an evaluation suggesting that the panopticon would generate net disorder, encourage perversion and moral degradation, facilitate the evils of despotism, and pay insufficient attention to the

spiritual reform of the sinner. Bentham's systematic efforts to describe
the panopticon in terms of the codes of the enlightenment as open, democratic, and progressive had failed.

To sum up, Foucault's account overreaches. Bentham's panopticon is
not identical with his. To be sure, surveillance and discipline were pivotal
to its functioning. But the panopticon had objectives other than reform,
exhibited diverse cultural themes revolving around ritual, pollution and
classification, was intended as a didactic signifier and came to be evaluated
according to a moral rather than utilitarian matrix. There is, of course, an
all-too-familiar defense for Foucault here, namely, that he has not really
been called to account, is not really "wrong" for his intention was to investigate the "history of ideas." In this rendition he is treating the panopticon
as an ideal type, as a fantasy for power, and as a paradigm or template
of exemplary techniques that were subsequently influential. His job was
never to provide an accurate reading of Bentham, but to extract from him
the essence of a new way of thinking about social control. As a theory
builder and philosopher of this kind he should be exempted from any
effort at routine empirical evaluation. So points of contradictory detail
about motivation or organization or reception even if found in Bentham's
own writings are simply empiricist quibbles that cannot undermine a more
general intellectual logic. Let's confront this position in an aggressive way.
Firstly, one cannot help but paraphrase Charles Tilly's acid remark on
Durkheim scholarship: There is always one more version of Foucault to
offer when the last one has failed.[56] Shifting avatars in this way is not a
form of debate, but usually a way of avoiding it.

More pointedly any such defection towards abstraction and away from
a verifiable propositional theory about real-world process directly contradicts Foucault's claim to be providing an account or "genealogy" with empirical traction or to be explaining a historical puzzle in the transformation of punishment. Power and knowledge are supposed to be interlinked,
remember, and it was this innovation that enabled Foucault to famously
transcend his own archaeological project and claim that he was not a
structuralist. It also allowed his apologists to assert he had gone "beyond"
structuralism because he had his feet on the ground of practices and not
in the realm of myth where cultural codes float free. Foucault's pivotal
methodological innovation was to realize that ideas are developed in the
laboratory that is the world of real institutions and real plans. This being
the case we should look at these very seriously and with an eye to detail.[57]
Precisely for this reason *Discipline and Punish* has been influential. It sits
on the impressive bedrock of evidence and is able to make broadly causal

claims about a substantive change in the organization of power in social life. "With *Discipline and Punish,*" he said, "I could perfectly well call my subject the history of penal policy in France."[58] This is not an argument from first principles that should be quarantined from unwarranted empirical examination but rather a grounded exploration of the logic of the social order. Foucault's inspiration is Nietzsche, not Descartes or Plato. If we give up on his insistence that we should tie ideas to history and process; if we no longer match bold theoretical statements to truth claims; if we no longer draw inferences from settings or test ideas against the sites where real power was actually created, reproduced, and imagined then we have, in a sense, betrayed his intellectual spirit.

Finally, for the sake of argument, let's give some ground here. Let's say Foucault set out to identify an intellectual model in a pure form and not to explain real outcomes nor to offer a faithful account of Bentham. He has made what might be thought of as a creative misreading for philosophical and methodological purposes. It has been said since Max Weber's time that such ideal types should be evaluated in terms to their pragmatic utility as investigative tools. They are the yardsticks against which we measure and understand the real. When put up against the *ground zero of Foucault's own choosing* we find this particular yardstick wanting. The method can only become useful to the extent that we can learn an honest lesson from the space between the ideal type of discipline and surveillance and this early empirical instantiation. The exploration of this epistemological gap then becomes a valid path for theoretical reflection and empirical inquiry. Next, new questions can and should be imagined and asked, how does the ideal type of disciplinary power intersect with broader systems of meaning? How does the civil sphere participate in surveillance? Under what circumstances might spectacle still play a role in social control?

The path taken here is closer to the timbre of Foucault's own work than many efforts to shield him from critique. It does not claim he has been "falsified" in any simple way. Rather it interrogates the past, looks both at what was imagined and what happened, and draws wider theoretical implications from this for others to use. It also treats his theory with respect but not deference. "The only valid tribute to thought such as Nietzsche's," said Foucault of his own interlocutor, "is precisely to use it, to deform it, to make it groan and protest."[59] By giving him a hard time we have discovered something new. Foucault explains a lot about the panopticon, but he does not explain everything. Coming to terms with this reality might be uncomfortable, but it is the start to a wider and constructive rethinking.

The Resonances of the Panopticon

The sins of the father, it is said, are visited on the son. And so we find the taint that stalked the original panopticon passed through time to each successive descendant carrying the gene that crosscodes observation with social control. Foucault's vision of surveillance triumphant fails to interrogate this possibility for the moral assay of a means of discipline. Had it done so he might have replaced a rendering of history (or even the "history of ideas") in which surveillance triumphs for one in which the very idea of surveillance is marked by symbolic pollution and so must continually struggle for legitimacy. We find its immediate traces in the efforts of intellectuals to evaluate Bentham's legacy. Gertrude Himmelfarb sees Bentham proposing not only an inspection device but also a proto-capitalist administrative system for extracting and exploiting labor, and takes this as evidence of the broader incompatibility of Benthamite utilitarianism with democratic ideals and human rights.[60] The historian Janet Semple takes a more benign view, flagging Bentham's whimsical moments and utopian aspirations. She reads the panopticon in the context of its time as a sensible effort and as a humanitarian improvement on its competitors. At the same time Semple agrees with Himmelfarb that Bentham was insensitive to the counterdemocratic implications of his invention.[61] Foucault, as we know, takes the panopticon as a normalizing technology with insidious consequences for individual autonomy of thought and action.[62] These forceful readings testify not only to the panopticon's ambivalence and multivocality but also to its totem-like ability to agitate sentiment. The panopticon is not simply a coin in an intellectual game, it is something intellectuals care passionately about.

And not only intellectuals. The academic critique of panopticism is simply a subset of a more generalized indictment of antidemocratic organized surveillance. Pivotal to this process, of course, was George Orwell's *Nineteen Eighty-Four,* a futuristic novel set in the grim state of Oceana whose imagining was fueled by the horrors of twentieth-century totalitarianism.[63] Thanks to high school reading curricula, an economy of style rendering the book accessible to middle-brow audiences, and memorable imagery, Orwell's thinking has not only tapped but helped to grow and sensitize a nerve in the collective conscience. Oceana is a world of political indoctrination, censorship and misinformation, ration books and compulsory optimism—and perpetual war. This is a garrison state whose interest seems to be on controlling its own citizens as much as destroying its enemies. It is also a place where social order is generated by surveillance and informants and torture. Records are kept, conversations utilitarian or furtive, and trust is thin. At home the panoptical "telescreen" sends out cheery propaganda and provides unseen officials with a one-way view into the domestic life of citizens. Privacy and autonomy of action are circumscribed. Observation centralizes power and obviates resistance. Realist in tone, *Nineteen Eighty-Four* is also gothic in inspiration. Although devoid of supernatural agency, Oceana is a world of darkness and horror, one where bureaucracy itself becomes an excess as it clamps down on authenticity in relationships and freedom in thought to the point where the cult of the individual is extinguished. It is no accident that Winston Smith was considered by Orwell to be the "the last man" and that he must be destroyed as an autonomous subject. In the world of 1984 surveillance is not just "dangerous" as Foucault would say—it is evil.

Orwell's fiction reflects not only his personal values and experiences, but also the wider current of British liberalism that could run the gamut from Fabian socialism to "Middle England" conservatism. For Edmund Burke and George Orwell alike, England's merit lay in a tradition of rough-and-ready organic constitutionalism—a belief in the virtues of privacy, critical inquiry, free association, and public debate that needed to be protected against authoritarian rationalism.[64] As we have seen Bentham himself tried to make use of this cultural pattern, taking great pains to integrate the panopticon within the social fabric beyond the state. He wanted to mobilize the public as fellow inspectors so as to solve the age-old problem for democratic society: *quis custodiet ipsos custodes,* or who will guard the guardians?[65] Yet in Orwell we find panopticism falling out on the wrong side of this imagining. It was evil because it was antithetical to civil society. Once such a belief became widespread it was hardly surprising that civil society would vigorously defend its perceived interests. Orwell's novel became itself an icon or emblem in this cause, working to encapsulate a set of concerns with considerable rhetorical and emotive force. From the middle years of the twentieth century onwards the tie of systematic observation to antidemocratic outcomes could be enciphered in four simple digits 1-9-8-4, relayed and amplified by means of simplistic contrasts between the free West and the Eastern Bloc. Indeed the fall of the Berlin Wall seemingly confirmed that surveillance societies were fundamentally antidemocratic as the miles of archives belonging to the East German Stasi and Soviet KGB were thrown open to inspection.

Once the Eastern Bloc was finished, the sign of panopticism attached

itself to a new target. The most vivid anxiety was now closed-circuit TV
(CCTV). By the 1980s such technology was affordable for local authorities, transport organizations, and shopping malls but implementation was
held back by popular concerns. For many CCTV in public spaces was a
form of illiberal spying. Orwellian metaphor became ubiquitous. During
the next two decades journalistic discussions of security cameras could be
guaranteed to drag Orwell onto the stage, using phrases such as "nightmarish visions of George Orwell's fictional and dystopian Big Brother
society," the "sinister Orwellian scenario" and "Big Brother-like power."[66]
Thanks to the free publicity provided by Michel Foucault they could also
wheel out Bentham's panopticon and expect the reference to be understood, the utilitarian's enlightenment idea now definitively encoded as
problematic.

It is telling and consistent with the theme of this book that the cultural
resistance thrown up by the polluted image of voyeuristic and controlling panoptical observation could only be overcome by incarnations of
even greater pollution: the terrorist, the pedophile, the stranger, the unruly teenager. In Britain historic resistance to CCTV surveillance took a
battering from IRA strikes on London and Manchester in the early-1990s.
Yet the substantial catalyst for change was the abduction and murder of
the toddler Jamie Bulger by two slightly older boys.[67] The only clue to his
disappearance was some footage from a shopping mall of the infant being
led away. Adding to the evil resonances of this crime was the fact that
Bulger's murder contained ritualistic elements. Details emerging through
the press were sketchy but it soon became rumored that the killers were
inspired by the horror film *Child's Play 3,* which had featured a demonic
doll, Chucky, who is possessed by the spirit of a serial killer.[68] Chucky met
his end on a haunted train ride in an amusement park. Bulger was found
dead on a rail line and was said to have been stuffed with batteries, his
face spattered with blue paint like Chucky's. If the killers thought they
were enacting the good, to the wider public they came to incarnate evil,
corrupted youth, the child devil. Death threats and a moral panic over
violent videos and ensued. Suddenly CCTV started to look like a blessing
not a curse and the Conservative and Labour governments of the mid-
1990s started to throw money into such systems. Within 10 years Britain
had over 2 million CCTV cameras, becoming the leader among developed
nations.

In the United States, public schools have proven the locus for such fears
centered on out of control youth and hence a particularly fertile ground

for cameras. With schools already widely seen as a den of ill discipline, violence, and drug taking, the Columbine High School shootings could become the straw that broke the camel's back. Although dubbed by some teachers' unions an "Orwellian intrusion on the sanctity of the classroom" parents wanted their kids saved from their evil schoolmates and administrators wanted to head off litigation for not exercising a duty of care.[69] Uptake of CCTV and the defeat of the "Orwellian vision" has been further facilitated in a creeping way by the growing fear of the unruly stranger in developed societies. The referent here is the dangerous Other of the public space—the homeless person, the wino, the youth gang—who challenge the ontological security of the "respectable citizen" in their daily round. Threatened with the potential loss of custom or a dent to civic image, retailers and local authorities have endorsed CCTV as a way to signal not danger but safety, and to promise not conformity, but rather a "risk-free" environment without such failed consumers.[70] The result has been a clamor for CCTV supported by various interest groups and gratefully accepted by a public fearful of antisocial behavior. When Miami Beach proposed installing "television monitors" back in 1981 the *New York Times* editorialized against this. It waxed Whitmanesque about the aesthetic pleasures and reveries of urban anonymity in places like Grand Central Terminal, where the flâneur could enjoy "the city's crowds and commerce gathered beneath a winking universe of ceiling-mural stars." Describing this anonymity as a form of privacy it hoped the "experiment fails."[71] Twenty years later the game would be up for such tender sentiment. The attacks of 9/11 had finally changed the rules, building on two decades of low-level attrition by fear of strangers. The perils of the Other as both local and global evil now outweighed and displaced the fear of centralized authority. CCTV was on *our* side.

These new realities, of course, have not gone unchallenged and attempts to repollute CCTV can be found from time to time. Jeffrey Rosen, the legal affairs editor of the *New Republic,* for example, argued in the *New York Times* that the benefits in the war against terror are minimal.[72] The cameras have never caught a terrorist, and facial recognition technology is primitive. Drawing on the work of the British criminologist and media researcher Clive Norris he notes that the bored men in control rooms apparently spend a large amount of their time leering at prostitutes, spying on teenagers making out in cars and tracking young black males. Further, the surveillance is insidiously dangerous. After some requisite discussion of Bentham and Foucault to set the tone Rosen moves into an analytic mode that is remarkably similar to that of organic English constitutional-ism. CCTV cameras have come to threaten not so much centralized state power as the multiple erosions of individualism and small-scale freedoms through their pledge of panopticon-like permanent visibility. The result is a retreat of the social. At the end of the day, he suggests, such technolo-gies are antithetical to a society where "people can redefine and reinvent themselves every day; a society in which people can travel from place to place without showing their papers and being encumbered by their past; a society that respects privacy and constantly reshuffles social hierarchy." Cameras, he says, are "not consistent with the values of an open society. They are technologies of classification and exclusion" and "a powerful in-ducement toward social conformity for citizens who can't be sure whether they are being watched." Citizens have already come to behave differently in the streets, trying to enact the respectable. The danger threatens in fu-ture to become universal and inescapable. Rosen warns: "In our digital age, once thousands of cameras from hundreds of separate CCTV systems are able to feed their digital images to a central monitoring station, and the images can be analyzed with face- and behavioral-recognition soft-ware to identify unusual patterns, then the possibilities of the Panopticon will suddenly become very real."

Likewise the left-wing U.S. magazine the *Nation* was worried about "D.C.'s Virtual Panopticon." Outlining an alleged plan to link 1,000 video cameras in Washington to a "NASA-style Joint Operations Command Center" the article voices fears through rhetorical questions:

> Who will monitor the video? When will the system be complete? How long will the tapes be kept and by whom? What agencies will get access to the tapes? And what steps will be taken to prevent video voyeurism or racist and antihomeless profiling? Nor are the ACLU's concerns merely hypothetical: Already, police in Detroit and DC have used CCTV to stalk personal foes, political opponents and young women.[73]

The article goes on speak of video surveillance in the Joint Operations Center during anti-NATO, anti-World Bank, and anti-International Mon-etary Fund demonstrations, of racial profiling, and the futility of the Fourth Amendment right against unreasonable searches. The item describes the subjective experience of being watched by CCTV as "chilling" and "creepy," terms that neatly capture the way that evil and indecency can still be fused in the indictment of surveillance.

So Main Street, USA, legitimacy has not convinced the critical left. Consequently social and aesthetic movements have eventuated oriented around getting surveillance out of our lives in the interest of freedom of expression, movement, and association. Like the electric chair (see chapter 6) the panopticon has become an attractive and malleable signifier for the *artiste engagé,* its polluted and ambivalent resonances offering a subversive piquancy to expressive statement. Over recent years ideas about reflexivity, the gaze, and observation have become more central to the thematics of conceptual art. Reference to panopticism and to power offers a way for this output to appear less self-indulgent and more immediately socially relevant. Hence the 1990s saw the emergence of a new genre. Well read in Foucault and Bentham, these "surveillance artists" seek to study the watchers or to foreground the surveillance processes in our society in other ways. This, says artist Julia Scher, is "art that watches back," perhaps by taking images of authority figures or by recording and displaying visitors to a surveillance art exhibit.[74] Consider the Institute for Applied Autonomy, whose roster includes programmers and artists. Its Web site, iSee,[75] documents Manhattan surveillance cameras and suggests de Certeau–like routes for avoiding them, insisting that dropping out of view is a form of cultivated everyday resistance.[76] Video artist Fiona Tan's 2005 exhibition at the New Museum of Contemporary Art in Manhattan's chic Chelsea district featured thirty-second-long clips of motionless prison inmates and guards displayed on video screens around central benches. According to the *New York Times* critic, the resulting "extended eye contact with strangers incites primitive transgressive feelings: it's a dare, it's a threat, it's erotic."[77] Here, then, the artist plays with the unseemly aspects of the panopticon, the indecent and threatening qualities of the gaze that Bentham tried to quarantine from the business of regulating inmates. Many high-end educational institutions now offer courses in surveillance art that are informed by the critical discourses on its aesthetic and political implications. That of the Art Institute of Chicago is representative. Students read works by Bentham, Foucault, and encounter works by Julia Scher, Steve Mann, David Rokeby, and the NYC Surveillance Camera Project. They watch Coppola's *The Conversation.* They become involved in projects mapping security camera locations and following people, they learn video surveillance techniques and video streaming for live webcams. The course outline makes it clear that the objective is to "investigate how and why artists have subverted traditional modes of surveillance for creative and critical discourse."[78] In short, panopticism has become a resource for reflexive aesthetic activity and, in our post-Marxist world, for the expression of a radical identity. This impulse finds its middle-brow expression in sites such as www.flickr.com, where a public bulletin board on the panopticon allows internet users to upload and discuss photos of surveillance cameras, recommend books to each other, and moot what is going on in our main streets.[79] One wonders if either Bentham or Foucault could have envisaged this possibility for civic critique.

If we are less interested in power and knowledge we might also care to think of the limitations of CCTV in terms of a humanist aesthetic and ponder the disjunction between systematic observation and the existential. Writing in the *Observer*, Peter Conrad notes with sensitivity the estrangement of the grainy, mundane images of CCTV surveillance from the human tragedies they reveal. Video footage taken shortly before the death of Diana, Princess of Wales, the toddler James Bulger discussed above, and other dead or missing persons seems "eerie and unsettling" because it plays in a "perpetual present tense" and without apparent regard for the tragedy that is about to unfold. It is jerky and records frozen moments of time such that "bodies look jittery and artificially animated from outside—not so much alive as undead."[80] CCTV, it seems, makes zombies. Like other banal and utilitarian social control technology it has unleashed the uncanny.

I will conclude this chapter with some illustration of reception right on the margins. This is the space where the panopticon as a signifier hovers on the border between sense and nonsense, where connotation outstrips any official denotation. There are associations with panorama or panoply or optic whose exact sense is hard to determine but that carry some of the residual energy of a powerful icon. When in 1983 the Polish government published an indictment of the Western media's allegedly false account of events in 1982—such as the strikes involving the union Solidarity—this was entitled "Panopticon of Nonsense" and referred to the "distorting mirror of the free press" that fed on rumor, slander, and sensationalist exaggeration.[81] In a more upbeat vein, a collection of author Anna Quindlen's commentaries and opinion pieces was described in the *Chicago Tribune* as "a panopticon of life in this decade, sure to be valuable to future historians. She touches on life, love, home, family, work, men, women, children, and issues large and small."[82] Fans of the low-budget BBC science fiction series *Dr. Who* call their North American Time Festival an annual panopticon.[83] The first of these usages feeds from the pollution of panopticism to conjure the image of insidiously propagandistic communication;

the second carries the positive meaning of a comprehensive survey; and the third amazingly enough helps us capture the mood of a futuristic opportunity for fun-seeking solidaristic activity. None of these applications will be found in a dictionary but each makes some kind of sense, for the panopticon has now become a public signifier without fixed abode.

This heterogeneity is to be expected for it mirrors the hybridity encoded in the original proposal. If the panopticon has been narrowly treated by Foucault and others as an efficient machine for observing, controlling, and normalizing humans, it has also and always been much more than this. We saw Bentham's plans show sensitivity to the diverse cultural concerns of his time, a desire to connect criminal justice to the community, a wish to eliminate pollutions, create penal theater, and make punishment meaningful. In all these respects the panopticon conforms to the Durkheimian vision of punishment as a communicative reflection of a collective conscience. Albeit that Bentham failed to build his inspection house, when all is said and done he did manage to create a powerful, enduring, collective representation. The panopticon lives on in the cultural imaginary. It is a useful symbol as much as a technology, a cultural resource to be decoded for its meanings, a rich, peculiar, and ingenious totem.

CHAPTER FIVE

The Guillotine

The trope through which Foucault begins *Discipline and Punish* is a now well-known contrast between the torture of the regicide Damiens in the middle of the eighteenth century and Faucher's prison timetable from early in the nineteenth. Like any rhetorical device, the Damiens/timetable couplet obscures as much as it reveals. Most importantly, it diverts our intellectual focus away from the exploration of capital punishment itself and the ways in which this too was transformed—in France and elsewhere—with the onset of modernity. After all, the prison did not simply replace capital punishment; rather, it augmented it.

Consider the case of the guillotine. This device is situated within the chronotopic domain marked out by Foucault and might, indeed, have provided an alternative starting point for his inquiry—a stillborn possibility confirmed by two short paragraphs in the first chapter of *Discipline and Punish*.[1] Here Foucault, like more orthodox historians before him, comments on its fit with a new juridical ethic and makes particular note of the guillotine's capabilities as a "machine for the production of rapid and discrete deaths."[2] He goes on to briefly observe the elimination of spectacle from French executions, with the operation of the guillotine eventually hidden from view within prison walls. The narrative Foucault briefly sketches in this case is consistent with the general thrust of his text, which traces a seemingly ineluctable march of the discourses and technologies of rationality and control into the heartland of the criminal justice system—a Spartan progress against the sybaritic displays of force that had characterized sovereign power. This chapter will show that the guillotine was indeed a "scientific" instrument, that its operations involved a routinization of bodily activity, and that an emergent professional gaze relentlessly interrogated its embodied effects. Yet it will also become apparent that none of these came at the expense of more profound symbolic resonance. Far from eliminating or replacing vital symbolisms, the guillotine and its bodies became, in Lévi-Strauss's term, *bonnes à penser*—material goods for a new set of mythologies.[3]

The first empirical component of this chapter shows that the invention of the guillotine—like those of the hidden execution, the prison, and the panopticon—was a response to cultural needs. Its design and material operation reflected the cult of reason, efficiency, novelty, and equality prevalent in revolutionary France. Hence its very Foucaultian qualities were themselves deeply meaningful expressions of an emergent and historically specific understanding of the sacred. The section following introduces expert debates about the impact of the guillotine on the bodies of its victims. The material here suggests that clinical discourses were infected by darker currents of fable and imagination. A Bakhtinian heteroglossia eventuated with the guillotine not only destabilized but also profaned by doubt and plagued by eruptions of the sacred in this transgressive representational modality. A brief final part hints at the enduring legacy of such a thematic and its movement from an elite public sphere towards the mass popular sphere—a progress from center to periphery.

The Guillotine, Rationality, and the Sacred

With the arrival of the French Revolution came an intense interest in law and justice. This priority arose from the desire of revolutionaries to sweep away not only the concrete and arbitrary power that they perceived to be the hallmark of the ancien régime but also its symbolic vestiges. Expressive, ritualistic, and religious as much as rational or goal-directed, this purge ran along an axis of binary oppositions that juxtaposed the old, arbitrary, corrupt, irrational, and sinister with the new, egalitarian, healthy, rational, and open.[4] Such Enlightenment values, when espoused by the revolutionaries, were advocated with a messianic zeal and surrounded by cultlike observances. Criminal and legal issues were far from exempt from this purifying, spring-cleaning exercise. Indeed, they took center stage in as far as despotic power was perceived to have been built upon a system of repression that had at its core the polluted symbol of the Bastille and the caprice of the king's *lettre de cachet,* which could condemn citizens to prison without due process.[5]

New criminological discourses such as those of Beccaria provided am-

munition for a rational rethinking of penal codes, including those relating to capital punishment. In a sequence of pathbreaking, passion-filled
debates in May and June 1791 it was decided, against fierce opposition,
to retain the death penalty, but in a form compatible with the new spirit
of the age. While the ancien régime had allowed class distinctions to be
demonstrated in the application of death (nobles were beheaded with
a sword, commoners hung), under the new laws each person would die
in exactly the same, egalitarian way. Arbitrary power, differential punishments, and torture were opposed in a binary manner to natural law.
M. Mougins de Roquefort explained this to the Assemblée nationale in
the spring of 1791:

> Aside from the uselessness of severe punishments, which affront nature and
> humanity ... there is no point of comparison between a fixed penalty, which,
> in certain cases, the crime deserves, and an arbitrary punishment, because the
> arbitrary often occasions a very real inequality in the uses that judges make of
> their power ... I allow therefore only the death penalty, that is to say, the simple
> privation of life, without torture, for all kinds of murder.[6]

With article 2 of *Code pénal* of 1791 declaring that the death penalty allowed only this equitable and universalistic "privation of life" without
pain inflicted on the body, a search emerged in the following debates for
the means of achieving this specific end. The option of beheading was consequently adopted in article 3, which explained that this was the swift-
est and least painful mode of death. However, the pragmatics of making
this policy workable required some attention. As Le Pelletier de Saint-
Fargeau pointed out, attempts at beheading could be themselves "arbitrary" in outcome, resulting in a polluted spectacle of butchery.

> There is one certainty from experience—the punishment of beheading requires
> a very advanced technique. There are many examples where one has seen the
> recipient of punishment executed with a very poor hand.[7]

The experienced celebrity executioner Sanson indicated some causes for
such eventualities in a letter to the Assemblée nationale.

> After each execution the sword is no longer in a condition to do another, it is
> absolutely necessary that it is sharpened again. If there are many persons to
> be killed at the same time, it is necessary therefore to have a sufficient number

of swords, all of them prepared ... [W]hen there are many condemned to be executed at the same time, the terror of the execution and the volume of blood that it produces gives fright and weakness in the spirit of the most intrepid of those who remain to be executed. ... we have seen the condemned fall ill on account of the sight of their punished companions, or at least show weakness and fear—all this counts against the execution by means of a head cut with a sword ... In other forms of execution ... it is not necessary for the condemned to remain firm and without terror, but in this one, if the condemned falters the execution will be flawed.[8]

Such unfortunate contingencies, Sanson pointed out, had been made clear in the case of the execution of the Duc de Lally, whose demise was still etched in living memory. It took several blows to cut off his head, the unfortunate victim being eventually turned onto his back as the sword was having trouble severing the neck. Decollation, then, could all too easily lead to indecorous, unsystematic spectacles coded as barbarous rather than civilized.

It is in this context of cultural pragmatics that the guillotine came to the fore. While primitive versions of the device had been around for at least two centuries, the invention had been improved and proselytized by Dr. Joseph Ignace Guillotin and Dr. Louis since 1789. Their technological solution to a cultural problem was finally authorized by M. Duport, the minister of justice, in 1792. From Foucault's perspective the machine they advocated can be seen as a technology that worked on the body in a predictable and reliable way, subjecting it to a routinized and coercive discipline. So efficient was this new device that it permitted the batch processing of up to twenty victims per hour during the Terror. Clearly then, *Discipline and Punish* has something to teach us here. Yet at the same time the guillotine can also be understood as a meaningful substitute for the more charismatic and capricious justice embodied in the executioner and his primitive technologies—themselves tokens of a now-defunct epoch. It was a means of execution that was not merely efficient but that also could be properly interpreted as enlightened.

These synergies between disciplinary logic and revolutionary values can be detected in the enthusiasms of the guillotine's advocates and in the logic of design. When the new technology of death was proposed by Guillotin to the Assemblée nationale, a fit was perceived between this innovation and the revolutionary and Enlightenment ideals of humanism, science, transparency, and efficiency—qualities we have already suggested revolutionaries regarded with an almost religious awe.[9] Viewed from a distance, the device has a certain clarity of purpose and modernist aesthetic appeal. The frame in which the blade runs is rectangular, the angled blade (*couperet*) appears triangular, and the head collar (*la lunette républicaine*) makes a circle. This geometrical combination of rectangle, circle, and triangle can be read as materializing an abstract, remote, and mathematical beauty that is consistent with Enlightenment ideals of reason and universality.[10]

Aside from this Euclidean felicity, the guillotine was supported by empiricist scientific discourses and procedures. These mobilized the knowledge bases of anatomy and natural science to attest to and celebrate a machinelike functionality in rational design. Experimental testing had established invariant efficacy. Louis, secretary to the Surgical Academy, had decapitated a bundle of straw, a sheep, and three corpses before witnesses in the Court de Commerce, which is behind the rue Saint André des Arts, and at the Bicêtre Hospital.[11] The arbitrary contingencies associated with human agency and human anatomy such as Sanson had observed were now obviated. As Louis himself pointed out in a report prepared for the Ministry of Justice:

> In considering the structure of the neck ... it is not possible to assure a prompt and perfect separation when leaving this task to a human agent susceptible to changing his technique and approach due to moral and physical causes. It is necessary for the certainty of the procedure, that it depend upon invariant mechanical procedures, whose cause and effect can be determined ... the body of the criminal is positioned with the throat between two posts crossed at the top by a beam, from whence a blade falls on the neck ... the instrument must be sufficiently strong and heavy to do the job effectively, as we saw with the sheep that was severed in the tests. We know that the force increases by reason of the height from which it falls.[12]

Cold as it may seem, this dispassionate discourse did not float free of substantive values—rather, it depended upon them for a wider legitimacy. As we saw with the panopticon, penal devices are more than just instruments that perform mundane functions. They can also be totems supported by and reproducing wider currents of meaning.[13] In some cases their evaluation hinges upon the sacred and profane symbolic codes through which they are situated as harbingers of a transcendent and dangerous world-ordering power. The guillotine fits this pattern especially well, for as Arnold van Gennep, Victor Turner, and others have argued, material instruments associated with rites of passage and other ritual interventions on the body usually carry enhanced, fetishistic, and magical properties that inspire awe and reverence.[14]

It has been often remarked that the guillotine became an unintended collective representation for the profanities of the Terror.[15] It was a flexible cipher for the unruly bloodlust of the crowd; the banal, machinelike justice of the state; the monstrous and remorseless energies of repressive power; and the unreason of revenge. Such tellings endured into Charles Dickens's *A Tale of Two Cities* as Madame Defarge clicks her knitting needles in the shadow of the scaffold.[16] It also provided a foil for the heroics of the Scarlet Pimpernel in the novel of the same name. Of more interest to us here, however, is the way that the mechanism of death became encoded as a sacred object that crystallized in a positive way the emergent ideologies of a new political order. Scientific and technical recommendations of the kind promoted by Louis were complementary to the association of the new device with revolutionary values of equality and progress. As Prudhomme expressed it, "one cannot imagine an instrument of death that better reconciles what is owed to humanity and what is demanded by the law." All that remained was to cleanse the ceremonial so as to "remove all taint of the ancien régime."[17] The hands-off technology was seen as representing the spirit of an age of universalism and role differentiation, one that was to replace a form of personalistic Kadi justice, which, according to historical sociologist Max Weber, "knows no rational rules of decision."[18] Hence a correspondent to a newspaper points out with enthusiasm: "The innovation of placing a mechanism in place of an executioner, who, like the law, separates the sentence from the judge, is worthy of the century in which we are going to live and the new political order into which we will enter."[19] Louis himself indicated the cultural appeal of the guillotine that came from its ability to provide instant, reliable, painless death: "It is easy to make such a machine whose effect is inevitable . . . decapitation will be accomplished in an instant [in] . . . the sprit and will of the new law . . . the apparatus will not give rise to any feeling and will be hardly discerned at all."[20] This vision was expressed in more graphic terms by Guillotin himself: "The blade hisses, the head falls, blood spurts, the man exists no more. With my machine I'll cut off your head in the blink of an eye, and you will feel nothing but a slight coolness on the back of the neck."[21]

The moral appeal of the guillotine is laid clear in these passages. It offered more than just an administrative convenience, an efficient and predictable means of carrying out the law. Hermeneutically it provided a truly "revolutionary" mode of execution in which the moment of fate dramatized the brisk, rational, precise, clean, and humanist spirit of the new France. The guillotine was a literal and metaphorical surgical intervention that could cut disease from the body politic through a severe and machine-like application of justice.[22] As James Whitman notes, it was also egalitarian, leveling up all executions to the aristocratic mode.[23] The technology played a telling counterpoint to the baroque grotesqueries of torture and the primitive dangling corpse. Like the Aboriginal Arunta's *churinga* so vividly described by Durkheim in *The Elementary Forms of the Religious Life,* the guillotine worked as a totem, as "the very type of sacred thing" that reflected the new collective social identity.[24] Is it any surprise, then, that the guillotine like the *churinga* came to be seen as a sacred avenging force possessed of almost supernatural powers? Capable of saintly and miraculous intervention in the new social order, it took on the qualities of an avenging Yahweh and inspired the awe and fear that Durkheim has argued is central to the sacred.[25] Hence we find one commentator during the Revolution writing enthusiastically from the field:

> Saint Guillotine is in most brilliant activity, and by reason of its philosophy, has produced a wonderful Terror here in an almost miraculous manner—something that one could not have hoped would come to pass for the next century.[26]

Reports exist of people dipping handkerchiefs in the blood around the scaffold and touching the apparatus or decapitated bodies in what some thought of as a "red mass." Many refused to visit the site of death, believing it to be haunted.[27] Such folkloric activities, which sought protection from sickness and other afflictions, find a precise counterpart in the cult of the Aboriginal sacred totems whose contact could cure illness, provide courage, and bring luck.[28] It should come as no shock to us to find that the guillotine, like the Aboriginal *churinga,* was protected by rituals of avoidance and respect. During the Festival of the Supreme Being, for example, the machine was hidden behind bolts of blue velvet and bouquets of roses, while dignitaries "processed peacefully before it ... with a religious solemnity."[29] In the same spirit we find that the guillotine was used to sever the heads of the saintly statues on the western façade of the Cathedral of Notre Dame.[30] Thus did a new divine power destroy the false idols of the old. With a new god in place, prayers could be said. For example, at the festival held on 21 January 1794, in the shadow of the scaffold we find the following litany read out:

Saint Guillotine, protectress of patriots, pray for us.

Saint Guillotine, the dread of aristocrats, protect us.

Gracious Machine, have mercy on us.

Admirable Machine, have mercy on us.

Saint Guillotine, deliver us from our enemies.[31]

The guillotine, to recap, was an invention emerging from the discourses of the Enlightenment and sustained by developing knowledge bases in medicine and anatomy. Yet here, as elsewhere during the Revolution, we find that these secular qualities were layered onto a spiritual base. Reason, justice, and science were themselves a sacred order. And so the Foucaultian logic of power and technological efficiency is embraced within a broader nexus of cultural codes. Paradoxically, this explicit, dramatic, and quasi-religious supportive frame was to work as a target for critics, opening up possibilities for its own destabilization by equally heady discourses. As we will now see, a counter-narrative emerged that layered natural science with the supernatural in reading the human body and its punishment. Only this time the guillotine was taken as polluting rather than as pure.

Uncanny Aspects of the Headless Corpse

In the discussion of the Damiens case, where a regicide was systematically tortured to death, Foucault correctly identifies how the body of the condemned was taken as a signifier in the premodern era. In his narrative of the subsequent period this possibility disappears from view. Instead of being a text that could be read for inscriptions of power, the body becomes the docile carrier of an internalized disciplinary logic. It is to be interpolated as a function not as a sign. The implication seems to be that as in the case of medicine,[32] a new scientific episteme was coming to replace an earlier kind of soothsaying forensic activity operating according to what Lévi-Strauss has termed the "science of the concrete."[33] In point of fact, during the late eighteenth and nineteenth centuries, the body of the condemned long continued to provide a locus for the interpretative operation of both popular and professional gazes.[34] Within discourses over the guillotine we find an intense interest in the body as a contexture of surfaces where underlying moral and metaphysical patterns were displayed. Such activities centered on readings of the severed head and the headless corpse. Just as the technology of the guillotine symbolized harsh but fair justice, thus providing a cipher that encrypted the sacred essence of a codified and purified revolutionary law, so did the headless body provide a resource for alternative readings of the technology and its implications. These can be thought of as a sphere-specific refraction of a widespread tendency during the Revolution. This was to take the body as a signifier and token with which to think through, and hopefully resolve, profound questions about the organization of the new society. Lynn Hunt, for example, has suggested that representations of the body of Marie-Antoinette served to reproduce the gender order, while Dorinda Outram considers how class dynamics influenced the bodily display of *homo clausus*.[35] In a similar vein, the bodies of the guillotine's victims were contested coins in the market-place of ideas about justice, science, and progress.

The debates in question came to a boil from May to November 1795 when a public controversy erupted about the reading of newly sepa-rated heads and bodies. These exchanges were between high-status, well-qualified figures in the emerging and slowly consolidating field of medi-cine. They are therefore analogous to the kinds of discourse that Foucault himself has studied. Yet far from being the internal talk of experts, these were exchanges directed toward the public sphere. The *Magasin encyclo-pédique* and the *Moniteur universel* were composite news, science, and arts publications pitched at an educated general audience. The supposition we can make is that there was a widespread interest, at least among literate elites, in the expert debates, and below I will account for this. First it is necessary to briefly review the discussions that combined abstract knowl-edge, personal experience, and common sense inference in a way that is typical of the period before the nineteenth-century professionalization of medical science.

Readings of the headless body were central to the influential attacks on the guillotine that were spearheaded by Professor Soemmering and citoyen Sue. Soemmering initiated the debate in a published letter in which he argued that the inventors of the guillotine had placed faith in their machine as "the most certain, most rapid and least painful mode of death" but had failed to reflect on the state of the "sensibility, which continues still after the punishment." He claimed that the guillotine con-stituted a "horrible mode of death. In the head, separated from the body of the victim, sentiment, and personality remain alive for some time, and feel the after-pain afflicting the neck."[36] Soemmering suggested the head was primary as a seat of pain. This was demonstrated by the phenomenon of phantom limbs. He pointed out that a patient would often "complain about pains that he believes can still be felt in a finger that no longer exists."[37] Citoyen Sue, in a similar move, pointed out that most persons who had undergone operations resulting in the removal of an arm, leg, eye, or male sexual apparatus "had such awareness of the existence of members that they no longer had—that they believed they could even make all kinds of movements, touch or feel foreign bodies: Persuade themselves that they could see with an eye they no longer had."[38]

Pivotal to the attack was a claim that the head could maintain its life force (*force vitale*) after being severed. This was supported by several sources of data. By far the most important of these related to the motions of the muscles to be observed in the severed head. Soemmering wrote that "[o]thers have assured me that they have seen teeth grinding after the head has been separated from the body; and I am convinced that if air still circulated through the organs of the voice, had they not been destroyed, the heads would speak."[39] He goes on to speculate that "if then the head of a man . . . remains sufficiently active to . . . move the muscles of the face, one cannot doubt that sensation (*sentiment*) and the faculty of perception remains at the same time."[40] How long could this last? According to Soemmering, "Judging from experience with the amputated limbs of living men, on which galvanic irritation has been attempted, it is reasonable to suppose that sensibility can remain for a quarter of an hour, due to the head, thanks to its thickness and round form, retaining its heat."[41] This point was reinforced by Sue, who suggested that a communicative urge was at hand: "One has observed many times in severed heads various movements of the pupils, the eyes, the lips, even movements of the jaws when the executioner holds up the still warm heads for people to see . . . We can hazard the supposition . . . this could have been to indicate by these conventional movements that they had awareness of their punishment . . . and for love of humanity . . . tried to turn this sad experience to the advantage of their fellow men."[42]

As Sue's words make clear, calls for imaginative identification with pain and suffering were a central motif of this argument. These can be seen, for instance, in claims that pain could persist in everyday life in the absence of motion or voice. Soemmering mentions that cold "freezes the fingers to a point where they are incapable . . . of writing, while feeling remains."[43] Similarly, Sue queries: "How many animals and plants suffer without making known their pain through any cry whatsoever? If it is evident that a living body can suffer without crying or speaking, then cries and speech when experiencing pain are not the surest signs. We can more or less consider them as accessory signs."[44] When it came to the experience of having a severed head, we are invited to imagine the utmost anguish. Soemmering's knowledge of anatomy led him to suggest that the guillotine struck at the most sensitive point on the human body. He writes: "The neck joins all the nerves of the superior organs with the spinal column, which is the source of all the nerves which are shared among the lower limbs. Consequently the pain of their separation . . . must be the most violent, the most acute, the most tearing that it is possible to devise."[45] Sue compounded this with reference to the existential anguish of being sensible after death: "[W]hat a terrible situation to have the perception of one's execution and at the same time a subsequent awareness of one's punishment."[46]

At the end of their reflections, Soemmering and Sue turn away from the body and reflect on the wider implications of their argument. The suffering of the individual, induced from a quivering jaw or thrashing limb, could be generalized into an indictment of revolutionary penal policy as neither sufficiently enlightened nor adequately humanistic. And it was not the mutilated body but identification of an aware mind that stood at the center of critique. By pointing to consciousness and pain, critics suggested that the guillotine could no longer be coded as sacred—as an instrument of civilization and progress. To the contrary it could now be seen as an indicator of barbarism and monstrosity, and its supporters as primitives who did not belong in a civil society.

> It is not necessary to point out to honorable souls how much this new form of punishment dishonors humanity. Those who can enjoy it and speak of it with a sort of delight, are monsters that a reasonable man cannot begin to convert; they must be deported to live amongst cannibals.[47]

> Such abominable spectacles should not take place among savages—yet here there are republicans who give and attend them.[48]

Defenders of the guillotine systematically addressed the points raised by critics. To begin with, every one of them suggested that the bodily motions should be seen as automatic responses—as natural signs that did not involve any higher order awareness or *sensibilité*. Consider the following statements by Cabanis, Le Pelletier, Sédillot, Gastellier, Wedekind, and Léveillé.

> Movement of a part of the body does not presuppose sensations, nor the ability to produce these motions, a conscious awareness . . . In some convulsive mala-

dies one can prick, pull, or cut the sick person without him giving any sign of *sensibilité* and when he comes round he remembers nothing of what happened during his fit.[49]

Soemmering ... attributes to the faculty of sensation all that which is only the automatic irritability to which our bodily parts are susceptible, as we know, for a long time after death and whilst functioning has ceased.[50]

I am convinced that the heads conserve the expression that they had at the moment of punishment and that the muscles of the face remain as they were. An unhappy victim, lying on the fatal plank [of the guillotine], waiting for the harsh instrument which is going to cut the thread of his days, can grind their teeth or have various other convulsions that remain even after the separation of the head from the body.[51]

One observes quite strong convulsions in the muscles of heads attacked by paroxysms of apoplexy, epilepsy, etc. . . . while consciousness is entirely lost.[52]

The (convulsions) that are given off in the face of the guillotine are the effect of the spontaneous retraction of muscles that have lost their point of attachment, etc. and not the effect of living pain, therefore the penalty of the guillotine is the most humane.[53]

These phenomena ... [are] the effect of shock to the entire body, of the unexpected upsetting of our functions that are destroyed, and finally of spasm and convulsive movement that must necessarily take place.[54]

An alternative deployment of medical knowledge is used here in an attempt to redescribe the phenomena noted by Soemmering and Sue. In this interpretative regime the motions of the victim's head and body do not indicate consciousness. The signals given off by the body belong to a different order from everyday communication. They are natural signs rather than motivated ones and are best seen as analogous to automatic convulsions. They indicate only themselves and should not be interpreted in terms of any higher-order semiotic system such as the codes relating to the expression of emotion. Indeed, such efforts can lead to paradoxical conclusions, as Dr. Gastellier pointed out:

To judge the absolute insignificance of these sorts of convulsions, consider the man who has received a sword blow to the nervous center of the diaphragm—it produces on the muscles of the face convulsions which we call the Sardonic laugh ... he dies laughing, or rather, with the appearance of laughing, and meanwhile we know he can hardly be happy. It is a purely mechanical convulsion and certainly the injured man dies without having awareness of what happens to him.[55]

Anatomical knowledge was also deployed in another way to confront claims about pain and consciousness. Cabanis urged that a state of shock would afflict the person whose head had been chopped off: "the violent hemorrhaging that follows decapitations ... deprives the brain of the blood required to maintain its proper functioning."[56] This argument was reinforced by Sédillot and Wedekind.

One knows that a simple hemorrhage ... can produce fainting, loss of consciousness, or loss of feeling.[57]

The loss of blood necessary to produce fainting can be very small if the blood drains with speed. The surgeon, who wants to avoid a patient falling into a faint while he is bleeding him, makes only the smallest cut in a vein. Can there be a bigger and faster loss of blood than from the severing of the vessels of the neck?[58]

And far from producing the most acute pain, severing the spinal column would produce instant death.

One sees ... the same phenomenon every day in our butcheries and in our kitchens ... one kills rabbits by hitting them behind the ears, chickens by wringing the neck: we have seen birds suddenly die when we introduce a needle into the spinal column. All these observations ... demonstrate that in the punishment of the guillotine the victim is killed before the complete section of all the tissue, that it is in the incalculable instant when the blade in falling hits the spinal column ... before cutting it.[59]

Medical supporters of the guillotine, then, tried to close down debate with alternative readings of the body and alternative suppositions on human consciousness. Even their best efforts, however, could never bring closure. As we will see, such counterarguments carried with them hidden themes and elements that unintentionally contributed to their own destabilization.

The Guillotine, the Body, and the Gothic Imagination

In his work on prisons, Foucault points to the fact that punishment in the modern era is predicated on an enduring connection between body and soul. In the case of the panopticon, the self-awareness of the inmate was the means through which they might come to regulate their own body. Other devices such as the treadmill worked in reverse, enforcing routines on the docile body in the expectation that these would lead to a normalized soul. The debates we have just looked at point to a completely opposing dynamic in capital punishment. Both advocates and detractors of the guillotine believed that executions could only be legitimate if they managed to effect a complete separation of body and soul. The latter was to be strictly quarantined from the former. Any connection between them, giving rise to pain or even awareness of the process of dying, would render a technology or procedure illegitimate. For this reason, critics of the guillotine attempted to establish just such a connection. Drawing on theories of anatomy and on philosophical reasoning about the relationship between body and mind, they suggested that bodily motions could be read upwards as traces of higher functioning. By contrast, supporters of the guillotine countered with their own range of expert knowledge. These attempted to downgrade the same observations, treating bodily movements as mechanistic responses of muscle and nerve that had no connection to higher levels of sensory direction and awareness. The resulting battle of stories and interpretations could only produce the Scottish verdict—"not proven."[60]

But this is not the end of the story. Looked at from Foucault's point of view, the debates we have considered can be thought of as typical of a power-knowledge discourse in an emerging modernity. They treat the body from an analytical stance and evaluate its interaction with technology using a clinical gaze. Had Foucault come across and worked on the documents and arguments we have briefly summarized, it is not difficult to imagine that he would have found them fertile material for his unique style of theoretical activity. Yet in this particular instance, disciplinary knowledge did not come at the expense of folk knowledge or popular discourse; rather, there was a strange hybridity linking scientific thought with the popular imagination.

Mikhail Bakhtin has spoken of the dialogical way in which culture works—an understanding that provides some purchase on thinking through the implications of our material.[61] He suggests that new concepts and intellectual templates can be seen as originating in a center, which tries to impose a fixed meaning. Yet once in circulation, meanings proliferate as symbol systems collide with each other—a situation Bakhtin has described as heteroglossia. Discourses now become layered and mutate in complex and unanticipated ways as formal models encounter folk models in the migration from center to periphery. In earlier chapters we saw the execution, the prison, and the panopticon become popular symbols unchained from any original disciplinary or signifying intent. Much the same game occurs here. If the technopolitical dimensions of the guillotine can best be understood using Foucault's theories, and Durkheim's model of the sacred and profane affords the most efficient mechanism for decoding its elementary semiotic logic, perhaps Bakhtin provides a superior tool for understanding its subsequent reception in the scientific and popular imagination. The revolutionary authors of the new penal technology, Drs. Guillotin and Louis, and their political backers attempted to confine possible meanings by offering what Bakhtin has termed an "authoritative discourse." This can be thought of as a package of ideas linked to political power and state institutions that worked as a "centripetal force" against semantic proliferation. Yet once set free in the public sphere, the guillotine was to become a multiaccentual sign whose definitive meaning was postponed and contested in an expanding universe of unlicensed images and symbols. The result was a cultural dynamic that has parallels with the existential analysis of the Terror as discussed by Maurice Blanchot.[62] According to Blanchot, the experience of routinized death, intended as a strategy of political control, unleashed as an unintended consequence a new sense of freedom. This found its ultimate expression in the unauthorized productive excess of the Marquis de Sade. Thus what Hegel had described in his *Phenomenology of Spirit* as an event "which has no inner dimension or resolution . . . the coldest and meanest of all deaths, with no more significance than cutting off a cabbage head or swallowing a mouthful of water" should, to the contrary, better be seen as the foundation for creative, unruly operations of the human imaginative faculty.[63]

Such a Bakhtinian story of unpredicted outcomes, unruly signs, and the volatile sacred can be traced through the medical material we have encountered above. To begin with, the medical discourses on the guillotine resonated with the thematics of symbolism and mythology as well as those of reason and knowledge. Soemmering's position, for example, embodies residual themes from the Pietist anatomical theory of Georg Ernst Stahl with its antimechanist insistence on an "organic body" whose every movement reflected the influence of an animating, mysterious soul. Stahl's broadly vitalist perspective, it has been noted elsewhere, offered a challenge to Newtonian and Cartesian rationalism and their atomistic (protodisciplinary) understanding of the body as a mere machine.[64] Other nonrational traces in the medical discourses were less systematic or organized, but perhaps more resonant, to the lay audience of the *Magasin encyclopédique* and the *Moniteur universel.* We can approach these with reference to the idea of the gothic genre, which is generally believed to have originated with Horace Walpole's *The Castle of Otranto* in 1764 and reached its peak of influence during the 1790s—the very era of the debates treated here. The genre played a central role in political language games of the time, operating as a code, metaphor, or trope for thinking through the structural transformations and ideological shifts of the era. Edmund Burke's *Reflections on the Revolution in France,* for example, depicted the Revolution as a depraved monster that endangered order throughout Europe, while the counter-narratives of Thomas Paine and Mary Wollstonecraft engaged the same imagery in attacking a feudal order of injustice, religious superstition, and decay.[65] The gothic, then, can be seen as a key component of the late eighteenth-century cultural imagination operating as a toolkit of symbols with which a rapidly changing and unstable environment could be understood.

In terms of its thematic content, the gothic genre is about terror, excess, ambivalence, transgression, and the speculative imagination.[66] The macabre and the bizarre take center stage, replacing the routine, knowable, and empirically certain as the objects of discourse. For this reason it has been widely claimed that "gothic figures have continued to shadow the progress of modernity with counter-narratives displaying the underside of enlightenment and humanist values."[67] This central theme sits, for example, behind the critique of science in Mary Shelley's *Frankenstein* or Robert Louis Stevenson's *Dr. Jekyll and Mr. Hyde.* Here the hubris of rational man is exposed, and technology and invention are denounced as threatening to human values. Ghoulish images populate the landscape of the gothic imagination—phantoms, madmen, corpses, and mad scientists. Ruptured, dismembered, and deformed bodies limp and stumble through gothic texts threatening ideas of progressive cultural and societal evolution and defying efforts at comprehension by reason and logic.[68] At work are supernatural powers —or as the science fiction writer H. P. Lovecraft puts it in his analysis of the genre, "unknown forces"[69]—whose comprehension lies in the realm of intuition rather than reason. Central to the power of the genre was the role of the human imagination. It worked by inspiring doubt, terror, and horror in the reader and by promoting anxious identification with protagonists. Within the gothic, ideas of doubling also play a crucial part. These circulate around the parallels that can be drawn between good and evil or point to the ways that evil can lurk behind a sacred façade. In sum, the result was a genre that questioned the ability of Enlightenment knowledge to produce closure, create the good society, or control elemental forces.

We are now in a position to return to our data. Consider again the quotations from Soemmering and Sue provided above. Here we find a gothic imagination immanent within the discourses of secular medical science. They speak of minds that are alive after death. They invite readers to use their imaginations and to identify with the horrors of pain, shame, and angst experienced by victims. They conjure up visions of amputations and talking heads. The images they raise, one after another, are ghastly, chilling, and disturbing. They suggest a doubling in which the apparently benign, rational, open technology has a darker side. In this vision the guillotine was a sinister monster whose ultimate effects were barbaric and unspeakable.

While attempting to deflect and refute such imagery, their critics come to repeat it. The gothic trumps the language of science, framing as spooky and disturbing that which is presented as matter of fact. Brusque analogies to epileptic fits and butchery, surgical procedures, automatism, scientific experiments, and the sardonic grimace of the defeated duelist become grist for the mill. Even efforts to describe the instantaneous qualities of death end up inviting a speculative imagination and identification. When Sédillot speaks of "the incalculable instant when the blade in falling hits the spinal column . . . before cutting it" or Guillotin himself of "a slight coolness on the back of the neck," we are in the same territory as Edgar Allan Poe's "The Pit and the Pendulum." Here audience sympathy, a sense of pleasing/repelling and ambivalent horror are generated by anticipating the precise moment at which the surface of the body is violated.[70] Ironically, because earlier discourses supporting the guillotine had spoken of the technology as extraordinary, sacred, miraculous, terrible, and transcendent rather than as plain, ordinary, routine, and boring, such heady imagery of the liminal and sinister fell upon prepared cultural soils. Public interest in the question grew to an extent that some thought of it in turn as unhealthy. The editors of the *Magasin encyclopédique,* for example, abruptly called off further debate in its pages.

In investigating further the qualities and force of these unruly bodies and gothic discourses, it is once again Bakhtin who provides a clue to guide our inquiry. Writing on Rabelais, Bakhtin draws attention to the thematic of the grotesque body.[71] Characterized by excess, openness, pain, pleasure, dismemberment, and profanity, such a body operated not only to celebrate the popular and carnal (as has often been noted) but also offered a counter-thematic and ironic commentary upon the closed and individualized body that emerged after the Renaissance as rationalistic knowledge replaced theological authority. In short, the grotesque body functioned to interrogate visions of perfection and rationality, order and discipline, with its coded affirmations of materiality, decay, and profanity.[72] The guillotine worked as an efficient technology, yet in its instrumental operation it produced not only dead bodies but also grotesque ones. There was the panoply of unintended bodily signs with which its own legitimacy could be undermined. Bakhtin points, for example, to dismemberment, dissection, and bodily fluids as pivotal emblems in the lexicon of the grotesque body—all core outputs of the guillotine. In particular, he argues for the centrality of the grotesque face and its gaping mouth in this symbolic universe. By operating on the head, which was held up to the crowd by the executioner, the mechanical and ritual operation of the guillotine served to focus attention exactly here at a crucial node of semiotic ambivalence. Soemmering and Sue, we remember, were most forcibly impressed by gnashing teeth and rolling eyes. In a similar vein Maurice Chardon was to later focus on the "human mask" in his poetic indictment of capital punishment: "One sees a mask that the executioner holds up, One sees a human mask, horrible, grimacing."[73] It is no accident that morbid popular interest peaked when the head of Charlotte Corday, Marat's assassin, was slapped by the executioner as he held it up for inspection. Primed by belief in the persistence of a *sensibilité* after decapitation, rumors spread throughout Paris that she had blushed out of shame at the infamy of this moral violation.[74]

The gothic motif and the Rabelaisian body, then, were able to run in parallel with and inform scientific discourses and at the same time touched a nerve with popular sentiments. They worked to destabilize brisk moral certainties by directing speculation toward the unknowable horror of the experience of decapitation. Following the debates of 1795, questions about pain and consciousness remained, persistent but incorrigible. It was this lack of resolution that allowed the now-questionable technology to remain minimally legitimate.

FIGURE 5. Michelangelo, *Moses*, 1515. Photograph by the author.

There was a heavy price to pay for this incorrigibility, for uncertainty and lack of closure prevented the routinization of charismatic technology within the social imagination. To help understand this we can turn to Freud's celebrated interpretation of Michelangelo's sculpture of Moses (see fig. 5). Intrigued by this masterwork, the centerpiece of the unfinished tomb of Pope Julius II, Freud would always visit it during his trips to Rome. He found puzzling the posture and expression of Moses as well as the position of the tablets containing the Ten Commandments. Why was Moses looking to his left? What were the tablets doing beside his right thigh? Why was one hand on his beard and pulling it to the side? Sherlock Holmes–like, Freud worked out a sequence of action that could explain this unusual composition but admitted that his answer was not definitive. He did, however arrive at a very important theoretical generalization that has been curiously ignored in cultural theory. According to Freud, cultural objects that are "unsolved riddles to our understanding" and refuse a simple, consensual explanation are often those which produce feelings of "awe."[75] They have a "magical appeal" and invite us to discover the source of "a power that is beyond them alone." Written around the same time as the *Elementary Forms of Religious Life,* these words echo Durkheim's belief that the sacred is always surrounded by mystery and ambivalence.

Just like body of Moses in Michelangelo's sculpture, the truncated bodies and severed heads of the guillotine's victims afforded a complex and somewhat fascinating discursive field for obsessive interpretation, with ambiguous gestures and movements tied to unknowable emotions. The guillotine sparked inquiries into the body for which resolution was impossible. Contending explanations, ordinary and extraordinary, produced the knife-edge of doubt that, as the literary critic Tzvetan Todorov has pointed out, is the engine behind the genre of the "fantastic." This requires the reader "to hesitate between a natural and a supernatural explanation of the events described."[76] Here is a marvelous contradiction: the very uncertainty that allowed the penal technology to continue provided fuel for a stubborn counter-discourse of wild speculation and morbid popular inquiry. This reached its apotheosis during the nineteenth century in popular narratives of Faustian scientific interventions on the grotesque body. The novelist Auguste Villiers de l'Isle-Adam, for example, published *The Secret of the Scaffold,* a best-selling fictional account of experiments conducted by one Dr. Velpeau on the head of murderer La Pommerais.[77] Many believed the book to be a report of true activities. Murky and unsubstantiated rumors continually circulated about such secret experiments. In his *Histoire de la médicine légale en France* (1880) Charles Desmaze provides a secondhand report of tests allegedly conducted on the severed head of one Prunier. Efforts were made to find signs of life, such as pupil dilation.[78] Conducted to put an end to public speculation and replace it with certainties, such scientific operations (if indeed they really took place) served only to drip feed a macabre popular thirst for fantastic stories. As late as the early twentieth century this genre of shady research continued to attract public interest. In 1907, for example, the populist newspaper *Le Matin* ran a front-page interview with a Dr. Dassy de Lignères, who, it claimed, had worked on the head of the murderer Menesclou in 1880.[79] Lignères spoke of connecting Menesclou's severed head to a supply of blood from a living dog in a bizarre act of vivisection. From here to the *Island of Dr. Moreau* it is but a short step. According to Lignères, color came to the face and life was regained for the space of two seconds. He concludes with a call for identification that, for all its Grand Guignol affectation, is remarkably similar to those of critics of the revolutionary period: "[W]hen the knife has done its work ... and the head rolls ... that head hears you well. That head separated from its body hears the noise of the crowd. The severed head feels itself dying in the basket."[80]

Perhaps more credible were the experiments on the head of Languille by Dr. Beaurieux reported in the *Archives de l'Anthropologie Criminelle*. The experimenter relates how the head opened its eyes when the name Languille was called and then how they "fixed in a precise fashion on mine and the pupils adjusted ... I had the impression that living eyes were looking at me."[81] Once again, then, the scientific account incorporates subjective elements that invite speculation and intersubjectivity rather than bringing closure. It is hardly surprising that these unnerving moments from a usually tedious academic journal were subsequently reported in detail and analyzed in the popular press. *Le Matin,* for example, ran a lengthy interview with a Professor Hartman.[82] Drawing analogies to his work dissecting frogs and other animals, Hartman concluded that the signs of life allegedly detected by Beaurieux were merely automatic reflexes. The truth of these debates, as well as the reality or otherwise of the experiments, is hardly at issue here. What is of interest is that the continuing circulation of fables documents a stubborn and persisting, morbid popular interest in the imagery of the severed head, the mad scientist, and the guillotine. Whether fact or fable, scientific attempts to resolve uncertainty merely generate a Bakhtinian heteroglossia, providing food for a popular imagination more attuned to the fantastic and uncanny possibilities of the penal technology on the body and soul than to its juridical logic and technological function. And trivial though such popular discourses may seem, they were to cycle back into elite debates. Thus in his polemical "Réflexions sur la guillotine," we find the usually innovative and skeptical Albert Camus reworking the familiar imagery of the blushing Charlotte Corday and Languille's eyes. He reports on a "new" set of scientific observations that suggested that the guillotine led to "a horrible experience, murderous vivisection followed by a premature burial."[83] So heterologous collective representation and iconography had oozed into the second half of the twentieth century in much the same form as at its inception at the close of the eighteenth.

It has long been recognized in cultural theory that death lends itself particularly well to symbolism. It is tied in complex ways to imageries of the body and to the emergence of discourses of pollution and salvation.[84] The guillotine stands, therefore, as a strategic research site for demonstrating in a rarified form the meaningful nature of penal technologies. It lends what I called in chapter 1 a "home field advantage." In chapter 6 I will replicate this methodological logic in a more recent context—the electric chair.

CHAPTER SIX

The Electric Chair

The history of the guillotine examined in chapter 5 is one that was to be curiously mirrored some one hundred years later in the case of the electric chair. Here we will see culture patterns replicating themselves as they unfold through time. First a technology is invented to cleanse judicially sanctioned death, to remove semantic irregularities and indignities. There is the intent to send out some kind of message about civilization and preserve the sacred dignity of the individual even as they are destroyed. Next we find this encoded, official narrative of what Bakhtin called the "center" received in uneven and unanticipated ways on the periphery. Decoding in civil society and popular culture mobilizes complex and unanticipated myths and regimes of figuration. The machinery of death is now an unknowable, ambivalent object. With its narration surrounded by ambiguous clues it becomes fascinating and mysterious, transcending any profane existence as a material artifact. Finally, official meanings become hopelessly contested and subverted as the technology transforms into a totem and signifier in a complex semiotic universe of sacred and profane iconography. In large part this is due to the unruly bodies that the electric chair produces and to the classificatory boundaries that it transgresses, such as the line between life and death. More than a simple tool or reflection of legal norms, the means of execution are reconfigured into an icon of barbarism, a symbol of oppression, a relic of the past, and the carrier of a ghoulish charisma. The chair's curtain call comes when it is abandoned as an anachronism, a cultural and legal liability that can continue to perform only as a star exhibit in wax museums or as a problematic one in more educational displays.

While the trajectory of the two technologies is largely identical, fine points of divergence are also visible. The electric chair offers a parallel but not precisely identical case to that of the guillotine. There is a far greater level of reflexivity at play. Right from the start, interested parties were more deeply concerned about signaling and meaning, so making more concerted efforts to regulate, control, and prevent alternative narrations. Partly for this reason the chair was hidden away. So long as citizens were prepared to get out of bed early they could witness the guillotine in action for themselves during much of its operative history. General inspection of the electric chair at work was impossible. The wider collective representation of the technology was indirect and mass-mediated through print and then film to a far larger extent than was that of the guillotine, a process that ironically aided the creation of mystique. Whereas the guillotine was the invention of the state, the early history of the electric chair is one where capitalist interests were very much at stake. Initially at least, meaning was tied to money in rather unsubtle ways. Yet for all these points of contrast the mythology of the electric chair, its wider totemic resonance, and its collective representation run remarkably close to the track of the guillotine. This convergence is methodologically useful, helping us to see the ubiquity and adaptability of culture structures to institutional and historical conditions as divergent as twentieth-century America and revolutionary France.

The Cultural Origins of the Electric Chair

Just as the guillotine replaced earlier botched, disorderly, and degrading punishments, just as the hidden execution was a response to the vice and carnival of the public death, and just as the Victorian prison emerged from the chaos and filth of the early-modern jail, the cultural origins of the electric chair lay in the perceived pollution of a prior punitive method, hanging. By the late nineteenth century there was widespread concern in the United States that this was undignified. It was seen as too unreliable and as sometimes lengthy and painful, such anxieties following upon a trend in newspapers from around 1850 onward to report in detail any chaotic twitching, gurgling, or facial contortion.[1] The case for reform was further accelerated by the growing influence of the humanitarian movement in the United States, which was intent upon reducing cruelty to animals and humans alike. Legitimacy for hanging was fragile, and morally offensive cases kept the pressure on right up to the moment of the electric chair's first use in 1890. For example, the execution of murderess Roxalana Druse in 1887 was an ugly affair. She took fifteen minutes to die at the end of the rope. Looking to set the pace in his State of the State address of 1885, New York governor Hill proclaimed that "the present mode of executing criminals has come down to us from the Dark Ages"[2] and urged the legislature to consider the issue of reform. In 1886 it responded, establishing a commission to review available methods. The panel's deliberations were a quest to locate a mode of death that was instantaneous and did not mutilate the body, or in Durkheimian terms, that did not confound embodied boundaries and that respected the cult of the individual. Electricity, the panel eventually decided, was the best answer.

For the most part the newspapers were in agreement with such reasoning. Hanging was looking abominable, and something innovative needed to be done. The *New York Times* editorialized in favor of change, suggesting that the "terrors of the law should be retained while the mere horrors are abolished," such as those involving "lingering struggles and contortions" at the end of the rope. The result of introducing electrocution—as it came to be called—would be to substitute a "civilized for a barbarous method."[3] Likewise the *New York Tribune* condemned the "brutal and barbarous practice of executing condemned prisoners by hanging."[4] The desired cultural binaries were beginning to fall into place. Hanging was premodern, unpredictable, and barbaric, while death by electricity scientific, reliable, and civilized. Electricity looked to be the status transformation force that could move an intact body and unconscious mind efficiently over the boundary between life and death. It symbolized the spirit of its age.

The novel choice of electricity as the solution to the problem of reconciling justice, death, technology, and meaning had been facilitated by vested interests of a curious nature. These were to play a crucial role in the evolution of the narratives for and against the electric chair, those that emphasized certainty and those that invoked mystery. When New York State first expressed an interest in electrocution as a mode of death, the inventor and entrepreneur Thomas Alva Edison had been only too keen to help. Edison was at this time in a competition with George Westinghouse over the supply of utility electricity and the construction of an electricity grid. Edison favored a direct current (DC) distribution system operating around 100 volts, yet this was handicapped by relatively large power losses during transmission, thereby requiring the expense of numerous local generators and thick copper cables.[5] Westinghouse, however, had developed an ingenious alternating current (AC) system that dramatically reduced power loss over distance. Resistance was reduced thanks to higher voltages, made possible by step-up transformers at the fewer points of generation and numerous step-down transformers near the point of consumption. Westinghouse's system was more efficient and therefore cheaper and threatened to dominate the market. Edison argued that such AC distribution was unsafe and could lead to fires or death by electricity in the home. Efforts to demonstrate this thesis saw Edison throwing his considerable financial, moral, social, and intellectual capital behind the development of a fatal device that made use of the AC current. Edison held such a technology to be "more certain and perhaps a little more civilized than the rope."[6] It could also serve as a powerful marketing tool. In the terms laid out by the semiotician Charles Peirce we can see it as a concrete and none too subtle "index" of danger that could dramatize time and again with each judicial death the perils of Westinghouse's AC systems in domestic contexts.[7] Edison was assisted in his efforts at such basic applied semiotics by the fact that the early AC systems in New York City that powered primitive arc lights were poorly maintained and operated. A tangle of wires, overburdened power poles, weak regulation, and poor training meant that accidental electrocutions were frequent, visible, and newsworthy. By contrast Edison's own DC generator in Pearl Street had functioned safely for several years.[8]

The Mystery of Electrical Power

Clean. Finite. Civilized. Knowable. Painless. Even before that alternating current ran through the body of its first juridical victim the seeds had been planted for a rather different narration of the electric chair, one that converted a material fact into an enigma and whose favored punctuation was the question mark. Clean? Finite? Civilized? Knowable? Painless? We have seen that within three years of its baptism the guillotine had become a problematic tool of justice thanks to the gothic imagination and tales of Faustian science. The electric chair was even quicker off the mark, made mysterious from the moment of a less than immaculate conception thanks to the semiotic spillover of long-enduring mythologies surrounding electricity. These saw the electric current as a medium connecting life and death, as an ambiguous and sacred force that could bridge this most fundamental classificatory boundary.[9] Early galvanic experiments such as those on twitching frogs' legs connected by wires to primitive metal and acid piles had suggested it should be understood as the very life force. Subsequent research on "animal magnetism," as mesmerism came to be known, hinted that the self could be accessed and adjusted by such currents. The later and related deployment of electrotherapy as a cure for "neurasthenia"—what we would now know as anxiety, listlessness, and depression—seemingly confirmed the existence of intimate if not fully understood ties between electric forces and the mysteries of the human soul.

Outside the field of medicine we find a similar cultural pattern. The telegraph, for example, was initially seen as a miraculous invention with belief widespread that thoughts were being transmitted along the lines via electrical pulses.[10] As for the telephone, its evolution had connections to spiritualism. Even Bell's assistant Thomas A. Watson saw it as speaking with an occult force.[11] Something of this exalted, mysterious view of electricity can be found in Walt Whitman. For the poet it was rather akin to a universal mind, a creative life force tying human souls together through the ether and animating the creative and unfolding activity of the "body electric."[12] We can use Durkheim to reinforce this point, but in the status of exhibit rather than expert witness. In his writings of the 1890s in particular he often speaks of nervous "currents" and of the moral "charge" of the collective conscience.[13]

This mythological complex where electricity embodies the occult finds resonance at the point of origin of the official narrative of the electric chair. Elbridge Gerry, the most important member of that commission set up by New York state legislature in 1886 to investigate and report on methods of execution saw it as communicatively appropriate for criminals to be eliminated by a "terrible but silent force to them unknown."[14] Dread and mystery, as Durkheim notes, are key indicators of the sacred. This particular discursive knot in which electricity, science, medicine, the body, the soul, the divine, and the supernatural were interlaced had of course reached an apogee much earlier in the century. The pinnacle of its thematic expression came in Mary Wollstonecraft Shelley's *Frankenstein*.[15] As a boy the well-meaning but misguided fictional doctor had been inspired by the utter destruction of a tree by lightening at Belrive. He later encountered a stranger, a "man of great research in natural philosophy," who explained his theory "on the subject of electricity and galvanism." At his moment of triumph Frankenstein narrates, "I collected the instruments of life around me, that I might infuse a spark of being into the lifeless thing that lay at my feet."[16] No act of pure imagination, Mary Shelley had been inspired very concretely by the real-life experiments of Karl August Weinhold involving the insertion of conducting materials into the bodies of dead kittens before subjecting them to galvanic irritation. She had also overheard the poets Byron and Shelley talking on the subject and speculating that a corpse could be reanimated using galvanism.[17] It was only a matter of time before such thinking saw real efforts made to raise the dead, Lazarus-like. In 1870, current was applied by means of a hand-cranked generator to Joseph Skaggs, who had been hanged in Bloomfield, Missouri. The *New York Times* reported violent twitching.[18]

For all his patents and for all the secular can-do mythology surrounding his collective representation, Edison himself was not insulated from this circuit of meaning that endlessly reproduced itself through the nineteenth century and that argued for mystery rather than closure in the case of electricity. Consequently in his endorsement of the electric chair he was simultaneously a source of scientific authority for its supporters and an ambiguous symbol from which counter-narrations could draw strength. Like other charlatans and snake oil vendors peddling the mysterious curative properties of electricity, in 1874 Edison had already developed an "inductorium." Endorsed by the discoverer of neurasthenia, George Beard, this electric shock machine was marketed as a fix for rheumatism. It was widely thought at the time that there was something uncanny about Edison's efforts to freeze the transience of sound with the phonograph, and it is entirely symptomatic that he was dubbed by his contemporaries the "Wizard of Menlo Park."[19] Edison was even inserted into the fiction of his time as a life-giver of miraculous abilities. From a Durkheimian perspective it is no accident that the Comte Villiers de l'Isle-Adam, briefly referred to in chapter 5, scripted him into his novel of 1888, *L'Ève future.*[20] In this curious precursor to twentieth-century cyborg literature, the British aristocrat Lord Ewald comes to visit Thomas Edison at his laboratories in Menlo Park, New Jersey. He relates his failures in love. Edison obliges Ewald's fantasies, using his scientific skills in the manner of Pygmalion to produce a female robot as an object of desire. Here Villiers generates and makes use of resonances between Edison, Faust, and those mad doctors of E. T. A. Hoffmann who tinkered with mesmerism and constructed lifelike automata.[21] Much the same can be said for the rival camp. Nikola Tesla, the genius who pioneered with Westinghouse the application of alternating current electricity, gave self-promoting magicianlike shows in which he harnessed the electrical power of what is now know as a Tesla-coil to generate thunder and lightening. Insulated with cork-soled shoes he would illuminate light bulbs in his hands and surround his body with the unearthly glow of Saint Elmo's fire.[22]

So even before the chair was born, the popular culture of the late 1800s was primed to see electricity as abnormal, supernatural, and as mediating life and death in complex and protracted ways. This perception could be confirmed and reiterated on a regular basis. For example, on 11 October 1888, when the Western Union lineman John Feeks was accidentally electrocuted atop a pole in downtown Manhattan before thousands of witnesses, the visual impression was of a body caught up in a web of wires. Supplied with current it looked half-alive, half-dead as it smoked and sparked. Cartoon illustrations that year likened electricity to an evil force out of control, and public agitation began for the removal of the AC current that crept through the city. A low-level panic ensued over the possibility of accidental electrocution in the course of daily life by this invisible force, for example by touching a door knob or railing that had accidentally become—and note the word—"live."[23]

Edison's own research unintentionally and indirectly reinforced such perceptions at the more mundane end of their spectrum by associating electricity with pain and a lingering demise, with the polluted imagining of a protracted, unknowable liminal condition between life and death. Intended to specify the type and strength of current required to kill, his experiments rather gave the impression that electricity was not infallible. Looking to influence the determinations of the New York State commission reviewing methods of execution, building on the earlier research of the Buffalo dentist and commission member A. P. Southwick, Edison commenced work on this topic in 1887, assisted by Harold Brown. The intent here as mentioned was one of elementary semiotics, namely, to create a strong association between AC and death. To underline the point Brown sent out a letter to municipalities and insurance companies dubbing AC in polluting terms as "the executioner's current" and alleging that Westinghouse was playing fast and loose with human life in the search for profit. Conspicuously using a Westinghouse generator Brown and Edison experimented upon stray dogs purchased from local urchins for 25 cents each, systematically increasing the current and meticulously noting the results. A subsequent public demonstration on July 31 at Columbia University saw a large black mongrel killed with just 500 volts of AC when it had already survived 700 volts of DC. Perhaps this was a convincing experiment. It was certainly a poor cultural performance. The association of electrocution with lingering death and torture began, and the American Society for the Prevention of Cruelty to Animals started to complain. Edison moved on to work with less sentimental material such as cows and horses.

Thanks in part to Edison's efforts, on June 4 1888 the New York State legislature agreed with the recommendation of its commission and established electrocution as the legitimate mode of death. On January 1 1889, the new law was to take effect. Harold Brown set about designing the necessary apparatus for killing humans, but Westinghouse refused to supply his generators to the state, forcing Brown to locate them through a backdoor route. Westinghouse further attempted to free his technology from symbolic contamination by funding the appeals of those condemned to die, arguing that the proposed new method of electrocution violated the Eighth Amendment and was a "cruel and unusual punishment." Edison and Brown testified against this, built the first electric chair, and sold it to the state for $8,000. A last-ditch Supreme Court challenge by the first convict scheduled for electrocution, a petty murderer named William Kemmler, was funded by Westinghouse. It was rejected, the court ruling that there was nothing cruel or unusual about death by electrocution. To the contrary, it insisted that a lower court had been correct earlier when it claimed it was "within easy reach of electrical science at this day to so generate and apply to the person of the convict a current of electricity of such known and sufficient force as certainly to produce instantaneous, and, therefore, painless, death."[24]

If electrocution got the green light through a court process that could proclaim in such unequivocal terms that electricity was knowable, controllable, and unmysterious, the diverse hearings required for the courts to reach this judgment did not bring closure to the matter in the wider public sphere. To the contrary, much of the evidence that was presented and relayed enthusiastically in the press simply raised doubt that the dividing line between life and death could be easily defined, doubt that electrocution was painless or electricity comprehensible by reason, and doubt that electricity could easily and definitively end life. And doubt, as noted in chapter 5, is the lifeblood of the uncanny. Witnesses were brought forward with extraordinary stories of having survived power line shocks and lightening strikes. They testified to pain and used words like "torture." The talented W. Bourke Cockran, who ran the case against the chair and was funded by Westinghouse, also raised the spectral possibility of living death. The chair might create only the appearance of death, he insisted, leading to a catatonic state followed by burial alive or death on the dissection table. Reference was made to Dash, a dog who had miraculously revived after being accidentally shocked by a fallen power line and had been assumed dead. It is indicative of the prevailing state of affairs that the *New York Tribune* came down in favor of electrocution, but at the same time confessed that this "new mode of capital punishment, departing radically from the customs of the past," depended "for its results on a mysterious agency of whose nature and operation those who know most confess that they know little."[25] It is an unstable legitimacy that is both modern and "mysterious."

The Kemmler Execution

The subsequent execution of William Kemmler on August 6 1890 was the first of some four thousand by electricity in American history. Looking to this event and its interpretation, we can see many themes that were to stalk the electric chair through the subsequent century. The pollutions of indignity and torture, the specter of a permeable and liminal zone separating the quick and the dead, the excess of a body that transgressed its own physical boundaries under the duress of the current and produced in its abjection a ritual of disgust. Even before the fateful day a counter-discourse had set in not simply against electricity in general but rather against the chair in particular. Details of the design were received with disappointment. The state's legislation had specified electricity, but not a "chair." There had been hopes that the condemned might simply step into a kiosk like a telephone booth or stand on a plate on the floor, rather as today protagonists in science fiction make use of "pods" and "transporters" to move unproblematically through time and space. Involving straps and damp sponges, the electric chair appeared simply humiliating and violated the autonomy and dignity of the sovereign individual. It looked like a medieval abomination, like one of those chunky, studded seats where the Inquisition would apply the thumbscrews to the helpless individual. The *Medical Record* caught the mood when it noted that the question was "one of aesthetics" and suggested that it was not scientific, civilized, or appropriate to "strap a condemned prisoner to a chair and throw him into a convulsion."[26] The medical experts, then, were more than the disinterested observers of bodies that Foucault depicts in his books. They were intensely aware that punishment was about meaning and appearances as much as biology and control and believed that scientific learning should be applied in line norms of decency and dignity as well as the quest for efficiencies.

Kemmler's death was a horribly botched affair requiring two jolts of electricity— what would subsequently come to be known as "death by installments." The first lasted seventeen seconds. Kemmler appeared dead. "We live in a higher civilization today," declared the electrocution enthusiast and commission member Alfred Southwick, to the assembled witnesses. But Kemmler was still alive. He could be seen breathing, there was foam on his lips, he moaned and strained against the leather straps.[27] Another shock was ordered. This went on for over a minute. Under the front-page banner, "Far Worse Than Hanging" the *New York Times* spoke the next day of a "sacrifice to the whims and theories of a coterie of cranks and politicians" and of a "disgrace to civilization." It reported singed flesh and hair, and that an "awful odour" had permeated the death chamber."[28] Some witnesses had fainted, and the spectacle "nauseated all but a few of them." The district attorney, for example, had "groaned audibly and rushed from the room." Journalists not present invented stories in which Kemmler had caught fire or cried out in pain—fables about him that have endured to this day.[29] An expert interviewed by the *Times* said that Kemmler was "literally roasted to death." Even the medical authorities seem to have shared this view that the workings of the chair were boundary-problematic rather than boundary-definitive. Prior to the execution it was agreed that the autopsy on Kemmler was to be delayed until three hours after his apparent death lest he come back to life or die for real under the scalpel, and permission was denied to one doctor to experiment with his new resuscitation device.[30]

So there was immediate ammunition for a new narrative of the chair as barbaric, mysterious, and disgusting that could run in opposition to the view that it was civilized, definitive, and humane. From the perspective of common sense this debate was all about whether there was pain and whether death was instant. Looking more sociologically and with the anthropologically strange viewpoint of Durkheimian cultural theory we see an activity centered on the pollution generated by the perforated, natural-sign-producing body and the evils attendant upon blurred rather than clear boundaries between life and death.

The Electric Chair Institutionalized — And Challenged

Inauspicious beginnings notwithstanding, the electric chair went on to be widely adopted by 1920 and to eventually become virtually synonymous with judicial execution in the United States. Its only challengers for supremacy in the twentieth century were the gas chamber from the 1920s onward and the lethal injection towards the end of that century. The official representation of the chair as the bringer of just retribution, painless but implacable, earnest and bureaucratic, was made more plausible over the years by improvements not so much in the basic technology as in protocol. Voltages were calculated more accurately. The use of the chair was revised in various ways to make invisible the signs of violation and to close up the unruly, messy body. Towards the end of its history the condemned would have a catheter to catch urine and a plug in the anus, as one inmate put it, "so you don't shit yourself in front of their witnesses, because that would just ruin the sterile effect."[31] A mask on the face came to offer privacy and also hold in the eyeballs. Specialist execution teams have been an innovation that has reduced Kemmler-type contingencies and accidents as far as possible.[32] Widely thought of as an effort to generate humane and efficient legitimate executions, their function can be simultaneously imagined as semiotic work oriented around the avoidance of spectacles of excess, the elimination of signs of horror such as the kicking, screaming, or weeping inmate, the body that smokes or does not die and sits on the border line of life and death, the machine that sparks out—the proliferating indicators of disorder. So the bureaucratic and impersonal qualities of the execution arise not only from the fact that we live in a society where capital justice has become routinized as a mode of "power," but also in part from this performative effort at controlling dangerous ritual signs.

There is plenty to suggest that the execution process involving the electric chair is more than some Foucaultian timetable of routinized procedures. Judicial death, like all sacrifice, seems to require special cultural preparations that minimize opportunities for the emergence of pollution and evil. In his ethnography of death row, Robert Johnson points to the emotion management functions of the death team, with the staff oriented around the goal of providing a "proper" or "professional" execution,[33] a "job to be done"[34] that is devoid of emotional input and that is conducted as quickly and efficiently as possible. For Johnson, teamwork and peer reinforcement of routinized norms serve as tools to this end. In the period of time leading to the execution, through surveillance, rehearsals, manipulative social interactions with the condemned, and the erection of psychological and social barriers the execution team transforms itself into a functional unit that can ensure a smooth delivery of service.

Yet reading against the grain we can find evidence for a more Durkheimian, less utilitarian understanding of what Johnson calls "death work." Durkheim speaks of the ways that the sacred is dangerous and so needs to be segregated from the profane or everyday. The death house is usually found on the periphery of the prison and is "removed from the daily ebb and flow of life in the penitentiary."[35] In the buildup to the execution the deathwatch teams are similarly separated from their colleagues. To invert a sentence from Johnson the team is symbolically and not just actually set apart from its peers.[36] Like members of a cult or a group of initiates they are sequestered, sworn to secrecy, keeping details of their tasks and the execution protocols to themselves, and refusing to discuss these with families, friends, or colleagues. They set up a camp, even sleeping and eating at the jail in the final days. Translated into Durkheimian terms this ritualized seclusion and intense interaction enables them to build up the emotional energy and symbolic power required to undertake their ritual duties in what is to all intents and purposes a rite of passage. For those hours theirs is a liminal social location. As Johnson himself reports, "there is a sense that on the deathwatch the officers are liberated from the mundane constraints of daily prison work."[37] This sense of ritual separation is reinforced by practical actions that have clearly ritualistic resonances—the last meal, the cleansing of the body, the prisoner changing into clean clothes for the execution like the novitiate about to undergo some induction. Consistent with anthropological theory on the special meanings of hair, shaving in particular seems to work as a ritual activity that transforms the man into a "dead man ... we take his identity; it goes with the hair."[38] In the final hours the deathwatch "takes on a distinctively funereal ambience." The officers are often silent, visiting officials are "quiet and reserved, even reverent. They speak in hushed tones, as though they were visiting a grave."[39] Discussions with the prisoner increasingly focus on the afterlife rather than this profane world, as if a journey had already begun.

Comments from death workers also suggest a worldview that is neither bureaucratic and mechanical nor just weakly inflected by humanitarian norms. For example, officers were sometimes required to be strapped and hooded in the chair during training drills. The resulting feeling was described as "weird," "peculiar." "It's kinda like puttin' you in another world," said one interviewee—a comment suggesting that even for the professional the chair has occult powers.[40] Jim Willett, the director of the Texas Prison Museum, makes us think of the divine evil of the left sacred when he speaks of his first execution experience as "awesome, but not in a good way."[41] Brother Cecil McKee used to walk condemned men to the electric chair in Huntsville, Texas. He reports feelings of disgust arising from the pollution of human death and the need for cleansing: "I closed my eyes ... You know, the flesh burns—it leaves a terrible odour. I'd go home and take my clothes off, leave 'em out, we'd go to sleep. Next day, I had to send my clothes to the cleaners. It was just part of the job."[42] As for the inmates themselves, not surprisingly the chair is understood superstitiously. According to prison lore a person who sits in the chair will also die in it.[43]

The chair found its highwater mark around the time of James Cagney's screams as he confronts his death in *Angels with Dirty Faces*.[44] The tide was to drop over the next fifty years. In the closing decades of the twentieth century, from the 1980s and accelerating through the 1990s, the kinds of collective representation present around the time of Kemmler's death made their reappearance. The chair became associated once more primarily with disorder and disgust, not only in obscure Amnesty International newsletters but now in the mainstream mass media. As the lethal injection became a viable alternative to the chair, the earlier method became the object of detailed reporting and public interest. In proportion as it was no longer the norm, it could become an object worthy of curiosity.

Ahead of the curve in bringing this sensibility to judicial reasoning was Justice William J. Brennan. In a 1985 dissenting opinion, and joined by Justice Thurgood Marshall, he cast doubt on the chair.[45] What is remarkable about his statement is the quantity of graphic description documenting the mutilation and violation of bodily boundaries and the existence of a protracted state between life and death. Brennan's approach is empirical, visual, and somewhat emotive, not dry and legal. The Supreme Court's decision in re Kemmler,[46] Brennan says, referring to precedent, was based on "factual assumptions that appear not to have withstood the test of experience." There was both pain and indignity in the electric chair. Brennan reports his belief that the electric chair routinely violated the Eighth Amendment. He speaks of the prisoner who "cringes, leaps and fights the straps with amazing strength"; who "defecates, urinates, and vomits blood and drool"; and of a "sound like bacon frying." Many scientists, Brennan says, implicitly inviting identification with the person in the seat, had testified to "unspeakable pain and suffering" and "pain too great for us to imagine." In short, the electric chair was anathema.

"The human organism conceals within its depths a sacred principle, which visibly comes to the surface in certain determined cases," wrote Durkheim when discussing the role of the body in religious activity.[47]

Within a few years of Brennan writing his opinion, the electric chair came to be more widely seen as violating that "sacred principle." Consistent with Durkheim's thinking some high-profile 1990s executions in Florida ("determined cases") were critical to this shift.[48] Critics of the electric chair pointed to deaths such as that of Allen Lee Davis and Pedro Medina, where there had been fire. Again, the imagery of the violated body was central. The case of Davis seems to have been particularly resonant because it involved blood, a substance that both Durkheim and Mary Douglas understand as having particular sacred powers.[49] The blood was visible in photographs released by the authorities, and these "struck a nerve" in the wider public and judicial sensibility.[50] The Florida Supreme Court Web site showing the pictures repeatedly crashed due to heavy traffic, and although this new ambiguity was dismissed by Governor Jeb Bush as a "nosebleed," newspaper stories fixed themselves leechlike on this rich bodily signifier. The *Economist* reported in dismay on the indignities of Davis "who was shown contorting and bleeding in pictures that were released to the world on the Internet."[51] Such episodes attest that fascination and horror accompany the chair in its concrete signifying particulars. These seem more compelling to the moral imagination than abstract legal arguments about justice and statute. When *Time,* for example, reported on the death of Jessie Tafero, we find it framing its critique through gruesome detail, not legal citation.

> The electric chair is supposed to be a quick and humane way to put a criminal to death. But when the executioner at the Florida State Prison threw the switch on cop killer Jessie Tafero two weeks ago, it seemed anything but. To the horror of spectators, fire and smoke shot out from the headpiece strapped to Tafero's skull. He nodded and gurgled for four minutes as his eyebrows burned and ashes fell from his head to his shoulders. The 2,000-volt current had to be turned off twice to keep the whole metal-and-leather headgear from bursting into flame.[52]

A further index of this narrative change polluting the chair is that by the late-1990s the words "gruesome" and "grisly" (not "clinical" or even "chilling") can be found routinely appended to discussions on the electric chair—for example, in reviews of recent books I found useful in researching this chapter. Provincial judicial statements came to increasingly mirror Brennan's agenda-setting 1985 opinion and were marbled with the same imagery of disgust and disorder. Dissenting from a 1990s Florida Supreme

Court decision retaining the legal status of electrocution, Justice Leander J. Shaw Jr. wrote that "execution by electrocution, with its attendant smoke and flames and blood and screams, is a spectacle whose time has passed."[53] Florida Justice Barbara Pariente suggested that conventions of cultural performance had been violated. Executions had become "something of a freak show ... a spectacle more befitting of a B Hollywood horror movie than a state-sanctioned execution."[54] As we saw with the chain gang and the public execution in prior chapters, the electric chair had crossed some invisible threshold and was producing signs that invited interpretation through an inappropriate and irreverent genre ("Dixie porn," "the B Hollywood movie," "the picaresque") or metaphor ("zoo," "freak show," "carnival"). Wider sensibilities also seemed to change in line with those of the judiciary and press, making the legal problem of nullification a very real possibility. In the early 1990s prosecutors in Louisiana, for example, began to suspect that getting a death penalty conviction from a jury was being made harder by the changing reputation of the electric chair and for this reason backed a mandatory switch to lethal injection.[55]

A significant problem for the chair's advocates in this changing cultural environment was that the technology could produce signs of disorder and leaky boundaries as a routine product of even the most textbook execution. The preventative ritual interventions of death row specialists had reached their ceiling of efficacy, yet outcomes such as those eventuating for Tafero, Medina, and Lee Davis were not unusual. They were what sociologist Charles Perrow calls "normal accidents."[56] These can be expected now and again thanks to the inherent complexities of certain systems linking humans with technology. For critics there would always be new material to work with. Fred Leutcher, a leading designer and builder of execution equipment, reports that even in an unproblematic case "people who have been executed smell bad, have burnt flesh, and are usually covered in urine and faeces."[57] This expected minimal production of disorderly signs can be amplified by opportunities for botches and malfunctions inherent to the technology and its overly temperamental interface with the body. The electric charge needs to be precisely calibrated. There must be sufficient juice to stop the heart and compensate for the adrenaline pumped out at the moment of the first shock. There needs also to be some extra power to kill off heavy inmates and compensate for voltage drop as heat builds resistance. Yet if more than 6 amps flow, the flesh starts to bake, creating a corpse that is much like "an overcooked chicken"[58] where the meat falls off the bone. So states cannot simply pump more and more electricity through the body to generate a surefire, sign-free kill. Such pragmatic and aesthetic concerns are tied to what Durkheim correctly identified as cultlike respect for the individual and their body in our time. They sit behind worries about barbarism and the intrusion of degrading metaphors such as "Frying Tonight." There seems to be no easy technological fix to this cultural peril. If the practice of giving several shocks at different voltages over a prolonged period reduces the risk of burning, it also opens up vulnerabilities to accusations of torture and the powerful trope of "death in installments." Add to all this the contingencies associated with the quality of contact of the electrodes on the body; new or worn-out connectors; overly tight, loose, cracked straps; and the result is a situation of high unpredictability in which there are risks of both over- and underelectrocution. The electric chair was quite simply difficult to get right.

In 1890 the Supreme Court upheld the constitutionality of the electric chair. Around 110 years later the counter-narrative finally became dominant with its subtext of the impure sacred and citation of leaky bodily boundaries, torture, and indignity. In 2001 Georgia's state supreme court ruled 4 to 3 against the chair citing in a manner similar to Brennan the cruel and unusual punishment clause and tying it to the *Trop v. Dulles* language of "evolving standards of decency."[59] In her majority opinion, Justice Carol W. Hunstein invoked the imagery that should by now be familiar to readers of this chapter. Although it was not possible to tell whether pain was experienced, there was "purposeless physical violence and needless mutilation" that resulted in the "spectre of excruciating pain and its certainty of cooked brains and blistered bodies."[60] In Nebraska Judge Robert Hippe made mention of torture arising from death in installments and pushed that state towards a rethinking.[61] By this point in time, however, such legal opinion was becoming increasingly irrelevant. States had long been defecting to the lethal injection.

The electric chair was slowly abandoned, phased out, or forgotten during the last two decades of the twentieth century by most of the twenty-six states that had used it. At the turn of the millennium the once fringe view that it was polluted and polluting had become mainstreamed to the point where it could be used emblematically to leverage wider arguments. For example, editorials homed in on the electric chair as a material crystallization of all that was wrong with the death penalty tout court. Rejecting capital punishment on the grounds that innocent people were put to death, the *Washington Post* opined that the death penalty was a vestige of a discredited way of thinking. It lamented "the naive belief in science, in perfection, in a criminal justice system that works so flawlessly that the wrong person is never executed. The electric chair itself was the fruit of such thinking, a device that was supposed to kill painlessly and quickly. It did neither, which is why it is now rarely used."[62] By 1999 only four states still had the electric chair as the sole method of execution.

Of course this move to judicial, popular, and civil centrality of a once peripheral discourse that polluted the chair and coded it as evil did not alone bring about its downfall. It was however a major precipitating factor. Other influences contributed to weaken resistance. Texas had started using the lethal injection in 1982, demonstrating it to be a practicable alternative. This was a life raft that made abandoning the SS *Electric Chair* a more convenient legal and political option than trying to plug the holes in a rusting hull. For once the decentralized nature of the U.S. justice system accelerated rather than retarded the effects of a cultural shift due to a collective action problem. Like rats leaving the sinking ship, one state after another dropped the chair or offered alternatives. Those that remained stood out in proportion as targets for stigma. Like the chain gang states we looked at earlier, these could be depicted as morally polluted anachronisms who had failed to evolve. By the same token each successive defection provided support for suits against the electric chair, drawing upon the claim that the Eighth Amendment should be interpreted in the terms laid down by Chief Justice Earl Warren in *Trop v. Dulles* of an "evolving standard of human decency that marks the progress of a maturing society."[63] When this statement was interpreted empirically (not abstractly, platonically, or religiously), demonstrable shifts in public opinion or legislation over the states of the union could be used to mobilize the argument that America had factually "evolved" or "matured" and that, if once acceptable, the electric chair had now become truly "cruel and unusual."[64] By the early 1990s a tipping point was reached leading rapidly to penal isomorphism. There was safety in numbers. For example, rather than being singled out to weather the legal storms over its allegedly faulty electric chair, Florida moved rapidly in its legislature to authorize the lethal injection. This headed off the embarrassing possibility of pleading the case before the U.S. Supreme Court and losing—something that had happened to Georgia in the Furman ruling. Although no court had ever upheld the claim that the electric chair was cruel and unusual punishment (the decision to suspend capital punishment in *Furman v. Georgia* related to the bureaucratically arbitrary application of the death penalty),[65] the writing was on the wall that such a ruling was nigh. The U.S. Supreme Court had

been giving indications to this effect for years and in March 2005 seemingly confirmed that the states had been right to abandon ship when it
outlawed the execution of those who were juveniles at the time of com-
mitting their crime. The majority opinion in that ruling ominously cited
Trop v. Dulles as a guiding precedent, pointed to the United States as
an international anachronism and indicated an evolving standard should/
could be measured empirically, referencing the fact that thirty of the states
now banned the execution of felons from this category.[66]

By 2005 Nebraska was the only state that did not offer the convicted
an alternative to the electric chair. The result was profound stigma and
contagious pollution. The Midwestern state could be described as regres-
sive, as "the last holdout for this universally rejected and condemned sole
means of capital punishment" by the lawyer behind the appeal of Carey
Dean Moore.[67] He also spoke of "the horror of death by internal burning
and shock." Just two years, before U.S. district judge Joseph Batallion of
Omaha had been prepared to apply the Eighth Amendment after being
shown photographs of blistered bodies from the three previous Nebraska
executions of the 1990s.

If on the ropes the electric chair was not yet down for the count. As late
as 2006 it was still on the books in seven states—an option rarely chosen
by the condemned but conspicuous by virtue of this fact. Its new discursive positioning as horrific, rather than bureaucratic, and the comparative
immunity of the lethal injection to negative symbolism had allowed death
in the chair to be strategically elected as a meaningful gesture or dramatic
speech act. Just as the changing racial composition of a neighborhood will
determine who stands out on the street, the electric chair was now the
marked rather than unmarked category. In 2003 in Virginia, sixty-one-
year-old Earl Conrad Bramblett argued that he was innocent of the crime
of murdering a family of four. Thinking of the victim's relatives who would
be witnesses to his death, he seemingly "chose electrocution as a form of
protest." "I hope the SOB's who put me here will never forget what they
see . . . if that's revenge then I suppose it is."[68] Likewise, the electric chair
could find supporters who were attracted to its new "incivil" symbolism
and so managed to gain support from victims' rights organizations for this
reason as a "compelling symbol of retributive justice."[69]

We have been looking for the most part at shifting legal discourse on
the electric chair. Seemingly based in black-letter, bookish judicial reason,
this sea change was grounded in visceral imagery and the use of a set of
bodily signifiers as relevant clues towards the interpretation of an ambigu-

ous object. The move was synergistically and indirectly reinforced by on-going wider popular imaginings that had long been reworking the electric chair, deploying it as a symbolic resource or appropriating it in creative ways that emphasized mystery, pain, disorder, and the sacred. The counter-myth that had started at the time of New York State's initial deliberations had never gone away. Consider the ways that diverse electric chairs were familiarized, turning them from technical abstractions into meaningful objects much as the naming of geysers in Yellowstone National Park transforms them from geothermal phenomena into bearers of personality and motivation. There was Old Smokey (New Jersey, Pennsylvania, Florida), Old Sparky (Texas, Florida, New York, Louisiana, Ohio, Kentucky, Georgia) Yellow Mama (Alabama), and Gruesome Gerty (Louisiana). No mere contraption of wood, leather, and copper, such names show the chair to be a morass of emotive contradictions: dread and familiarity, the mother and the sexualized avenging angel. We can also meditate on how the negative association with torture and terror became further cemented through Stanley Milgram's infamous psychology experiments from the early 1960s on obedience to authority. Here the experimental subjects—believing they were participating in a study on learning—administered what they thought were electric shocks to other subjects when they answered questions wrongly. Relentlessly prompted by a scientific authority figure many continued to turn up the amps and gave more powerful shocks despite hearing agonized screams and pleas from an invisible "learner" (in fact a research collaborator) in another room, a person they had seen being strapped into an electric chair. Although nobody was actually given electric shocks, the popular belief is still to the contrary. Such negative publicity for electrocution was only reinforced by the never-ending controversy over whether the experiment was ethical, the real issue of legitimate deception of experimental subjects being hopelessly and for all time confounded with the bogus matter of whether Milgram should have "tortured" people in the name of science. Milgram's culturally incompetent insistence that his experiments were consistent with Hannah Arendt's "banality of evil" thesis did little to help the reputation of the electric chair or his work. Arendt had claimed that the Holocaust was not the product of twisted and sick minds but rather of ordinary people operating with a bureaucratic mentality and with a blinkered moral awareness. When Milgram brought this up he simply established a resonance with evil Nazis doctors and the inhuman medical experiments they conducted during the Holocaust.[70] The connection with

torture was repeated in the Abu Ghraib prison scandal. Photographs released in the wake of the war in Iraq showed U.S. troops humiliating and
intimidating Iraqi inmates. It is no accident that the most notorious and
iconic came to be of an eerily hooded, Inquisition-like figure standing on
a box holding electric cables with outstretched hands.

Such cases suggest that electrocution has proven stubbornly resistant
as a signifier, demonstrating in the clearest possible fashion that the judicial use of a penal technology does not encompass its range of meaning.
The electric chair is both an object and a mythology. Like a fading actor
it has continued to trade on past glories but has been problematic to cast.
The chair is the charismatic object of spectacle, but at the same time it is
dangerous, morally polluted, and evil. Due respect is called for even after
it has been unplugged. Consider what happened when in 2005 Westchester
County put proposals to the Empire State Development Corporation for
a tourist initiative at Sing Sing Prison, estimating that this would bring in
$10 million every year to the local economy along with 120,000 visitors.
The prison, it argued, was well suited to such intervention, enjoying "an
especially dark mystique" thanks to the execution of 614 people from 1891
to 1962 (more than any other prison) including the Rosenberg "spies" in
1953 and the serial killer cannibal Albert Fish. Further, Sing Sing had been
mythologized in films such as *Angels with Dirty Faces* and *Castle on the
Hudson*.[71] The news release cited the electric chair and the famous villains
put to death there as major cultural assets for a profitable initiative. The
proposal included a replica of the death house and electric chair. Visitors
could interact with a condemned prisoner, played, one presumes, by a suit-
ably desperate actor.

Proponents of the museum were placed in the difficult position of advocating an attraction but also managing the genre. "Would a museum
turn prisoners into an attraction and sensationalize the electric chair?"
asked *USA Today*.[72] Efforts were made to hose down fears of populism.
According to a spokesperson for the company designing the experience,
the encounter with the death chamber would be "pretty sombre and fairly
chilling." Visitors could sit in "what are like pews and read witness accounts."[73] "It'll be tastefully done . . . we're certainly not ghoulish and morbid," claimed Westchester Country Executive Andrew Spano in an effort
to show that this was a reflective, educational activity.[74] Critics thundered
that the result would be "like Madam Tussaud's Wax Museum" and argued
the need for a serious interpretative exhibit rather than a "freak show."[75]
The *New York Times* conjured up the horrifying image of trash tourism.

There was something "repellent and cruel about cashing in on the lurid impulses of throngs of people with Slurpees and fanny packs."[76] Durkheim remarks that "human blood is so holy a thing that . . . it frequently serves to consecrate the most respected instruments of the cult."[77] Sanctified by the blood of those who had died, the Sing Sing chair needed to be treated with respect, as did the memories and dignity of those who had suffered.

The problems of managing a charismatic, evil-tainted artifact encountered by proponents of a Sing Sing museum are by no means unique. When the used electric chair from Tennessee, along with a certificate of authenticity, went up for sale on eBay there were howls of protest. It was bid up to $25,100 on eBay before being withdrawn from sale and bought by Ripley's Believe it or Not![78] It is interesting to think counterfactually about this. Would there have been an outcry if it had been just a replica chair up for auction on the internet? I think not. There is an auratic quality to a real electric chair that is bestowed by death.

Genre problems and ambivalence are also evident at the Texas Prison Museum. Located in Huntsville, Texas, this attracts not only "American families on vacation and looking for roadside fun" but also schools that "bring busloads of students."[79] Here Ol' Sparky stars in the exhibit Riding the Thunderbolt. As if drawn by some magnetic or charismatic property of the object, visitors repeatedly ignore the signs telling them not to sit in the chair. One visitor, Arnold, reported to a journalist that "seeing Ol' Sparky and knowing so many people died in it" was the highlight of his trip. The museum shop sells a book of "Meals for Die For" that includes "Ol' Sparky's Genuine Convict Chili" and "Uh-Oh I'm Dead Meat-Loaf." If this is gallows humor, the artifact itself is treated more reverentially. A New York Times treatment describes it as "set in a dimly lighted alcove." It continues in a more sinister vein, "the chair might fit into a slightly offbeat living room were it not for the eerie leather straps and the thick black cord that snakes from a brace below the seat."[80]

The hypnotic, iconic, left-sacred inflected pulling power of the electric chair noted by the proponents, managers, and visitors of prison museums has also been detected and used in the artistic community. Andy Warhol's diversely colored screen prints known as the Little Electric Chair represent the most famous such appropriation and provide for us a kind of natural experiment (see fig. 6). Begun in 1963 they were derived from an official photograph of the Sing Sing chair released at the time of the execution of the Rosenbergs and were part of his wider series entitled American Death, Death and Disaster, or Death and News that also in-

FIGURE 6. Andy Warhol, *Little Electric Chair*, 1963. © 2007 Andy Warhol Foundation for the
Visual Arts/Artists Rights Society (ARS), New York.

cluded images of riots, car crashes, and suicides rendered as puzzlingly
banal. Warhol did not provide commentary on his own work, and art critics are usually unable to decide on the meaning of the items. Are they
about the banality of death or its horror? Do they make voyeurs of view-
ers, or do they encourage mature reflection on the direction of our civilization? The modal solution has been to waffle about the difficulty of interpretation when confronted with such images and then suggest Warhol
is challenging the viewer to locate their own meaning. Not so the electric
chair prints: Strongly confirming our Durkheimian reading of the chair
as an object always already inserted into a complex mythology, the critics
seem for once amazingly confident that something to do with the sacred
is afoot, notwithstanding the autistic, realist, and documentary qualities of
the art work. Alain Jouffroy writes, "The traditional feelings attached to
death are banished. In front of these pictures we are cleansed. The paintings become the holy scenes of a godless world."[81] When the chair was
in the frame other commentators too found it easy to locate profound
and sacred meanings in the usually depthless art of Warhol. Peter Halley

describes the fifteen Little Electric Chair paintings as "haunting works" and as "an almost Mosaic tablet of empty revelation." He speculates that Warhol's "intimate experience of the language of Easter icons allows him to make small paintings that speak in almost mystical terms."[82] Likewise the usually scaly and cynical Robert Hughes spoke of Warhol's "Golgotha, envisioned in repeated views of an execution chamber with its electric chair and its sign enjoining silence" and tied the works to the artist's Polish Roman Catholic upbringing.[83] The point is echoed by Eleanor Heartney, who sees Warhol as part of a tradition in Catholic art that links mysticism, eroticism, and death, as does Jane Daggett Dillenberger, who likens the electric chair to the cross of the Crucifixion in her study on *The Religious Art of Andy Warhol*.[84]

That the chair touches off religious symbolism and related interpretations has been most clearly demonstrated in British artist Mark Wallinger's installation *Prometheus* from 1999. Prometheus, it should be remembered, mediated the sacred and profane worlds by stealing fire from the gods. He was punished with eternal torture by Zeus. We should also mind that Frankenstein was dubbed the "modern Prometheus." He was a man who tinkered with the secrets of life and death only to create a monster. In the installation visitors pass from a dark room to a brightly lit execution chamber. There is the hum of electricity from a metal circle, and an electric chair protrudes from the wall opposite. This gives us what the art critic Carol Kino tellingly calls a "god's eye" perspective, or perhaps that of a "departing soul."[85] Next the viewer encounters monitors showing Wallinger in the chair, humming Ariel's song from *The Tempest,* screaming and twitching. The overall effect is unsettling. The chair is the focus for an ambiguous drama, a play of signs and connotations linking torture, life, and death, the sacred and profane.

For all its erudition, Wallinger's imaginary can be understood as a highbrow specification of a cultural complex tying the chair to the supernatural, mysterious, and evil that has long been playing out in low-brow genres. In 2002 you could spend $5,000 on an unusual Halloween decoration, the Deep Fryer. This was a "full sized model of a man in an electric chair who writhes and smokes."[86] You might wish to take a visit to the award-winning Skull Kingdom in Orlando, Florida. In this "Haunted Family Attraction" or "twisted world of fright and fun you won't forget," you could watch a show or have a birthday party complete with beer, pizza, interactive ghouls, and electric chair.[87] Likewise Miami's walkthrough House of Terror could be whimsically reported around Halloween as featuring an electric chair that "shakes and spits out sparks and smoke" and "zaps a new victim every 15 minutes."[88] The singer Madonna's 2004 Re-Invention Tour featured not only the usual seminudity, erotic dance, and simulated sex but also a sequence in which she rises onto the stage bound to an electric chair to sing the James Bond movie theme "Die Another Day."[89] Madonna escapes, leaving behind some kabbalistic sacred symbols on her seat. It is entirely consistent with my reading that in her Confessions tour of 2006 the diva appeared not in the chair, but Jesus-like on a crucifix. During the singing of "Live to Tell" she descends from the cross. It would seem the two technologies are substitutable symbols.[90] Exactly what Foucault would have made of Madonna is not clear, but for our purposes her show well illustrates the matrix the chair inhabits in popular culture: torture, excess, mystery, the sacred, life, death, transgression and even sexuality.

Such interpolations with the supernatural are more explicitly signaled in *The Green Mile,* a 1999 film based on a story by Steven King.[91] Set in a 1930s death row environment, it involves the relationship between an unusually sensitive prison guard, Paul Edgecomb (played by Tom Hanks), and African American inmate John Coffey (Michael Clarke Duncan), a seven-foot gentle giant. In the course of the movie it turns out that Coffey, who is condemned to die for the murder of two white girls, has been wrongly accused. *The Green Mile,* then, is partly about race and justice and in this context the electric chair becomes a lynching machine. Yet such political themes are overridden by supernatural ones, for Coffey has mystical powers to cure the sick that are seemingly electrical in nature. When he lays hands on Edgecomb to cure a bladder infection, fuses blow and sparks fly—as they do for his wife later that evening when Paul discovers new sexual capabilities. At the end Coffey makes what one critic describes as "a sacrificial, Christ-like exit in the electric chair."[92] It is not by chance that John Coffey's initials are J. C. nor that Paul Edgecomb seemingly lives to be one hundred years old having been given the gift of immortality by the death row inmate.[93]

The decision of Steven King, Madonna, Mark Wallinger and other creative specialists to situate the electric chair into a drama of supernatural forces and redemption; the curious ability of art critics to decode Warhol's work with confidence; the appearance of the chair alongside the ghouls and zombies of the wax museums—all these are made possible by its mythology, this being derived in turn from a deeply rooted symbolic connection to themes of sacrifice and the sacred. For Durkheim's students Henri Hubert and Marcel Mauss the sacrifice served as a "means of communication between the sacred and the profane worlds through the mediation of a victim, that is, of a thing that in the course of the ceremony is destroyed," but which "remains indifferent to the direction of the current that passes through it."[94] The sacrifice, in other words, is a medium for a two-way flow connecting the known and the mysterious. If the person in the chair is a criminal in the eyes of the law, their body and soul are a sacrifice in the eyes of myth. There follows a train of cultural logic, for the sacrifice is part of a "whole complex of sacred things . . . the system of consecration."[95] Regardless of bureaucratic intent or the material wrongdoing of the criminal, we have seen how the electric chair and its victim become inevitably caught up in a complex web of symbolism affect, awe, and contagion. They are the bridge between life and death, the sacred and the profane that has been consecrated by thousands of victims. This is why the electric chair is America's most powerful totem.

The Lethal Injection — A Brief Postscript

The closing of the curtains on the electric chair and its ascent into myth brings us to our last technology, the lethal injection. This was first used by Texas in 1982 and within ten years had become dominant in thirty-seven of the thirty-eight states that retain the death penalty. Consistent with the theme of this book, the poison injection can be understood as a defensive reaction to the semiotic excess of the electric chair, working not so much to remove cruelty as to limit the production of signs of disorder and degradation. This was yet another housekeeping action in which efforts were made to eliminate pollution. As a *New York Times* editorial explicitly put it, it was a way to "purify an indecent duty."[96] It was hoped that a dead body could be produced with no more signs of disorder than a pinprick, no more degradation than that experienced for a tonsillectomy.

Nevertheless, the injection has its own vulnerabilities and produces its own disorders and myths, and it is useful to conclude this chapter with a brief account and explanation of these. We could begin by noting that like all other penal technologies the lethal injection can be renarrated in positive terms and recoded within the carnivalesque. If death in the electric chair can be likened to a sideshow thrill, to "riding the thunderbolt," then the injection can be described as the drug user's nirvana, "the ultimate high."[97] By the same token victims' rights advocates suggest it is not punishment enough. More serious for implementation and legitimacy is the confounding of basic cultural categories: "medicine" is used to produce "death." Sometimes, as in Missouri, the execution would take place in the prison medical unit thus eliminating the spatial boundaries of the old death house. Reports consistently use medical terminology in their descriptions, reinforcing this uncomfortable juxtaposition.

> Brooks was taken into the death chamber and strapped to a *hospital stretcher.* At that point a *medical technician* inserted an *intravenous catheter* into Brooks' arm.[98]

> As the shades fall the witnesses shuttle out. As they leave *nurses in white uniforms* stare at them. In the courtyard the *ambulance* waits to take Blair's body away.[99]

Although physicians have long been involved in executions, conducting post mortems, certifying death, caring for inmates on death row, and so forth, the semiotics of the injection served to bring their complicity in the process to the fore, leading to a new round of debate and deliberation on their role that had not been present with the electric chair.[100] If medical intervention could help to purify the death penalty, the price might be a stigma that ran the other way and contaminated the medical profession. Not surprisingly physicians moved to excuse themselves from the act, speaking of it as a violation of their sacred Hippocratic Oath. As one doctor wrote:

> Street drug addicts, of course, are adept at making intravenous injections. Furthermore, it does not take a doctor to determine that a person is dead. Still, society has made us doctors responsible for things like ordering drugs, making intravenous injections and pronouncing death. Since we physicians have collectively stated that physicians should not participate in executions, why are we doing so?[101]

Worse, those physicians who cooperated could be caught up in a form of torture. We have seen how the guillotine had given rise to speculation on sensibility in the severed head, and the electric chair to imaginings of protracted agony for the helpless and inarticulate body in its grip. History repeated itself with the injection, conjuring up the specter of the strapped-down zombie situated in the nonplace between life and death. We find the *Economist,* for example, writing that those who have witnessed executions by lethal injection say the deaths appear almost hauntingly serene, more evocative of an operating theatre than the gallows. But now it is argued this tranquility could be deceptive: if insufficient sodium thiopental has been administered, a paralyzed yet wide-awake patient could find himself unable to speak, cry out or indicate his distress in any way as he first slowly suffocates and then suffers a massive heart attack.[102]

A widely reported study published in the *Lancet* not long after this statement indicated that anesthetic doses were too low to generate unconsciousness before chemicals intended to generate paralysis and stop the heart were introduced. Autopsies from Arizona, Georgia, North Carolina, and South Carolina showed in many cases the levels of anesthetic were consistent with awareness. The result, according to the *Chicago Tribune,* would be an experience of "asphyxiation, a severe burning sensation, massive muscle cramping, and finally cardiac arrest."[103] Fuelled with such speculations the Eighth Amendment was easily invoked. Critics could further point out that the execution of humans was painful and degrading because it involved the use of chemicals banned for putting down pets. Already by May 2004, opinion polls suggested some 21 percent of Americans believed that the lethal injection was a "cruel and unusual punishment."[104] In June 2006 the U.S. Supreme Court declared it would allow a challenge to the procedures involved. In December 2006 the botched execution of Angel Nieves Diaz in Florida saw the chemicals delivered into tissue and not the blood stream. He took thirty-four minutes to die in an event widely described as torture. Over in California, executions went on hold when doctors could not be found to supervise the procedure as a federal court ruling required. The lethal injection, then, has an uncertain future. Like other forms of death, it produces a surfeit of pollutions and uncertainties which cannot be easily managed.

CHAPTER SEVEN

Punishment and Meaning

With the fall from grace of the electric chair and the lethal injection we have traveled far from the birth of the prison and even further from the spectacle of the scaffold. More than just an empirical tour through shifting modes of punishment, our journey had as its goal the theoretical task of developing and illustrating a new Durkheimian theory of this sphere of social life. This guiding intellectual project generated some surprises, for the cultural codes we have uncovered differ radically in structure, content, and spirit from what we might expect after reading the standard literature. They have an imaginative, emotional, and symbolic valence whose orbit has never been observed in the earnest documents of policy-relevant criminology, the dustbowl empiricism of positivist inquiry, the bone-dry legalisms of law school jurisprudence, or even in the incisive ironies of critical theory. Punishment, we have seen, is only partly about program efficiency, inky statutes, or the armatures of power for it is also a form of expressive, communicative, ritualistic activity whose reach and grasp are shaped in decisive ways by meanings. These can be considered as collective representations, as nonmaterial social facts that transcend interests, slip through the fingers of those who seek to control them, and reproduce themselves in similar ways time and time again. As they do so they come to propel and direct not only the imaginative but also the concrete human activities of formal social control.

Of course this book has not been the first to argue that punishment is tethered to a greater or lesser extent to meaning. However, as I suggested in chapter 1, it is perhaps more wide-ranging and ambitious in its aspirations than the product of most of my fellow travelers. Many of the studies that I have recruited to my cause in this text take the form of a case study and situate meanings in geographically local and historically

specific determinants. These find their expression in the particular outcomes of a given site—the expressive repertoire of the French revolutionaries, the cultural politics of the Supreme Court, the endogenous history
of nineteenth-century prison design, and so forth. The impulse in this book
has been towards a more general kind of cultural argument, one that can
weld such conjunctural specifications of penal culture into a broader intellectual project and account for continuities over the centuries. For this
reason our inquiry has moved over a range of locations so as to construct
and furnish a comprehensive and transposable toolkit of Durkheimian
propositions and insights. It has also done this the hard way, by simultaneously confronting the most developed and compelling intellectual alternative, the deep thinking of Michel Foucault. He has been challenged not so
much through the normal channel of critique on points of detail but rather
by the mapping out an alternative logic for understanding punishment in
our time.

   If diverse case studies have enabled us to pursue this objective in multiple arenas the risk has been run that an atomized presentation of self-
contained essays will obscure the bigger project, that we admire the speci-
men trees, and not the wider landscape of the arboretum. For this reason
it is useful to summarize the findings of our empirical investigations and
to pull together the scattered illustrative materials through reference to
some basic propositions. If not a tight, inferential weave, these nevertheless capture the essence of our new Durkheimian way of understanding
criminal justice activity. Such propositions have been the cords that have
been plaited together through each of our historical inquiries, even if some
studies have given more prominence to one thread of imagery, symbolism,
or myth than another. The resulting product is I hope a book wherein
the whole is more than the sum of the parts just as the tensile strength of
a rope surpasses that of its constituent fibers measured individually and
summed.

   My first set of findings related to the theme of *pollution,* a concept to
which we were sensitized by Durkheim's thinking on the need to separate
the sacred from the profane, Robert Hertz on the evil "left sacred," and
Mary Douglas on the classificatory origins of disgust and abomination.
Punishment is not simply about regulating the politically dangerous or
economically costly nor even maintaining the "social order" and ensur-
ing system stability as the old-fashioned functionalist Durkheimians used
to assert. Rather it is about eliminating the disgusting and unruly, effecting the decontamination of the spiritually and morally offensive, banish-

ing evil, and enforcing cultural classifications and boundaries by shutting down liminal possibilities. This imperative to purge and exorcise finds its expression in a peculiar, tougher-than-Kyoto obligation—punishments can only be fully legitimate if they produce zero net emissions. If punishments put out more cultural pollution than they are deemed to eliminate, they are in trouble. The public execution disposed of a criminal but was accompanied by whoring, gambling, alcohol abuse, and ugly crowds; it had to go. The early prison was the antithesis of a civil society. Reformers saw themselves cleaning up this mess in which the potentially virtuous were all too easily contaminated by contact with vice. Newer, more closely regulated prisons, from Pentonville to the supermax, have tried to impose greater levels of order and enforce boundaries. Yet these have come in turn to be seen as factories of disorder churning out madmen and making unpredictable evil recidivists from petty criminals. A converse discourse saw "soft" prisons as a boundary-defying monster that generated pleasure and thereby endangered the binaries that divided the prison from everyday life, just as the public execution had failed to distinguish itself from the bacchanalian excesses of carnival. The guillotine and the electric chair were introduced as progressive attempts not simply to be more "scientific" but rather to be so in order to eliminate the evils of hanging and beheading—twitching bodies and the liminal in-between time joining life and death. In due course these too came to face the accusation that they polluted by situating the condemned in a boundary-breaking zombie-like state of living death, producing in the process degraded, cooked, and broken bodies and offensive noxious fluids. Efforts to introduce panoptical technologies have long been challenged by claims that they are morally problematic and facilitate totalitarian or voyeuristic evils, that they breach the boundary that separates private and public spheres. We have seen that to remain legitimate punishments have to be able to fend off such criticisms. They must show not simply that they punish and prevent crime, that they are humane or conform to the law, but also demonstrate that they work within rather than over cultural boundaries and can sustain only authorized closed narrations, that they are hygienic, that they do not threaten some form of moral or spiritual contamination.

A second recurrent motif in the penal imaginary has been the *sacred,* a force that Durkheim understood as the true foundation of social life. As I illustrated at the very outset, in social and legal theory alike punishment and its technologies are overwhelmingly taken to be utilitarian activities guided by efficiency and protocol. They are knowable, finite, and amenable to calculation. What our investigations have discovered is that punishment is a volatile, unpredictable compound. Like sex, death, and religion, punishment is a field of human activity that is vulnerable to eruptions of the primal, mysterious, and awe-inspiring, to the emergence of powers understood as beyond human control. Importantly we have seen that the form of the sacred encountered in punishment is not simply the "good" side associated with civic virtue or the majesty of the law, nor indeed the regal display of Foucault's sovereign power. To the contrary, punishment activity frequently conjures the uninvited spirit of the malevolent, enraged "left sacred" that represents the theme of holy terror screwed to its highest pitch. Such a motif was most clearly expressed in the cultural histories of the guillotine and the electric chair, these being seen even as avenging forces with sacrificial connections to some sinister supernatural realm. The electric chair was empowered by the mysterious force of electricity, the guillotine by the new cult of reason thrown up by the French Revolution in its initial millennial euphoria. Even the prison with its austere design and monotonous routines could not escape from such overcoding. Pentonville's inmates were described as ghostlike, the supermax prison likened to a high-tech hell, the panopticon to the all-seeing eye of some malevolent god. Mettray, the alleged apotheosis of disciplinary society was read by its contemporaries as a quasi-monastic institution run on sectlike lines. Punishment-based tourism and leisure, the day trip and wax museum, the novelty hotel—these thrive upon and make money from the half-life of such charismatic energy as does the highbrow art that seeks to channel the radioactivity of the impure sacred into valued expressive activity. So punishment is very much inflected with the nonrational, unpredictable, and ambivalent. The authorities must strive to keep the genie of surplus meaning in the bottle.

This brings us to our third set of Durkheimian findings, these relating to the volcanic fecundity of punishment as it spews forth *mythologies, collective representations,* and *totems.* Thanks to its imaginative engagement with the sacred and profane, with possibilities for pollution, with the mysteries of death and the body and with the universal dialectic of freedom and constraint—thanks to all these the universe of punishment is a realm of powerful, important, and somewhat unruly signifiers. Although nonmaterial these products of the mind and of our cultural systems loop back to their referents and constrain as they knot onto concrete technologies, practices, and institutions, binding them with layers of meaning. Legitimacy, reform, and innovation can hang in the balance as particular totemic shortcuts tell us not only what a punishment does but also what it means or how we should think about it. With the rise of mass communications and the public sphere such surplus meaning has become more, not less, central to the fate of punishment modalities. The guillotine ran hot when it was seen as a sacred symbol of the revolution, but sentiment cooled and the blade dropped less frequently once unanticipated resonance with the gothic set in. Efforts to revive the chain gang stumbled against the poisoned iconography of slavery. The electric chair proliferated while it symbolized science, reason, and progress but later had to fend off metaphors related to cooking and suggestions of torture. The federal minimum-security prison had to be reformed once it was embarrassingly rebadged in popular mythology as a country club and Pentonville's food quality went downhill once word got out that it served the best cocoa in London. The panopticon, in Orwell and Foucault, is a metaphor and index of a dangerous surplus of social ordering that must be stopped and not just a clever and expedient device or design. The fate of punishments is never just about their efficiency or cost or humanity. Of course these play a part, but decision making and destiny is also influenced by the semiotic spin that attaches to objects and policies as mythologies of the kind Roland Barthes identified gather and breed. Contra Wittgenstein and the Foucault of *Discipline and Punish*, "use" does not determine or exhaust "meaning." To the contrary, meanings determine uses and then feed upon these endlessly, insatiably, unpredictably.

These thoughts about the role of a *collective conscience* that thinks in terms of myth bring us to the idea of *civil society*. Although conventionally thought of as a sphere of cool and "rational" debate, the idea of civil society can be transposed into the Durkheimian idiom once we realize that efforts towards reason are always normatively inflected and that we think by means of myth.[1] Further, it is clear that Durkheim's model of social life as informed by diffuse, shared moral inputs and emotions is one that is highly consistent with understandings of an active and critical, morally evaluating public sphere that is in dialogue with the more concretely institutionalized state. Even in his rather structural essay "Two Laws of Penal Evolution," for example, Durkheim briefly speaks of the constraint that religion and tradition can place on centralized political authority suggesting that these could temper punitive urges.[2] Treated in the analytical (not normative) sense of a sphere of open dialogue and debate that exerts regulatory pressures on state activity, the concept of civil society can be thought of as a way of concretizing and updating Durkheim's rather psychologistic understanding of how cultural inputs might come to shape penal activity. Civil society theory points in particular to the role of mass communications and moral debate, to pressure groups and to information exchange, and most important of all to the narrative process through which substantive justice is evaluated.[3] In this book we have seen time and time again that punishment is never left to the experts. It is a relentless topic for civil debate, and not only in its generality but also in its particulars. Indeed civil society seems to be more concerned with the *how* of punishment that Foucault invokes than the abstractions of the *why* so beloved of moral philosophy and jurisprudence.[4] Talk about the purpose of punishment—retribution, rehabilitation, and so forth—is amazingly rare. It is technologies, policies, and institutions that catch the eye and spark the collective imagination. Administrative reason is encouraged to toe the line thanks to the ever present reality or threat of scandal, humiliation, disgust, and ridicule. Opinion slowly tilts, talk embarrasses, and the state responds. The cocoa ration ends, the chair is mothballed, the prison closed down, the execution held at dawn. Sometimes this process favors the advance of disciplinary society, at others not. Panopticism and the separate system of confinement, for example, were both held back by civil critique. Such findings suggest that the impulse towards practical reason is filtered through cultural codes and emotive symbolism. There is only limited deference in the public sphere to cool science and expert knowledge. Within the collective conscience, reasoning makes use of totemic representations as much as measurement, calibration, and protocol. By the late twentieth century the electric chair could be understood as a bad idea even in the centers of judicial and political life because it was already keyed into discourses of bodily pollution and transcendent evil on the periphery. Newgate was an icon of disorder, not simply a place that was disorganized. The guillotine was ambivalent rather than knowable because of its Faustian resonance. The realm of civil discourse is one where myth—understood in the sense of layered symbolism and narrative not necessarily "false understanding"—plays a hand, pressing the pans of the scales of policy in ways sometimes subtle and sometimes unmistakable.

Finally we should acknowledge the omnipresence of the *cult of the individual.* Durkheim saw this as the "religion" of our age and Goffman expanded upon this theme, talking of the ways that the self is a sacred thing protected by displays of deference and demeanor.[5] Although much work in criminology has documented the status degradation rituals that accompany the transition from citizen to felon, the studies in this book have highlighted a converse process notwithstanding the rise of penal populism. Punishments have increasingly needed to preserve the dignity of the individual, and so authorities have become acutely sensitive to problems of meaning in this sphere. When they are narrated as failing in this end punishment modalities begin to look problematic and are understood as propagating pollution by profaning the self. In neglecting status boundaries and encouraging disorder, Newgate had humiliated its more respectable inmates, especially those not yet convicted. Pentonville and the supermax prison transformed autonomous criminals into nonhuman lunatics. The electric chair and the guillotine did not respect the integrity of the body, even if the elaborate ritualized preparations for the former usually enabled the condemned to slip through their last hours without losing self-control. The panopticon transgressed privacy by snooping and spying. The circus crowd at the public execution did not permit the condemned a dignified end and encouraged counter-hegemonic cults of the individual that revolved around the antihero and the martyr. The chain gang made slaves of prisoners and exhibited them like animals in a roadside zoo. All these critiques have been effective. The range and extent of disciplinary possibilities have been as severely constrained by the sacred status of the sovereign human being as they have been energized by the quest for the docile body.[6]

Such a model of strong cultural inputs into the punishment process goes a long way towards keeping what was best about Durkheim's thought and leaving behind that which was problematic or unacceptable. As discussed in chapter 1, the legacy of evolutionism and functionalism, the shadow of Saint-Simon and Comte marked much of Durkheim's early writings on the theme of punishment. These have been further burdened by a problematic and distracting vision of punishments becoming less harsh over the centuries, simplistic analyses of cultural and psychological process in "primitive societies," causal models that focused on needs for system stability and the repair of damage to the collective conscience through the expression of anger. Once stripped of this excess weight we are left with the empty baggage of a theory whose merits lie chiefly in abstraction. Punishment is about meaning and emotion, there are diffuse societal inputs, it is expressive and so forth. Rather than attending to this imprecision most efforts to rebuild Durkheim in whichever field insist on the need to bulk up on questions of class and power.[7] Here I have called for a different kind of workout in the intellectual gym, suggesting that more not less attention needs to be given to meaning. What we have done is to repack those suitcases of useful generalities from the earlier writings with middle-range resources derived from Durkheim's later work and that of kindred spirits. Now punishment becomes encoded through discourses about purity, pollution, ordering, and the sacred. The emotional register includes not only anger as Durkheim originally proposed but also disgust, shock, pity, and contempt. Societal inputs come via a witnessable civil discourse on punishment, not invisible psychological currents in a collective conscience. This is a full set of luggage, but of course it does not contain clothes for every eventuality we might encounter. There are limits to the reach of our approach. It must be admitted that much regulatory activity remains intractably dull and is seemingly resistant to symbolic rescripting. Durkheim himself noted that the collective conscience could respond to crimes differentially: "[W]e feel no urge to protest against fishing and hunting in the close season, or against overloaded vehicles on the public highway."[8] Parking tickets, it should be said, are annoying but not evil, mysterious, degrading, or polluting.[9]

Sometimes, as Freud allegedly remarked, a cigar is just a cigar. But only "sometimes"—and recognizing this possibility for symbolic layering offers a real challenge to currently dominant understandings of the administration, evolution, and logic of punishment under modernity. In particular the vision of punishment outlined by Foucault in *Discipline and Punish* begs for critique. To understand the full implications of *my* book I need to recap *his* one last time. Foucault understood modern criminal justice as fundamentally rational and bureaucratic, and as a largely cold and routinized expression of growing administrative control. Within such a perspective the sacred, mysterious, and affective elements that once ornamented the criminal process can be consigned to the cabinet of curiosities that is the past. The historicist stance adopted by Foucault is one in which the instruments and instrumentalities of punishment have become progressively denuded of the affective responses, substantive value inputs, and improvised rococo embellishments that flourished under the regime of sovereign power. According to Foucault the "social play of signs" that occurred during an earlier "representative, scenic, signifying" mode of punishment has been decisively replaced by a disciplinary power driven by surveillance, training, and isolation.[10] This is embodied in technological innovations that are characterized by machinelike operation, uniformity, and calculability. Within such a vision the relationship of modernity to mythology is hydraulic and opposed. Passionless technologies and protocols are unable to carry a substantial didactic and eschatological weight.

Their rise to authority sees richer and more mysterious textures of symbolism wither on the vine of disciplinary power/knowledge, even if these can hang on for a while as anachronistic survivals of a prior epoch.[11] Bodies, meanwhile, lose their ability to communicate as potent signifiers in the morality play of judicial theodicy, becoming merely the docile and robotic carriers of external and coercive power/knowledge regimes. For Foucault, the brute, mundane facticity of the docile body replaces the eschatological, liminal, more mysterious corpse that was exposed to sovereign power. Hence in just one page Foucault speaks of "Man-the-Machine," of the "useful body," the "analyzable body," the "manipulable body," and the "intelligible body."[12] As for the soul, Foucault is able to make an explicit contrast with an earlier and more religious conception of the kind discussed by Ernst Kantorowicz.[13] The new soul of the disciplinary society is finite and mundane, not invested with any inherent mystery of dignity. It is no longer the carrier of the sacred. It is "unlike the soul represented by Christian theology, is not born in sin and subject to punishment, but is born rather out of methods of punishment, supervision and constraint."[14] The soul, in fine, is a place where we find "articulated the effects of a certain type of power and the reference of a certain type of knowledge, the machinery by which the power relations give rise to a possible corpus of knowledge."[15]

In Foucault's account, then, primordial symbols and mythologies no longer play a significant part in punishment discourse. Punishment is now explicable as a rational and instrumental application of social control, not an expression of any symbolic imperative. Insofar as substantive value commitments and patterns of belief do survive in the brave new world of *Discipline and Punish,* they eke out a precarious and impoverished existence as mantralike incantations of predictable humanist principles by reformers and professionals.[16] There is neither enduring reference to the immanence of the sacred in punitive operations nor an invocation and appreciation of the heady *tremendum* of redemptive expiation. And even these remaining meager scraps of meaning can be dismissed as the products of false consciousness. Foucault makes it clear that the dead hand of disciplinary power is the puppeteer tweaking the heart strings of the reformers and making them dance to its dexterous bidding. This vision, rather like Max Weber's disenchantment thesis, is one in which a formal and passionless instrumental rationality infects modernity, replacing a richer life world of signification and protean mythology with which it is incompatible.[17] This triumph of reason has been facilitated by parallel changes to the social structure. In the era of the "spectacle of the scaffold" the mob participated in a collective social drama. Even Foucault acknowledges it was able to subvert the rhythm if rarely the exercise of sovereign power. Regrettably this popular authority diminished with the rise of the "carceral continuum" and the emergence of a world composed of institutions organized around the circulation and training of bodies. Here there is no civil sphere or dissent, merely closed expert systems, a weblike archipelago of buildings and bureaucracies that reproduce disciplinary power and churn out docile bodies, passing them around the city in a meaningless and grim procession through the life course.

Further, there are methodological implications to this vision. Foucault's worldview is one in which aggressive bodies of power/knowledge colonize and annihilate weaker and less-organized opponents. In this rendering, institution building and rationalistic information systems provide a competitive advantage over localized, fragmented, primordial, and ad hoc traditions. As discipline replaces semiosis as the logic of practice, so must genealogy replace hermeneutics as a mode of inquiry.[18] Cut off by the scissorlike intersection of Nietzschean theoretical logic and fatalistic historicism, decoding a thick and potent cultural system becomes irrelevant to the explanation of punishment activity. Scholars can give up on interpretation and look simply to process and effects.

We live in a society where the range of relevant meanings has been closed down, where what the public thinks or says cannot make a difference to the conduct of punishment, and where there is no pressing need for critique to start with a hermeneutic moment. Or so Foucault would have it. He is wrong. We have seen that his position seriously underestimates the resilience of the sacred, which Durkheim correctly recognized as the most powerful, necessary, and indestructible of all social forces. He further neglects or ignores the historical emergence of a public sphere in the period between the death of Damiens and the publication of *Discipline and Punish*. With his commitment to a vision of routinized and rationalized culture under the control of experts, Foucault fails to come to terms with the unpredictable, rhizomic properties of semiosis and the flexible qualities of myth that make alternative, contending, plural narrations of penal process not just likely but inevitable. The Durkheimian story told in this book has challenged his grim thesis on theoretical and empirical grounds. Time and time again we have seen that punishment is a deeply meaningful activity that still needs to be interpreted if it is to be understood. Newer, more "modern" forms of punishing are efforts at ordering driven by the urge for purification, decontamination, and dignity. The sacred keeps showing up unbidden and unexpected in technologies, procedures, and institutions. Bodies continue to be read for signs. Powerful emotional reactions influence judgment on punishment. Legitimacy is contested by a vibrant and autonomous civil sphere that is suspicious of expert knowledge, rather than deferential, defeated, or indifferent. Far from eliminating or replacing vital symbolisms, the new punishments of modernity became themselves, in the anthropologist Lévi-Strauss's term, *bonnes à penser*—that is to say, materiel for renewed myth-making activity. As for, among other things, efficiency, control, and rationality, we have seen that these Foucaultian coin are generally ranked low in the priorities of civil discourse and indeed that they can be censured if their implementation violates some more symbolically charged evaluative criterion such as the sacred dignity of the individual or the requirement for genre consistency.

If the mission of constructing an alternative has made it convenient to bear arms against Foucault's reductionist position the time has now come to bring about reconciliation. Foucault sets out to demonstrate an all-or-nothing thesis whose hyperbolic arc parallels that of Nietzsche's own vigorous prognoses. I have tried to avoid this kind of foreclosure. Although this book has pushed a claim against Foucault as a more visible agenda, careful readers will have noticed that I have written in a path to compromise here and there. It is most fruitful perhaps to understand the relationship between disciplinary knowledge and mythology as additive rather than necessarily substitutive or antithetical. This requires a more subtle and layered understanding of how culture works. If we think of society as composed of both expert systems and wider publics, then space is opened for parallel narrations, each beholden unto the rules of its own sphere. The logic of discipline and surveillance will find its most stark expression in the handbooks, reports, architectural diagrams, and reasoned proposals of experts. We might perhaps fairly understand this as a hermeneutically thin world where bureaucratic rationality trumps. For it is true that criminal justice administration has become more professional and less informal over the past two hundred years and that efforts to plan, calculate, regulate, and control have become more central to its routine activity. It would be foolish to deny this process of rationalization, and we must tip our hat to Foucault here. But it must also be acknowledged that there has been a simultaneous and massive expansion of the public sphere and in the circulation of information and opinion that is more strongly inflected by broader social values and mythologies. The rationalization of penal activity does not kill off more affective and symbolic meanings, it simply moves in parallel with them. A "How to Run a Prison" manual will have a different agenda and genre from a satirical newspaper cartoon or a newspaper editorial on the latest imprisonment statistics. Studying public discourse is not an irrelevant exercise precisely because as we have seen there is interchange between spheres of evaluation, or as the political philosopher Michael Walzer would have it, "spheres of justice."[19]

There is another path to compromise that is more ambitious than this model of societal differentiation and cultural interchange. Rather than perpetuating a binarism that sees rule-driven formal organizations responding to nonrational external pressures with reluctant and calculated actions, we might understand the distinction between disciplinary and symbolic discourses as an analytic possibility rather than as an empirical reality. This is closer to the "turtles all the way down" position of Geertz, which emphasizes that there is no bedrock outside of culture in which to ground explanation, no final resting place for inquiry as all actions and institutions are built up from bottomless layers of meaning, whether convention or code.[20] Taking this perspective we can interrogate administrative and professional understandings of specific techniques for the skeins of symbolism and narrative that are woven into a seemingly passionless tapestry. As the criminologist David Garland pointed out some years ago in an oft-repeated statement, "the instrumentalities of penal power, which Foucault describes, always and necessarily take place within a framework of social values, culture and *mentalité*."[21] Hence we can understand that "particular styles of punishment" embody not only "power and strategies of control" but also "social values, sensibilities, conceptions of justice, and social policy goals."[22] In effect culture is written deep into the practices of the center in ways that are prereflexive and profound rather than being a kind of spin control that is reluctantly superimposed after external pressures have eventuated. Recasting this position in a stronger and more Durkheimian form, we can argue that the sacred, the symbolic, and the mythological can be found at the core of authorized discourses and practices and not only in the chattering anxieties of those sensitive souls peripheral to the exercise of disciplinary power. This is most obviously the case when science, progress, and reason are fetishized as forms of transcendent value within the culture of modernity. As I demonstrated, Pentonville was not simply a defensive response to the disorder of Newgate; rather, it was a temple where disciplinary practices served at the altar of the god of order. Mettray was an austere institution because this very austerity was an expression of the sacred and pure. The electric chair and the guillotine were conceived as illustrations of the triumph of enlightened reason that harnessed the power of the sacred through the rites of technology. The panopticon incarnated Bentham's paradisiacal aspirations for an ordered and productive society. In short discipline, order and rationality can be seen as propelled by mythology internally as well as responding to it externally. The cult of reason is one where rationality is an end in itself and not just the means to some more earthly power.

So I have not been arguing that Foucault's position is "wrong" or needs to be discarded in any simple way but rather that there is no necessary antimony between instrumental reason within the disciplinary complex and affective mythology. Although separable as ideal types, in the messy practice of social life we find diverse forms of coexistence, interchange, and hybridity. Spread over differentiated social spheres and layers of culture, this relationship gives rise to a sometimes competitive, sometimes symbiotic ecology of ideas that requires careful decoding. An account that is able to recognize these possibilities for paradox and the continuing, ambivalent, and unstable force of the sacred can also have a small normative force. Foucault's image of modernity is of a hermetic *dispositif.* Bryan Turner has likened this to a dominant ideology thesis.[23] Disciplinary power and its younger sibling, "bio-power" (a term invented by Foucault a few years after the writing of *Discipline and Punish* to describe population control through systems related to sex and demography), are seen as colonizing, subordinating, and exterminating alternative ways of thinking. This is a nightmarish ordered and self-organizing society from which there can be no escape towards authenticity or virtue. What we might think of as modes of resistance or the loosening of controls or ethical injunctions, Foucault tells us, are really just circuits in the production of power as the governed become self-governing in preprogrammed, predictable ways. According to the social theorist and Foucault scholar Arpad Szakolczai, the French master liked to think of himself as a parrhesiast, as a person who spells out dangers, speaks the truth, or "tells it like it is."[24] Yet with such vivid thinking Foucault has come to be seen as a prophet who has first traced the writing on the wall and then told us what it means for our future. The result can be a kind of self-fulfilling prophecy in which a fatalistic spirit generates apathy and subjects absolve themselves from responsibility for outcomes once it is believed the runaway train of disciplinary society cannot be stopped.

Here again is a situation in which an olive branch can be extended, for it would seem that in his last years the dying Foucault came to a startling realization of just this kind. We find clues in his final writings that he repudiated *Discipline and Punish* as a mistake and dead end. He tried to bring meaning and responsibility back into a social theory that once sought to replace these with the antihermeneutics of genealogy and archaeology. As another Foucault scholar, Eris Paras, put it following an exhaustive reconstruction of his later notes and lectures, "Foucault's model of the individual changed from 'determined' to 'partially self-constituting,' whilst his model of the exercise of power changed from absolutism to liberalism."[25] Foucault had been impressed by the agency demonstrated in the Iranian Revolution of 1979 and by writings from antiquity on the formation of the self, and so he moved towards a perspective of liberal governmentality in which subjects can make both themselves and their history. Richard Sennett confirms this shift in the sensibility and theoretical logic of his friend: "in the notes he made for the volumes he did not live to complete, he tried to explore the bodily pleasures which are not society's prisoners. A certain paranoia about control, which had marked much of his life, left him as he began to die."[26]

If this volte-face is ethically attractive it is regrettable that Foucault came to seek meaning within the trajectory of the individual who engages in the cultivation of the self as a life project. His belated humanism overburdens the individual subject with normative responsibility. He seems no longer to have faith in the less concrete and personal, amplified, transformative, and societywide reordering powers of discourse, signification, and classification—a communicative perspective that he had championed in earlier works such as *The Order of Things*.[27] Nor does he return to offer a compelling rewriting of the history of punishment or modernity. Foucault's newfound existential perspective rescues us from the prison of the docile body but does little to confront a wider vision of societal rationalization peppered with stoic, individual islands of aesthetic resistance.[28] It is Durkheim, Foucault's distant intellectual ancestor,[29] who has allowed us to go where Foucault could not in his last years and to put a wedge between culture and control. Durkheim splits the atom of power/knowledge and so opens the space for public critique and reflexivity that does not privilege or require the heroic subject. We have seen that a shared civil discourse really can constrain the administration of power, subjecting even the most technical and bureaucratic of activities to moral evaluation. Further, we have observed that potential counter-discourses will spring forth weedlike from the fertile, symbol-rich soils of punishment. This is not a field where authority can easily plough under unwanted meanings. Culture will make trouble whether or not we take the time to plant the seeds of some deliberately chosen counter-myth. Should we feel ethically compelled, our findings have indicated some effective pathways for such critical activity. We might invoke and mobilize sacred awe to counter the dominance of reason, or show the existence of disorders and degradations and call for a cleanup, or raise doubt and ambivalence where certainty seemed to rein, or flag category violations that abuse the primitive classifications of our civilization. Through all these means a braking influence can be exerted on that runaway train of disciplinary society. Many years ago Durkheim claimed that society could not only understand but also reconstitute itself through its collective representations. If he is correct, as I have been arguing, then coming to terms with the symbolic logics of culture should be the first and not the last step in any analysis and reform of criminal justice.

Notes

Chapter One

1. Paul Kahn, *The Cultural Study of Law* (Chicago, University of Chicago Press, 1999).

2. Karl Marx and Friedrich Engels, *The German Ideology* (Moscow: Progress Publishers, 1964). See also Friedrich Engels, "Letter to Conrad Schmidt, October 27, 1890," in Lewis S. Feuer, ed., *Karl Marx and Friedrich Engels: Basic Writings on Politics and Philosophy* (New York: Anchor, 1969), 439–45. As Engels explains here the formal and logical qualities of the law guaranteed that its true intent and function were veiled. "In a modern state the law must not only correspond to the general economic condition and be its expression, but must also be an internally consistent one" (442). Consequently the law could never be a "blunt, unmitigated, unadulterated expression of the domination of class" (442–43).

3. Georg Rusche and Otto Kirchheimer, *Punishment and Social Structure* (New York: Columbia University Press, 1939); Louis Althusser, *Lenin and Philosophy* (New York: Monthly Review Press, 1971); Michel Foucault, *Discipline and Punish* (London: Penguin, 1975); Malcolm Feeley and Jonathan Simon, "The New Penology: Notes on the Emerging Strategy of Corrections and Its Implications," *Criminology* 30, no. 4 (1992): 449–474; and Loïc Wacquant, "Deadly Symbiosis: When Ghetto and Prison Meet and Mesh," in *Mass Imprisonment: Causes and Consequences,* ed. David Garland (London: Sage, 2001), 82–120.

4. Nils Christie, *Crime Control as Industry* (London: Routledge, 2000); Zygmunt Bauman, *Modernity and the Holocaust* (Cambridge: Polity Press, 1989). This bleak vision provides a ready mandate for a humanistic critical theory. Christie, for example, writes: "[P]oliticians invariably attempt to give the impression theirs are rational tasks in a field where utility thinking is of obvious importance. Our counter-idea as cultural workers ... is to puncture this myth and bring the whole operation back to the cultural arena" (202). My worry is that such a critique will be misplaced if it is launched from a false premise. Rather than bringing meaning

back in as a white knight, we might do better to understand how it remains deeply implicated in the reproduction of cruelty in the criminal justice system.

5. The term is taken from David Garland, *The Culture of Control* (Chicago: University of Chicago Press, 2001). See this text for further discussion of late-twentieth-century transformations in thinking about crime.

6. David Garland, "Concepts of Culture in the Sociology of Punishment," *Theoretical Criminology* 10, no. 4 (2004): 419–440.

7. John Pratt, "Norbert Elias and the Civilized Prison," *British Journal of Sociology* 50, no. 2 (1999): 271–296, and idem, *Punishment and Civilization* (London: Sage, 2002).

8. See, for example, Katherine Beckett, *Making Crime Pay* (New York: Oxford University Press, 1997); also Wacquant, "Deadly Symbiosis."

9. Erving Goffman, *Asylums* (London: Penguin, 1968); Gresham Sykes, *The Society of Captives* (Princeton: Princeton University Press, 1958); and James Q. Wilson, *Varieties of Police Behavior* (Cambridge: Harvard University Press, 1968).

10. David Garland, *Punishment and Welfare* (Aldershot: Gower, 1985); Pratt, *Punishment and Civilization.*

11. Bernard Harcourt, for example, cautions that imprisonment might encourage rather than reduce the attractions of gun ownership for young offenders. It can magnify a broader association of guns with "protection" and with status in the symbolic systems of the gang imaginary. See *Language of the Gun* (Chicago: University of Chicago Press, 2006), 233–234.

12. Austin Sarat and Christian Boulanger, eds., *The Cultural Lives of Capital Punishment* (Stanford: Stanford University Press, 2005); Austin Sarat, *When the State Kills* (Princeton: Princeton University Press, 2002); and Franklin Zimring, *The Contradictions of American Capital Punishment* (Oxford: Oxford University Press, 2003).

13. Jeff Ferrell and Clinton Sanders, *Cultural Criminology* (Boston: Northeastern University Press, 1995). For all its ingenuity and creativity this literature remains hobbled by the longstanding Achilles Heel of cultural studies—the tendency to see culture as an expression first and foremost of power, or resistance to power. This has prevented a forceful argument for the autonomy of culture. It has also headed off a full blown attack from this quarter on the penology of Foucault, the French master being an iconic figure for critical social science discourse.

14. David Garland, *Punishment and Modern Society* (Oxford: Oxford University Press, 1991). I should acknowledge here that the seeds of this book lay in Garland's analysis, which I first encountered in 1993 when working on early drafts of the material that appears in chapter 2. I'm not certain my study could have been written without his field-constructing, foundation-digging activity. Kudos!

15. See Philip Smith and Jeffrey Alexander, "The New Durkheim," in *The Cambridge Companion to Durkheim,* ed. J. Alexander and P. Smith (Cambridge: Cambridge University Press, 2005), 1–37.

16. See Michelle Perrot, *L'impossible prison* (Paris: Éditions du Seuil, 1980).

17. Michel Foucault, *Discipline and Punish* (London: Penguin, 1975).

18. See Perrot, *L'impossible prison.*

19. For these critiques see, respectively, "Table ronde du 20 mai 1978," 40–56; and a polemic against Foucault by Jacques Leonard, 'L'historien et le philosophe," 9–28 in Perrot, *L'Impossible prison.*

20. See Leonard, "L'historien," 16; "Table ronde," 43.

21. Foucault in Perrot, *L'impossible prison,* 80.

22. Paul Rabinow and Hubert Dreyfus, *Michel Foucault: Beyond Structuralism and Hermeneutics* (Chicago: University of Chicago Press, 1983). Ironically Foucault tried to return to meaning in his last years with a treatment of the self and ethics. I discuss this shift in the final chapter but cannot resist noting here that it seems he eventually judged his effort to go "beyond" meaning to be a failure.

23. See Philip S. Gorski, *The Disciplinary Revolution* (Chicago: University of Chicago Press, 2003); also Garland, *Punishment and Modern Society.*

24. Note, for example, that Foucault (*Discipline and Punish,* 68–69) sees the detective novel as an irrelevance or distraction from the serious business of thinking about the deviant, as an aesthetic indicator of the rump status of a prior romantic conception of the criminal in today's world. One could argue the contrary. The continuing success of this genre in print, television, and film attests to the growing influence of popular culture and folk models not their residual status. Moreover, the law and order politics that marks out serial killers and pedophiles as its most evil other has been fueled by such a genre of literary and televisual output. As critics of penal populism have pointed out, such representations have fed into quasi-Foucaultian modes of penal practice such as Megan's Law and indefinite postrelease surveillance.

25. See Garland, *Punishment and Modern Society.*

26. Émile Durkheim, *Suicide* (1897; Glencoe: Free Press, 1951).

27. Of course this is not the first book on Durkheim and legal regulation, social control, or punishment. The new territory covered here is in developing a theory *inspired by* Durkheim, taking him in a more cultural direction and applying this perspective broadly. Existing studies in the field by Durkheim scholars tend to be concerned more with detailed matters of intellectual biography and the history of his ideas. They often seek to explicate his "true" thought and map its contemporaneous academic and philosophical contexts. See, for example, Steven Lukes and Andrew Scull, *Durkheim and the Law* (New York: St. Martin's Press, 1983); or Roger Cotterrell, "Constructing the Juristic Durkheim?" *Durkheimian Studies* 10 (2004): 56–69. A minority strand looks to systematize or test Durkheim's thinking, treating it in a more propositional and positivistic manner. See Jack P. Gibbs, "A Formal Restatement of Durkheim's Division of Labor Theory," *Sociological Theory* 21 (2003): 103–127.

28. Émile Durkheim, *The Rules of Sociological Method* (Chicago: University of Chicago Press, 1938).

29. Émile Durkheim, *The Division of Labour in Society* (1893; Basingstoke: Macmillan, 1984), quotation on 44.

30. Durkheim, *Division of Labour,* 47.

31. Durkheim, *Division of Labour,* 45.

32. Durkheim, *Division of Labour,* 46.

33. Durkheim, *Division of Labour,* 49.

34. Durkheim, *Division of Labour,* 50.

35. Durkheim, *Division of Labour,* 56.

36. Durkheim, *Division of Labour,* 56.

37. Durkheim, *Division of Labour,* 57.

38. Durkheim, *Division of Labour,* 63.

39. Durkheim, *Division of Labour,* 63.

40. For an earlier formulation of this theme, see Garland, *Punishment and Modern Society.*

41. For a history of Durkheim's interpretation, both positive and negative, see Smith and Alexander, "The New Durkheim." A surprisingly parallel assessment from a rival camp can be found in Randall Collins, "The Durkheimian Movement in France and in World Sociology," in *The Cambridge Companion to Durkheim,* ed. J. Alexander and P. Smith (Cambridge: Cambridge University Press, 2005), 101–135.

42. Émile Durkheim, "Two Laws of Penal Evolution," in *The Radical Sociology of Durkheim and Mauss,* ed. Mike Gane (London: Routledge, 1992), 21–49.

43. Kai Erikson, *Wayward Puritans* (New York: Wiley, 1966).

44. From "L'individualisme et les intellectuels," in the *Revue bleue* 10 (1898). Part of this essay is reprinted as "Individualism and Freedom," in *Durkheim on Politics and the State,* ed. Anthony Giddens (Stanford: Stanford University Press, 1986), 79–83, quotation on 81.

45. Erving Goffman, *Interaction Ritual* (Chicago: Aldine, 1967).

46. Durkheim, "Individualism and Freedom," 81.

47. Émile Durkheim, *L'éducation morale* (1902–3; Paris: Alcan, 1938), quotation on 200, emphasis added.

48. Durkheim, *L'éducation morale,* 201.

49. Jeffrey Alexander, "The Inner Development of Durkheim's Sociological Theory: From Early Writings to Maturity," in *The Cambridge Companion to Durkheim,* ed. J. Alexander and P. Smith (Cambridge: Cambridge University Press, 2005), 136–159.

50. Émile Durkheim, *The Elementary Forms of Religious Life* (1912; London: Allen and Unwin, 1968), Émile Durkheim, and Marcel Mauss, *Primitive Classification* (1903; Chicago: University of Chicago Press, 1963).

51. Henri Hubert, and Marcel Mauss, *Sacrifice: Its Nature and Function* (London: Cohen and West, 1964), quotation on 101.

52. Robert Hertz, *Death and the Right Hand* (Glencoe: Free Press, 1960).

53. For the analysis of the scapegoat, see Hubert and Mauss, *Sacrifice,* 53. For death, see Hertz, *Death and the Right Hand.* An extended discussion of the left sacred is provided by Alexander T. Riley, "Renegade Durkheimianism," in *The Cambridge Companion to Durkheim,* ed. J. Alexander and P. Smith (Cambridge: Cambridge University Press, 2005), 274–301.

54. Goffman, *Asylums;* Arnold van Gennep, *The Rites of Passage* (1908; London: Routledge and Kegan Paul, 1960).

55. Martha Grace Duncan, *Romantic Outlaws, Beloved Prisons: The Unconscious Meanings of Crime and Punishment* (New York: New York University Press, 1996).

56. Stanley Cohen, *Folk Devils and Moral Panics* (London: Paladin, 1973); and Howard Becker, *Outsiders* (New York: Free Press, 1966).

57. Harold Garfinkel, "Conditions of Successful Degradation Ceremonies," *American Journal of Sociology* 61 (1956): 420–24.

58. Jack Katz, *The Seductions of Crime* (New York: Basic Books, 1988); Hertz, *Death and the Right Hand;* and Georges Bataille, *The Accursed Share* (New York: Zone Books, 1988).

59. James Q. Whitman, *Harsh Justice* (New York: Oxford University Press, 2003), quotation on 194.

60. Pieter Spierenburg, *The Spectacle of Suffering* (Cambridge: Cambridge University Press, 1984); V. A. C. Gatrell, *The Hanging Tree* (Oxford: Oxford University Press, 1994); also Pratt, *Punishment and Civilization.* The literature awaits a telling intellectual comparison of Durkheim and Elias. Notwithstanding the fact that Elias comes out of the tradition of Freud and Weber, his findings can be subsumed into the Durkheimian master narrative. For Durkheim modernity (organic solidarity) is associated with higher levels of tolerance, greater levels of fellow feeling across social boundaries, and more respect for the Other. Elias captures some of the causal, institutional, and macrolevel dynamics of this broader process through his examination and identification of a civilizing process. This involves microrituals of deference, a cooling of hot sentiments, a net reduction in cruelty, the invention of privacy, the growth of sympathy, and the emergence of disgust as a regulatory emotion. The obvious synergies between Elias and Mary Douglas further attest to this kinship. Both talk of disgust and disorder as central to cultural life. In short, I would contend that Elias provides an elaboration to Durkheim rather than a rival hypothesis. Consequently much of the Elias-inspired literature on punishment can be reread through a Durkheimian lens.

61. For elaboration on this point, see Riley, "Renegade Durkheimianism"; and Smith and Alexander, "The New Durkheim."

62. For extended discussions on how Durkheimian theory has been retooled over the past two decades, see Philip Smith, "The Durkheimians," chapter 5 in *Cultural Theory* (Oxford: Blackwell, 2001); also Smith and Alexander, "The New Durkheim."

63. Briefly, some seminal and representative references for this intellectual perspective: Jeffrey C. Alexander, Bernhard Geisen, and Jason Mast, *Social Performance: Symbolic Action, Cultural Pragmatics, and Ritual* (Cambridge: Cambridge University Press, 2006); Jürgen Habermas, *The Structural Transformation of the Public Sphere* (Cambridge: MIT Press, 1989); Roland Barthes, *Mythologies* (Paris: Éditions du Seuil, 1957); Edward Shils, "Center and Periphery," in *Center and Periphery: Essays in Macrosociology* (Chicago: University of Chicago Press, 1975), 3–16; and Victor Turner, *The Ritual Process* (Ithaca: Cornell University Press, 1977). My book *Why War?* (Chicago: University of Chicago Press, 2005) can also be situated in this movement.

64. Again, see Smith and Alexander, "The New Durkheim."

65. Garland, *Punishment and Modern Society.* I might add here that around the same time John Braithwaite's *Crime Shame and Reintegration* (Cambridge: Cambridge University Press, 1989) also missed an opportunity to trigger a Durkheimain revival. In this highly influential book Braithwaite follows a Durkheimian line in explaining the failure of conventional criminal justice. In effect he claims it consists of the application of stigmatizing (polluting) rituals and identities to delinquents and criminals. These compound anomie and marginality and so amplify deviance. Braithwaite calls for "reintegrative shaming" rituals that signify wrongdoing and then welcome the individual back into the community. The result would be greater net moral integration. For all this focus on morality, solidarity, and ritual, Braithwaite is reluctant to move Durkheim to center stage.

66. Mikhail Bakhtin, *The Dialogic Imagination: Four Essays* (Austin: University of Texas Press, 1981).

67. Habermas, *Structural Transformation of the Public Sphere;* Raymond Williams, *The Long Revolution* (London: Chatto and Windus, 1961).

68. Collins, "The Durkheimian Movement"; Smith and Alexander, "The New Durkheim."

69. Barthes, *Mythologies.*

70. Mary Douglas, *Purity and Danger* (London: Routledge and Kegan Paul, 1966). My book is about criminal justice process and not the history of Durkheimian social theory. For this reason I sidestep here a series of internal debates on the nature of the profane and its relationship to the evil "left sacred" as well as the routine or mundane. I further avoid discussion of Douglas's own relationship to Durkheim, the vexing question whether the logic of her "grid/group" social theory is too deterministic, and if so, whether this might undercut the more Geertzian deployment that I am making here that liberates cosmology from morphology. Shortly before her passing we exchanged on this point. Her feeling was that theory today should try to connect the social system with mind and culture. My perspective is that we need still better illustrations of cultural autonomy.

71. The philosopher Karl Popper suggested that knowledge grows by means of efforts to disprove theory. See *The Logic of Scientific Discovery* (New York: Basic

Books, 1959). This scientific vision does not sit well with the imperative to interpret and reconstruct systems of meaning in cultural research.

Chapter Two

1. Anthony Giddens, *The Nation State and Violence* (London: Polity Press, 1985), quotation on 188.

2. Giddens, *Nation State and Violence,* 188.

3. Norbert Elias, *The Civilizing Process* (1939; Oxford: Basil Blackwell, 1978); Pieter Spierenburg, *The Spectacle of Suffering* (Cambridge: Cambridge University Press, 1984); John Pratt, *Punishment and Civilization* (London: Sage, 2002).

4. The historian V. A. C. Gatrell's account of changing bourgeois sentiment is consistent with the Elias paradigm, suggesting that revulsion at violence and identification with the victim had a role in driving punishments out of sight and out of mind. His account, however, is a little more sensitive to the theatrical class dynamics of execution ritual and its associated range of emotions and narratives. Sadly from a sociological point of view, he avoids generalizing theory. In an interesting example of independent convergence from two fields, the year 1992 must have seen Gatrell finishing up his seminal study just as I was starting work on the far more modest paper that underpins this chapter. See V. A. C. Gatrell, *The Hanging Tree: Execution and the English People, 1770–1868* (Oxford: Oxford University Press, 1994).

5. Gatrell, *Hanging Tree,* 17.

6. Michel Foucault, *Discipline and Punish* (London: Harmondsworth, 1977), see 3–31.

7. Foucault, *Discipline and Punish,* 60–69. For another scholar in agreement with my reading of Foucault, see Spierenburg, *Spectacle of Suffering,* 108–109.

8. Émile Durkheim, *The Division of Labour in Society* (Glencoe: Free Press, 1984); also "Two Laws of Penal Evolution," in *The Radical Sociology of Durkheim and Mauss,* ed. Mike Gane (London: Routledge, 1992), 21–49.

9. For an example, see David Kertzer, *Ritual, Politics and Power* (New Haven: Yale University Press, 1989); and Robin Wagner-Pacifici, *The Moro Morality Play* (Chicago: University of Chicago Press, 1986).

10. Victor Turner, *The Forest of Symbols* (Ithaca: Cornell University Press, 1967).

11. J. A. Sharpe, "Last Dying Speeches: Religion, Ideology and Public Execution in Seventeenth-Century England," *Past and Present* 107 (1985): 144–167; Louis Masur, *Rites of Execution* (Oxford: Oxford University Press, 1989); and Gatrell, *Hanging Tree.*

12. David Garland, *Punishment and Modern Society* (Oxford: Oxford University Press, 1991), quotation on 253.

13. See, for example, J. Edgar Hoover, "Statements in Favor of the Death Penalty," in *The Death Penalty in America,* ed. Hugo Bedau (Chicago: Aldine Publishing Company, 1964); and Arthur Koestler, *Reflections on Hanging* (New York: Macmillan, 1957).

14. See Foucault, *Discipline and Punish;* Sharpe, "Last Dying Speeches"; Gatrell, *Hanging Tree;* and Masur, *Rites of Execution.*

15. This invocation of the sacred could find its echo in popular practices and superstitions. Contact with the dead or with the gallows, for example, was believed by some to cure illness while the ill-timed arrival of a storm might signal divine disapproval of the execution. See Gatrell, *Hanging Tree,* 81.

16. G. Wilkinson, *The Newgate Calendar* (London: Thomas Kelley, 1816), quotation on 127–128. V. A. C. Gatrell also zeros in on Fenning as an exemplary case. See *Hanging Tree,* 353. With reason he speaks of her "beatification."

17. Wilkinson, *Newgate Calendar,* 125–128.

18. Wilkinson, *Newgate Calendar,* 298.

19. Wilkinson, *Newgate Calendar,* 310.

20. Wilkinson, *Newgate Calendar,* 312.

21. *London Evening Post,* 16–19 August 1746.

22. Wilkinson, *Newgate Calendar,* 212.

23. *London Evening Post.*

24. Wilkinson, *Newgate Calendar,* 212; *London Evening Post.*

25. Richard Sennett, *The Fall of Public Man* (Cambridge: Cambridge University Press, 1977).

26. John Barrows, *Knights of the High Toby* (London: Peter Davies, 1962), 156.

27. Barrows, *Knights of the High Toby,* 263.

28. Wilkinson, *Newgate Calendar,* 191.

29. *Oracle,* 10 August 1790, quoted in Leon Radzinowicz, *History of English Criminal Law* (London: Stevens and Sars Limited, 1948), 167.

30. G. T. Crook, *The Complete Newgate Calendar* (London: Navarre Society Limited, 1926), quotation from 269–270.

31. Erving Goffman, *Interaction Ritual* (New York: Pantheon, 1967), see especially 229–233.

32. Goffman, *Interaction Ritual,* 91.

33. Harold Garfinkel, "Conditions of Successful Degradation Ceremonies," in *Symbolic Interaction,* ed. Jerome Manis and Bernard Meltzer (1956; Boston: Allyn and Bacon, 1972), 201–208.

34. Émile Durkheim, *The Elementary Forms of Religious Life* (London: George Allen and Unwin, 1976), quotation on 271.

35. See Douglas Hay, ed., *Albion's Fatal Tree* (New York: Partner Books, 1975).

36. Sennett, *Fall of Public Man.*

37. For the importance of sensationalism in the early press, see Larry Sabato,

Feeding Frenzy (Oxford: Oxford University Press, 1991); and John Stevens, *Sensationalism and the New York Press* (New York: Columbia University Press, 1991).

38. Hay, *Albion's Fatal Tree;* Radzinowicz, *History of English Criminal Law;* Gatrell, *Hanging Tree;* and James Heath, *Eighteenth-Century Penal Theory* (Oxford: Oxford University Press, 1963). See also the contemporary writing of Jonathan Swift, *The Poetical Works of Jonathan Swift* (London: William Pickering, 1853).

39. Bernard Mandeville, *An Enquiry into the Causes of the Frequent Executions at Tyburn* (1725; Los Angeles: Augustan Reprint Society, 1964).

40. Mandeville, *Enquiry,* 19.

41. Mandeville, *Enquiry,* 25.

42. Mandeville, *Enquiry,* 29.

43. Mandeville, *Enquiry,* 20–22.

44. Mandeville, *Enquiry,* 36–37.

45. Mandeville, *Enquiry,* 41–42.

46. Henry Fielding, *An Enquiry into the Causes of the Late Increase of Robbers* (1751; Oxford: Clarendon Press, 1988).

47. Fielding, *Enquiry,* 167.

48. Paul Ricoeur, *The Symbolism of Evil* (Boston: Beacon Press, 1969).

49. James Joyce, *A Portrait of the Artist as a Young Man* (Oxford: Oxford University Press, 2000), 172.

50. James Boswell provides an example of just the kind of emotional response Fielding was tying to eliminate. After witnessing the execution of the attractive young highwayman Paul Lewis, he found himself surprisingly afflicted with both horror and depression. He could not sleep easily and tried vainly to cure himself through whoring and other forms of dissipation. "I was in a manner convulsed with pity and terror," he wrote. This was not the desired impact for the execution. As Gatrell notes, Boswell had achieved a deep identification with Lewis. Pity, it seems, had not been separated from terror, leading to a complex and ambivalent response to ritual. See Gatrell, *Hanging Tree,* 288–289.

51. Fielding, *Enquiry,* 169.

52. Fielding, *Enquiry,* 171.

53. Fielding, *Enquiry,* 170.

54. William Paley, "Of Crimes and Punishments," in *The Works of William Paley* (1785; Edinburgh: Thomas Nelson, 1831), 131–136.

55. Anon., *Hanging Not Punishment Enough* (London: Printed for A. Baldwin in Warwick Lane, 1701).

56. See *Parliamentary Debates (Authorized Edition)* (London: H. M. Stationery Office), quotation from Sir Stephen Lushington (934) and Mr. Goulburn (938) for March 5, 1840.

57. Quoted in Gatrell, *Hanging Tree,* 605.

58. Robert Frederick Opie, *Guillotine: The Timbers of Justice* (Phoenix: Mill. Sutton Publishing, 2003), quotation on 5.

59. Robert Johnson, *Death Work* (Belmont: Wadsworth, 1998).

60. For a more detailed analysis of the "defensive" qualities of contemporary executions and their vulnerabilities, see Herb Haines, "Flawed Executions, the Anti-Death Penalty Movement and the Politics of Capital Punishment," *Social Problems* 39, no. 2 (1992): 125–138; also Austin Sarat, *When the State Kills* (Princeton: Princeton University Press, 2002), and chapter 6 below.

61. Goffman, *Interaction Ritual,* 92.

62. "Murderer of 11 Executed by U.S.," *San Francisco Chronicle,* 6 September 1930, 1.

63. Peter Strafford, "Gilmore Dies in First U.S. Execution for 10 Years," *Times,* 18 January 1977, 1.

64. Bill Hazlett, "Killer Dies in Nevada Gas Chamber," *Los Angeles Times,* 23 October 1979, section 1, pp. 3, 24.

65. L. Marks and T. van den Bergh, *Ruth Ellis* (London: Penguin, 1990), quotation on 184–185.

66. Frederick Bywaters, *The Trial of Edith Thompson* (Edinburgh: W. Hodge and Co., 1923); L. Broad, *The Innocence of Edith Thompson* (London: Hutchinson, 1952); and Peter Aykroyd, *Evil London* (London:. Wolfe Publishing, 1973).

67. See, for example, opinion poll data in Elizabeth Hastings and Philip Hastings, *Index to International Opinion Polls* (Westport: Greenwood Press, 1992).

68. H. Hertzberg, "Premeditated Execution," *Time,* 18 May 1992, 49.

Chapter Three

1. Michel Foucault, *Discipline and Punish* (London: Harmondsworth, 1977); Michael Ignatieff, *A Just Measure of Pain: The Penitentiary in the Industrial Revolution, 1750–1858* (London: Macmillan, 1978); David Rothman, *Conscience and Convenience* (Boston: Little, Brown and Company, 1980); also William Forsyth, *The Reform of Prisoners, 1830–1900* (London: Croom Helm, 1987).

2. For an illustration of this perspective in the field of literature, see Victor Brombert, *The Romantic Prison* (Princeton: Princeton University Press, 1978).

3. See John Pratt, *Punishment and Civilization* (London: Sage, 2002). Pratt comprehensively demonstrates the pressures that prison administrative regimes come under to live up to public expectations of "the prison."

4. For more on this process, see Pratt, *Punishment and Civilization.*

5. See also Randall McGowen, "The Well Ordered Prison," in *Oxford History of the Prison,* ed. Morris Norval and David Rothman (Oxford: Oxford University Press, 1995), 79–109.

6. The boundary between criminal and law enforcement officer could be further perforated in more dramatic ways, as we find in the case of the celebrated thief-taker turned highwayman Jonathan Wild.

7. Daniel Eaton, *Extortion and Abuses of Newgate* (London: D. I. Eaton, 1813), quotation on 5.

8. Eaton, *Extortion and Abuses of Newgate*, 12.

9. In Anthony Babington, *The English Bastille* (London: Macdonald, 1971), quotation on 140.

10. Martha Grace Duncan, *Romantic Outlaws, Beloved Prisons* (New York: New York University Press, 1996), quotation on 173.

11. In Arthur Griffiths, *The Chronicles of Newgate* (London: Chapman and Hall, 1986), quotation on 204.

12. In June Rose, *Elizabeth Fry* (London: Macmillan, 1980), quotation on 92.

13. Sarah Anderson, "Imagining the Prison" (Ph.D. thesis, Victoria University, 2005), quotation on 61.

14. In Babington, *English Bastille*, 175–76.

15. Griffiths, *Chronicles of Newgate*.

16. Anderson, *Imagining the Prison*.

17. In Babington, *English Bastille*, 140.

18. Griffiths, *Chronicles of Newgate*, 150–151. Much the same sanitary obsessions, I should also note, can be found in the writings of commentators in France. The historian Patricia O'Brien notes that "pestilence and disease, darkness, dampness, and noxious air, were repeatedly cited by reformers of old-regime prisons." See *The Promise of Punishment* (Princeton: Princeton University Press, 1982).

19. Duncan, *Romantic Outlaws, Beloved Prisons*.

20. Rose, *Elizabeth Fry*, 92.

21. In Babington, *English Bastille*, 105.

22. McGowen, "The Well Ordered Prison," 88.

23. Howard in Babington, *English Bastille*, 108.

24. Howard in Babington, *English Bastille*, 109.

25. Howard in Babington, *English Bastille*, 110.

26. Sir Thomas Buxton, *An Inquiry Whether Crime and Misery Are Produced or Prevented by Our Present System of Prison Discipline* (London: John and Arthur Arch, 1818).

27. *Report of the Inspector of Prisons in Relation to the Gaol of Newgate,* as related in Babington, *English Bastille*. See also Parliamentary Papers, "Report of Committee of Court Aldermen, on Report of Inspectors of Prisons, in relation to Newgate," Houses of Parliament, 1836 (London: H. M. Stationery Office). This was a subsequent investigation into the abuses detected by the Inspector of Prisons.

28. July 1900, in Babington, *English Bastille*, 235.

29. Babington, *English Bastille*, 236.

30. Ignatieff, *Just Measure of Pain,* 3; W. Hepworth Dixon, *The London Prisons* (London: Jackson and Walford, 1850).

31. In Babington, *English Bastille*, 206.

32. Duncan, *Romantic Outlaws, Beloved Prisons,* 176. We can find the raw data

reported in Henry Mayhew and John Binny, *The Criminal Prisons of London and Scenes from Prison Life* (1862; London: Frank Cass, 1971). On pages 103–104 they draw on data from the prison inspectorate to indicate rates of lunacy at Pentonville ran at 62 per 10,000 prisoners, compared to 5.8 in the wider prison population.

33. Terence Morris, Pauline Morris, and Barbara Barer, *Pentonville* (London: Routledge and Kegan Paul, 1963), 12.

34. Pratt, *Punishment and Civilization,* 43.

35. Joshua Jebb, *Report of the Surveyor General of Prisons on the Construction, Ventilation and Details of Pentonville Prison* (London: HMSO, 1844), 6.

36. Jebb, *Report,* 33, emphasis added.

37. This nexus was also to ideologically inform nineteenth-century colonialism. Anne McClintock provides a fascinating account of how ideas of whiteness and cleanliness went alongside empire. See her *Imperial Leather: Race, Gender and Sexuality in the Colonial Conquest* (New York: Routledge, 1995).

38. Jebb, *Report,* 13.

39. Jebb, *Report,* 18.

40. Jebb, *Report,* 18.

41. Jebb, *Report,* 29.

42. Jebb, *Report,* 16.

43. Jebb, *Report,* supplement, 21.

44. Pratt, *Punishment and Civilization,* 46.

45. Hepworth Dixon, *The London Prisons: With an Account of the More Distinguished Persons Who Have Been Confined in Them* (London: Jackson and Walford, 1850), quotation on 157–158.

46. "The Model Prison," *Times,* 28 November 1842, 4.

47. Mayhew and Binny, *Criminal Prisons of London,* 120.

48. Mayhew and Binny, *Criminal Prisons of London,* 120, 128.

49. Thomas Carlyle, "Model Prisons," in *Latter Day Pamphlets* (London: Chapman and Hall, 1850), 1–108.

50. For example, "The Model Prison," *Times,* 26 November 1842, 6.

51. Dixon, *London Prisons,* 153.

52. Mayhew and Binny, *Criminal Prisons of London,* 130.

53. Dixon, *London Prisons,* 157.

54. Mayhew and Binny, *Criminal Prisons of London,* 141.

55. McGowen, "The Well Ordered Prison," 79.

56. The quotes are from Foucault, *Discipline and Punish,* 293, 295, 296.

57. Sydney Turner and T. Paynter, *Report on the System and Arrangements of "la Colonie agricole" at Mettray Presented to the Committee of the Philanthropic Society,* 19 August 1846 (London: James Truscott, Nelson's Square, 1846).

58. Société paternelle pour l'education morale, agricole et professionnelle des jeunes détenus, *Foundation d'une colonie agricole de jeunes détenus à Mettray, départment d'Indre-et-Loire* (Paris: Librairie de B. Duprat, 1839), quotation on 4.

59. Félix François Jean Cantagrel, *Mettray et Ostwald: Étude sur ces deux colonies agricoles* (Paris: Librarie de l'École Sociétaire, 1842), quotation on 47.

60. Turner and Paynter, *Report*, 5.

61. Turner and Paynter, *Report*, 4–5.

62. Turner and Paynter, *Report*, 8.

63. Cantagrel, *Mettray et Ostwald*, 25.

64. Société Paternelle, *Foundation d'une colonie agricole*, 19.

65. Société Paternelle, *Foundation d'une colonie agricole*, 8.

66. Paul Huot, *Trois jours à Mettray: Rapports lus au Congrès scientifique de Tours* (Paris: Imprimerie Claye, Taillefer etc, 1848).

67. Société Paternelle, *Foundation d'une colonie agricole*, 4, 6.

68. Anon., *Application du système de Mettray aux colonies agricoles d'orphelins et d'enfants trouvés* (Paris: Imprimerie J. Claye, 1850).

69. Société Paternelle, *Foundation d'une colonie agricole*, 7.

70. Société Paternelle, *Foundation d'une colonie agricole*, 6. I should note that statistics seem to prove Demetz got it right. Far from being a breeding ground for recidivism like most prisons, Mettray at this point in its history had a recidivism rate of around 10 percent (see Jeroen Dekker, *The Will to Change the Child* [Frankfurt: Peter Lang, 2001], 67). But more importantly, Mettray was a huge success in cultural terms. As we are seeing it was a legitimate and influential institution less because of efficiency and more because of its collective representation.

71. Huot, *Trois jours à Mettray*, 56.

72. In Dekker, *Will to Change the Child*, 61.

73. Dekker, *Will to Change the Child*, 61.

74. Paulin Gillon, *Rapport sur la colonie pénitentiaire de Mettray: Fait au Comité du travail, le* 20 Octobre 1848 (n.p., 1848), 4.

75. Gillon, *Rapport*, 2.

76. Huot, *Trois jours à Mettray*, 22, 19.

77. Turner and Paynter, *Report*, 18.

78. Turner and Paynter, *Report*, 27.

79. Contagrel, *Mettray et Ostwald*, 42.

80. Turner and Paynter, *Report*, 27.

81. Turner and Paynter, *Report*, 27.

82. Turner and Paynter, *Report*, 28.

83. Turner and Paynter, *Report*, 33.

84. Cantagrel, *Mettray et Ostwald*, 42.

85. Cantagrel, *Mettray et Ostwald*, 42.

86. "Genet—Rebel with a Cause," *Guardian Weekly*, 8 November 1992, section "Le Monde," 15.

87. Jean Genet, "Miracle de la rose," in *Oeuvres completes*, vol. 2 (Paris: Gallimard, 1953).

88. Genet, *Miracle de la rose*, 261.

89. Richard N. Coe, "Traps and Allegories: Miracle de la rose," in *Genet: A Collection of Critical Essays,* ed. Peter Brooks and Joseph Halpern (Englewood Cliffs: Prentice-Hall, 1979), 76–97, quotations on 76, 78.

90. Peter Annin, "Inside the New Alcatraz," *Newsweek,* 13 July 1998, 35.

91. Robert A. Shepperd, Jeffrey R. Geiger, and George Welborn, "Closed Maximum Security," *Corrections Today,* July 1996, 84.

92. A "Maryland official" quoted in Jessica Gavora, "The Prisoners' Accomplice," *Policy Review,* September 1996, 6.

93. "Latest in Incarceration Outdoes Alcatraz," *Los Angeles Times,* 11 December 1994.

94. Jan Hoffman, "Testing the Limits of Punishment," *New York Times,* 26 October 1997, 31.

95. "The Prisoners' Accomplice." Also see Spencer P. M. Harrington, "Caging the Crazy," *Humanist* 57, no. 1 (1997): 14–20.

96. Sasha Abramsky, "Return of the Madhouse," *American Prospect,* 11 February 2000, 26–29.

97. Sasha Abramsky, "When They Get Out," *Atlantic Monthly,* June 1999, 30–36, quotation on 32.

98. Thomas Dumm, "Enlightenment as Punishment," *Social Justice* 27, no. 2 (2000): 237.

99. "We Have a Strong Suspicion," *Times,* 5 January 1844, 4.

100. Charles Dickens, *American Notes and Pictures from Italy* (London: Chapman and Hall, 1842), quotation on 83.

101. John Galsworthy, "Patient or Criminal?" *Pall Mall Gazette,* 26 February 1910. Also, *Justice* (London: Duckworth, 1910). For an outstanding and detailed treatment of Galsworthy's position on criminal justice see Anderson, *Imagining the Prison.*

102. "Inside the New Alcatraz," 35

103. "When They Get Out," 33

104. Joe Hallinan, "Poor Town Welcomes 'Supermax Prison,'" *Times-Picayune,* 10 December 1995, A30.

105. Maura Dolan, "Judge Orders End to Brutality at High-Tech Prison," *Los Angeles Times,* 12 January 1995, 1.

106. Associated Press, "Famed Country Club Prison Is to House Violent Inmates," *New York Times,* 31 July 1990, A14.

107. Joseph Henslik, John Shinners, and John Molenda, "An Insider's Guide to America's Top Ten Jails," *Playboy,* July 16 1992, 16. See also "Rating Some of the Best Places—Behind Bars, That Is," *New York Times,* 24 July 1992, B7.

108. Kurt Eichenwald, "In Danbury, Prison Is Just Too Inviting," *New York Times,* 14 September 1986, 11CN.

109. Strat Douthat, "Federal Prison Camp Houses White Collar Criminals," *Los Angeles Times,* 23 April 1989, 14.

110. Carol Leonard, "Caviar Porridge," *Times,* 31 March 1988.

111. Pratt, *Punishment and Civilization,* 147.

112. Charles Elmore, "Lawmaker Sees Road Chain Gangs as Tourism Boost," *Palm Beach Post,* 25 April 1997, B6.

113. John Leland and Vern Smith, "Back on the Chain Gang," *Newsweek,* 15 May 1995, 58.

114. "Tough Sheriff Puts Women in Chain Gang," *Los Angeles Times,* 20 September 1996, 19; "Sheriff in Arizona Uses Female Chain Gang," *Washington Post,* 20 September 1996, A2.

115. Brent Staples, "The Chain Gang Show," *New York Times Magazine,* 17 September 1995, 62.

116. William Booth, "Link to the Past," *Los Angeles Times,* 8 January 1996, 1.

117. Tracey Meares, "Let's Cut Chain Gangs Loose," *U.S. Catholic,* July 1997, 20–22.

118. "Shackled to the Bad Old Days," *Kansas City Star,* 14 February 1996.

119. John David Morley, "Back on the Chain Gang," *Times,* 5 August 1995, 24.

120. Henry Weinstein, "Ga. High Court Relegates Electric Chair to History," *Los Angeles Times,* 6 October 2001, A21.

121. Pratt, *Punishment and Civilization,* 51.

122. Pratt, *Punishment and Civilization,* 53.

123. P. Watson, "Anyone for a Night Behind Bars?" *Business Review Weekly,* 8 December 1997, 108.

124. Carolyn Strange and Michael Kempa, "Shades of Dark Tourism," *Annals of Tourism Research* 30, no. 2 (2003): 386–405.

125. Strange and Kempa, "Shades of Dark Tourism."

126. The quote is from http://www.alcatrazhistory.com/rs1.htm, accessed January 2007.

127. Quoted in Strange and Kempa, "Shades of Dark Tourism," 398.

128. "Death Is Texas Growth Industry," *Baltimore Sun,* 24 April 2001.

129. Sun Wire Services, "The Best Prison Hotel Bar None," *Ottawa Sun,* 13 August 2004, 18.

130. "Checking into a Prison with Only Minibars," *Mail on Sunday,* 14 April 2002.

131. Vitali Vitaliev, "Masochists Welcomed Here," *Sunday Telegraph,* 1 April, 2001, 11.

132. "Gut Reaction," *Sunday Times,* 10 March 1996.

133. Paul Wright, "The Cultural Commodification of Prisons," *Social Justice* 27, no. 3 (2000): 15ff.

Chapter Four

1. Gertrude Himmelfarb, "The Haunted House of Jeremy Bentham," in *Victorian Minds* (London: Weidenfeld and Nicolson, 1968), pp. 32–81, quotation on 33.

2. Janet Semple, *Bentham's Prison* (Oxford: Clarendon Press, 1993).

3. See Christopher Dandeker, *Surveillance, Power and Modernity* (Cambridge: Polity Press, 1990); and David Lyon, *The Electronic Eye: The Rise of Surveillance Society* (Cambridge: Polity Press, 1994). Written from a neo-Weberian and analytic perspective, these two books are somewhat cool in tone and can be contrasted with another component of this tradition, namely, a voluminous radical literature emerging from a fusion of Foucault with cultural studies. The latter engages in a more clearly normative critique using words such as hegemony, resistance, normalization, and exclusion.

4. For example, Brandon Welsh and David P. Farrington, "Effects of Closed-Circuit Television on Crime," *Annals of the American Academy of Political and Social Science* 587 (May 2003): 110–135.

5. Michel Foucault, *Discipline and Punish* (New York: Pantheon Books, 1977), quotation on 205.

6. In the early 1990s the celebrity O.J. Simpson was on trial for murder. A key exhibit was a bloody leather glove said to have been used by the killer in the case. Simpson's lawyer Johnnie Cochran daringly had him attempt to put the glove on in court. It was too small. In summing up the case Cochran famously said, "If it doesn't fit, you must acquit."

7. It is notable that Foucault relies heavily on Bentham's initial minimalist twenty-seven-page proposal, more or less ignoring the hundred or so pages of detailed elaboration, modification, and concession in two extended postscripts written in later years. Nevertheless, we cannot explain away his reading simply as a faithful rendition of his chosen, more limited source material. When I presented this research at the University of Chicago, an interesting issue was raised: to what extent was the "'cultural" component of the panopticon (identified later in this chapter) an aspect of Bentham's "true" or personal beliefs and to what extent a concession to an audience of critics and potential sponsors? Perhaps Foucault had accurately captured the essence and intent of the plan in its early and more pure form, and I had merely tapped into ad hoc spin management and marketing. A comparison of proposal and postscripts would allow a determination to be made. The hypothesis is intriguing, but it turns out to be false. The original proposal contains the germs of the cultural themes elaborated in the later postscripts. There is reference to the need to protect privacy and decency during toilet activity (42); the need for economic self-sufficiency (50); the problem of promiscuous association (44); the advantages for visiting inspectors of avoiding direct and degrading interpersonal contamination (45); the recruiting of a curious popular gaze (46) as well as that of the keeper's family in need of entertainment (45); the importance of publicity as a check on abuse of power by the powerful (46); provision for religion (47); and the superior deterrent value of panopticism over transportation (58). We should also note that Bentham's ideas on the primacy of deterrence as the end of punishment and the importance of theater and spectacle to penal logic extend back

to the 1770s and his *Rationale of Punishment.* The panopticon postscripts, then, are better thought of as an expansion rather than as a revision or contradiction of any earlier thoughts Bentham might have had.

8. Jeremy Bentham, "Panopticon; or, The Inspection House Containing the Idea of a New Principle of Construction Applicable to Any Sort of Establishment, in Which Persons of Any Description Are to Be Kept Under Inspection," in *The Works of Jeremy Bentham,* vol. 4 (Edinburgh: William Tait, 1843), 37–175.

9. Bentham, "Panopticon," 40–41, 44.

10. Foucault, *Discipline and Punish,* quotations from 201, 203, 205, 210, 211, and 208, respectively.

11. Bentham, "Panopticon," 122.

12. John Pratt, "This Is Not a Prison: Foucault, the Panopticon and Pentonville," *Social and Legal Studies* 2 (1993): 373–395.

13. Bentham, "Panopticon," 122.

14. Bentham, "Panopticon," 80.

15. Patrick Colquhoun, *A Treatise on the Police of the Metropolis* (London: H. Fry for C. Dilly, 1796), xi.

16. Bentham, "Panopticon," 174.

17. Bentham, "Panopticon," 174.

18. Bentham, "Panopticon," 39.

19. Jeremy Bentham, *The Works of Jeremy Bentham,* vol. 10 (Edinburgh: William Tait, 1843), quotation on 224.

20. Bentham, "Panopticon," 54.

21. Bentham, "Panopticon," 47–55; also Himmelfarb, "Haunted House."

22. Jeremy Bentham, *The Rationale of Punishment* (1775; London: Robert Heward, 1830).

23. Bentham, "Panopticon," 72.

24. Bentham, "Panopticon," 74.

25. Bentham, "Panopticon," 74.

26. Bentham, "Panopticon," 76. The formidably erudite Bentham makes the perfect reference here to Luke 13:4 (New International Version Translation): "[1] Now there were some present at that time who told Jesus about the Galileans whose blood Pilate had mixed with their sacrifices. [2] Jesus answered, 'Do you think that these Galileans were worse sinners than all the other Galileans because they suffered this way? [3] I tell you, no! But unless you repent, you too will all perish. [4] Or those eighteen who died when the tower in Siloam fell on them—do you think they were more guilty than all the others living in Jerusalem? [5] I tell you, no! But unless you repent, you too will all perish.'"

27. Michel Foucault, "The Eye of Power," in *Power/Knowledge: Selected Interviews and Other Writings* (New York: Pantheon, 1980), 146–165, quotation on 152.

28. Bentham, "Panopticon," 45.

29. Bentham, "Panopticon," 43.

30. Bentham, "Panopticon," 136.

31. Bentham, "Panopticon," 161–162.

32. Foucault later noted that Bentham's ideas went down well in Revolutionary France due to an elective affinity between ideas of visibility and the Rousseauist themes of transparency that were "the lyrical note of the Revolution." The problem remains that he understands Bentham himself as proposing and exemplifying a purely instrumental fix devoid of such cultural inputs. His was "the technical idea of the exercise of an all seeing power" which could be "grafted onto" this more meaningful foundation. See "The Eye of Power," quotation on152.

33. In Semple, *Bentham's Prison,* 269.

34. Bentham, "Panopticon," 46.

35. Bentham, "Panopticon," 45.

36. Semple, *Bentham's Prison,* 295–96.

37. Bentham, "Panopticon," 79.

38. Bentham, "Panopticon," 79–80.

39. Bentham, "Panopticon," 78.

40. Bentham, "Panopticon," 79.

41. Bentham, "Panopticon," 79.

42. Bentham, "Panopticon," 79. The idea of using masks for didactic purposes had been earlier proposed in his *Rationale of Punishment,* 135. Here Bentham had proposed that punishments be exemplary and publicly understandable. "Let the offender . . . be made to wear a mask . . . . The masks may be more or less tragical, in proportion to the enormity of the crimes of those who wear them. The air of mystery which such a contrivance will throw over the scene, will contribute in a great degree to fix the attention by the curiosity it will excite, and the terror it will inspire."

43. Foucault, *Discipline and Punish,* 217.

44. Foucault, *Discipline and Punish,* 203.

45. *The Yale Edition of Horace Walpole's Correspondence,* vol. 37 (New Haven: Yale University Press, 1974), 164. Bentham's initial plan was for a building of 100' diameter (later 120') and two stories of forty-eight cells. This seems in keeping with the case for Ranelagh.

46. M. Cavadino and J. Dignan, *The Penal System: An Introduction* (London: Sage, 1992).

47. Foucault, *Discipline and Punish,* 225.

48. Semple, *Bentham's Prison,* 254.

49. Semple, *Bentham's Prison,* 255.

50. Semple, *Bentham's Prison,* 272.

51. Semple, *Bentham's Prison,* 257ff. The following newspaper quotes are taken from this source. I am grateful to the late Janet Semple for collecting this information.

52. *Morning Chronicle,* 1 April 1799.

53. *Morning Herald,* 2 April 1799.

54. *Courier and Evening Gazette,* 2 April 1799.

55. *Morning Chronicle,* 1 April 1799.

56. Charles Tilly, "Useless Durkheim," in *As Sociology Meets History* (New York: Academic Press, 1981), 95–108, see in particular 107.

57. As Maurice Blanchot puts it: "*Discipline and Punish,* as is well known, marks the transition from the study of isolated discursive practices to the study of the social practices that constitute their underpinning. It is the emergence of the political in the work and life of Foucault." Or put another way, the book is all about how doing informs thinking in a context of power. This makes it distinctive from the earlier works. See "Michel Foucault As I Imagine Him," in *Foucault/Blanchot* (New York: Zone Books, 1987), 61–109, quotation on 83.

58. Foucault, *Power/Knowledge,* 56.

59. Foucault, *Power/Knowledge,* 53–54.

60. Himmelfarb, "Haunted House."

61. Semple, *Bentham's Prison.*

62. Foucault, *Discipline and Punish.*

63. George Orwell, *Nineteen Eighty-Four* (London: Secker and Warburg, 1949).

64. Gordon Marsden, "Orwell and Burke: Strange Bedfellows?" *History Today* 53, no. 7 (July 2003): 22–24.

65. Bentham, "Panopticon," 45.

66. Chris Wood, "The Electronic Eye View," *Maclean's,* 19 November 2001, 94.

67. Christian Parenti, "D.C.'s Virtual Panopticon," *Nation,* 3 June 2002, 24–26.

68. *Child's Play 3: Look Who's Stalking* (1991, Universal Pictures), directed by Jack Bender.

69. Sam Dillan, "Cameras Watching Students," *New York Times,* 24 September 2003, B9.

70. M. McCahill, *The Surveillance Web: The Rise of Visual Surveillance in an English City* (Cullompton: Willan, 2002).

71. "Privacy in Public," *New York Times,* 20 November 1981, A39.

72. Jeffrey Rosen, "A Watchful State," *New York Times Magazine,* 7 October 2001, 38. The quotations that follow are from pages 85 and 93.

73. "D.C.'s Virtual Panopticon," 25.

74. Sarah Boxer, "Beating Surveillance: Don't Care, Just Laugh," *New York Times,* 4 July 1998, B7.

75. The French theorist Michel de Certeau suggested that everyday life could be lived as a form of resistance to routinization and power. Seemingly trivial acts like walking down the street with a jaunty step or cutting corners were ways to assert the existence of an autonomous self in the face of modernity. Organizations like the Institute for Applied Autonomy (www.appliedautonomy/isee.html) try to offer practical ways to achieve this objective. See de Certeau, *The Practice of Everyday Life* (Berkeley: University of California Press, 1984).

76. Patrick Justo, "Protests Powered by Cellphone," *New York Times,* 9 September 2004, G4.

77. Philip Gefter, "Is That Portrait Staring at Me?" *New York Times,* 10 April 2005, D2, 32.

78. "The Art of Surveillance," http://www.artic.edu/~tholme/surveillance_course/ m/, accessed January 2006.

79. At http://www.flickr.com/groups/panopticon/, accessed January 2006.

80. "The All-Seeing Eye That Understands Nothing," *Observer,* 10 December 2000, Review, 2.

81. "Polish Government Booklet on Media Coverage," *BBC Summary of World Broadcasts,* 14 January 1983.

82. Stevenson Swanson, "Writing the Book on Life in the 1980s," *Chicago Tribune,* 17 October 1988, section 5, 3.

83. "The Nation," *Los Angeles Times,* July 15 1985, OC 2.

Chapter Five

1. Michel Foucault, *Discipline and Punish* (London: Allen Lane, 1977), 13–15.

2. Foucault, *Discipline and Punish,* 15.

3. Claude Lévi-Strauss, *The Savage Mind* (London: Weidenfeld and Nicholson, 1966).

4. Lynn Hunt, *Politics, Culture, and Class in the French Revolution* (Berkeley: University of California Press, 1984); Mona Ozouf, *La fête révolutionnaire, 1789–1799* (Paris: Gallimard, 1976).

5. For an extended analysis of the symbolism of the Bastille over the past three centuries, see another study in the spirit of this book: Philip Smith, "The Elementary Forms of Place and Their Transformations: A Durkheimian Model," *Qualitative Sociology* 22, no. 1 (1999): 13–36.

6. M. Mougins de Roquefort, Assemblée National transcript for 31 May 1791, in *Archives Parlementaires de 1787 à 1860. Recueil complet des débats législatifs et politiques des chambres françaises,* 1st ser. (1787–1799), vol. 26 (Paris: Société d'Imprimerie et Librairie Administratives, 1887), 639.

7. Le Pelletier de Saint-Fargeau, Assemblée National transcript for 3 June 1791, in *Archives Parlementaires de 1787 à 1860,* 721.

8. Reported in Pierre Quentin-Bauchart, *Le docteur Guillotin et la guillotine* (Paris: Éditions de la Nouvelle Revue, 1905), quotation on 22.

9. Hunt, *Politics, Culture, and Class.*

10. Daniel Arasse, *La guillotine et l'imaginaire de la terreur* (Paris: Flammarion, 1987).

11. Yves Saint-Agnes, *Guide de Paris révolutionnaire* (Paris: Musée et Perrin, 1989).

12. Dr. Louis, report to Ministry of Justice, reproduced in *Journal de Paris,* 22 March 1792, 332.

13. See also Jeffrey Alexander, "The Promise of a Cultural Sociology: Technological Discourse and the Sacred and Profane Information Machine," in *Theory of Culture*, ed. Neil Smelser and Richard Munch (Berkeley: University of California Press, 1992), 293–323. In this pathbreaking paper, which is only now starting to attract attention, Alexander shows that the computer—seemingly the most rational of all devices—has never been understood in fully rational ways. To the contrary, it is narrated through apocalyptic and utopian narratives.

14. Victor Turner, *The Ritual Process* (Ithaca: Cornell University Press, 1977); and Arnold van Gennep, *The Rites of Passage* (London: Routledge, 1960).

15. Arasse, *La guillotine et l'imaginaire de la Terreur;* Daniel Geroud, *Guillotine: Its Legend and Lore* (New York: Blast Books, 1992).

16. Charles Dickens, *A Tale of Two Cities* (London: Macmillan, 1905).

17. L. Prudhomme, "On a mis la dernière main à la guillotine," *Révolutions de Paris* 198 (20–27 April 1793): 224–25, quotation on 224.

18. Max Weber, *Economy and Society* (Berkeley: University of California Press, 1978), 979. Weber here refers to what he saw as the capricious decision making of traditional Islamic magistrates.

19. Letter to Moniteur dated 18 December 1789, quoted in Quentin-Bauchart, *Le docteur Guillotin et la guillotine.*

20. Louis, report to Ministry of Justice, 332.

21. Guillotin, reported speech in Assemblée National transcript for 21 January 1790, , in *Archives Parlementaires de 1787 à 1860*, 278.

22. Arasse, *La guillotine et l'imaginaire de la Terreur,* 77–78.

23. James Q. Whitman, *Harsh Justice* (New York: Oxford University Press, 2003).

24. Émile Durkheim *The Elementary Forms of Religious Life* (London: Allen and Unwin, 1968), quotation on 119.

25. For more discussion on this point, see Alexander, "The Sacred and Profane Information Machine."

26. Letter of 27 Brumaire, Year II by Citoyen Gateau, administrator of military subsistances, quoted in Gilles Lenotre, *La guillotine pendant la révolution* (Paris: Perrin, 1893), 307.

27. Arasse, *La guillotine et l'imaginaire de la Terreur,* 111; and Lenotre, *La guillotine pendant la révolution,* 310.

28. Durkheim, *Elementary Forms,* 121.

29. Lenotre, *La guillotine pendant la révolution,* 309

30. Lenotre, *La guillotine pendant la révolution,* 299.

31. Gilles Lenotre, *The Guillotine and Its Servants* (London: Hutchinson, 1929), 208.

32. Michel Foucault, *The Birth of the Clinic* (1963; London: Tavistock, 1973).

33. Lévi-Strauss, *Savage Mind.*

34. Laurence Guignard, "Les supplices publics au XIXe siècle," in *Le corps violenté,* ed. M. Porret (Geneva: Droz, 1998), 157–184.

35. Lynn Hunt, "The Many Bodies of Marie-Antoinette," in *Eroticism and the Body Politic,* ed. Lynn Hunt (Baltimore: Johns Hopkins University Press, 1991), 108–130; and Dorinda Outram, *The Body and the French Revolution* (New Haven:. Yale University Press, 1989).

36. Professeur Soemmering, "Lettre de M. Soemmering à M. Oelsner," *Magasin encyclopédique* (1795): 468–478, quotation on 469.

37. Soemmering, "Lettre," 470.

38. J.-J. Sue, "Opinion de J-J. Sue sur la douleur qui survit à la decolation," *Magazine encyclopédique* (1795), 170–189, quotation on172.

39. Soemmering, "Lettre," 471.

40. Soemmering, "Lettre," 472.

41. Soemmering, "Lettre," 472.

42. Sue, "Opinion," 179.

43. Soemmering, "Lettre," 473.

44. Sue, "Opinion," 173.

45. Soemmering, "Lettre," 473.

46. Sue, "Opinion," 177.

47. Oelsner, "Oelsner aux redacteurs du *Magasin encyclopédique,*" *Magasin encyclopédique* (1795): 463–467, quotation on 467.

48. Soemmering, "Lettre," 476–477.

49. Citoyen Cabanis, "Note adressee auz auteurs du *Magasin encyclopédique,* sur l'opinion de Messieurs Oelsner et Soemmering et du Citoyen Sue, touchant le supplice de la Guillotine, par le citoyen Cabanis," *Magasin encyclopédique* (1795), 155–174, quotation on 161.

50. Jean Sédillot le Jeune, *Réflexions historiques et physiologiques sur le supplice de la guillotine* (Paris: L'Imprimerie de Pain, Passage-Honoré, 1795), quotation on 19.

51. Réné-Georges Gastellier, *Que penser enfin du supplice de la guillotine* (Paris, 1795), quotation on 15.

52. Georges Wedekind, "Sur le supplice de la guillotine," *Le Moniteur universel,* 11 November 1795, 198.

53. Le Pelletier, "Melanges: Au Redacteur," *Le Moniteur universel,* 15 November 1795, 213–214, quotation on 213.

54. J. B. F. Léveillé, "Dissertation physiologique par J. B. F. Léveillé, chirurgien a l'Hotel-Dieu de Paris," *Magasin encyclopédique* (1795), 453–462, quotation on 460–461.

55. Gastellier, *Supplice de la guillotine,* 15.

56. Cabanis, "Note," 169.

57. Sédillot, *Réflexions historiques et physiologiques,* 14.

58. Wedekind, "Sur le supplice," 198.

59. Sédillot, *Réflexions historiques et physiologiques,* 22.

60. In Scotland a trial may result in a verdict of guilty, not guilty, or not proven,

the last being generally known as the "Scottish verdict." It is used when there is not enough evidence to convict but a strong presumption of culpability. The Scottish verdict allows for acquittal but results in stigma.

61. Mikhail Bakhtin, *The Dialogic Imagination* (Austin: University of Texas Press, 1981).

62. Maurice Blanchot, "La littérature et le droit à la mort," in *La part du feu* (Paris: Gallimard, 1949), 293–331.

63. G. W. F. Hegel, *Phenomenology of Spirit,* translated by A. V. Miller (Oxford: Clarendon Press, 1977), 360, translation slightly modified.

64. For a discussion of this hybrid, see Roger French, "Sickness and the Soul," in *The Medical Enlightenment of the Eighteenth Century,* ed. Andrew Cunningham and Roger French (Cambridge: Cambridge University Press, 1990), 88–110. It should be noted that vitalism also influenced Mary Shelley's thinking, this philosophical/scientific system providing an easy bridge into the Gothic genre.

65. Fred Botting, *Gothic* (London: Routledge, 1996),see especially 86.

66. George Haggerty, *Gothic Fiction/Gothic Form* (College Park: Pennsylvania State University Press, 1989).

67. Botting, *Gothic,* 2.

68. Kelly Hurley, *The Gothic Body* (Cambridge: Cambridge University Press, 1996).

69. Howard P. Lovecraft, *Supernatural Horror in Literature* (New York: Dover Press, 1973), see 15 for a discussion of "unknown forces."

70. Edgar Allan Poe, "The Pit and the Pendulum," in *Works of Edgar Allan Poe* (New York: Gramercy Books, 1985), 344–354; see also Haggerty, *Gothic Fiction/ Gothic Form,* 88.

71. Mikhail Bakhtin, *Rabelais and His World* (Austin: University of Texas Press, 1984).

72. For a useful discussion on this point, see Peter Hitchcock, "The Grotesque of the Body Electric," in *Bakhtin and the Human Sciences,* ed. Michael Meyerfeld Bell and Michael Gardiner (London: Sage, 1998), 78–94.

73. Maurcie Chardon, *Les nuits de l'échafaud* (Paris: Librairie Generale, 1878).

74. See Outram, *Body and the French Revolution,* 119.

75. Sigmund Freud, "The *Moses* of Michelangelo" [1914], pp. in Sigmund Freud, *Standard Edition,* vol. 13 (London: Hogarth Press, 1955), 211–236, quotations from 211, 213.

76. Tzvetan Todorov, *The Fantastic* (Cleveland: Press of Case Western Reserve University, 1973), quotation on 33.

77. Auguste Villiers de l'Isle-Adam, *Le secret de l'échafaud* (Paris: Marpin and Flammarion, 1888).

78. Charles Desmaze, *Histoire de la médicine légale en France* (Paris, 1880).

79. Georges de Labruyere, *Le Matin,* March 3, 1907, 1–2.

80. *Le Matin,* March 3, 1907, 2.

81. Dr. Beaurieux, "Exécution de Languille: Observation prise immédiatement après décapitation," *Archives de l'Anthropologie Criminelle* 20 (1905): 643–648, quotation on 645.

82. "Après Le Couperet," *Le Matin,* 30 June 1905, 1.

83. Albert Camus, "Réflexions sur la guillotine," in Albert Camus and Arthur Koestler, *Réflexions sur la peine capitale* (Paris. Calman-Lévy, 1957), 125–238, quotation on 133.

84. Georges Bataille, *The Accursed Share* (New York: Zone Books, 1991); and Robert Hertz, *Death and the Right Hand* (1907; London: Cohen and West, 1960).

Chapter Six

1. Mark Essig, *Edison and the Electric Chair* (New York: Walker and Company, 2003), see 84.

2. In Craig Brandon, *The Electric Chair: An Unnatural American History* (Jefferson: McFarland, 1999), quotation on 49.

3. "Capital Punishment," *New York Times,* 17 December 1887, 4.

4. Quoted in Brandon, *Electric Chair,* 76.

5. Frank Wicks, "Full Circuit," *Mechanical Engineering-CIMF* 122, no. 9 (2000): 76.

6. Quoted in Essig, *Edison and the Electric Chair,* 202.

7. For Peirce, an "index" was a sign linked to its referent by causality or by an existential connection. Smoke, for example, is an index of fire. See Peirce, *Peirce on Signs* (Chapel Hill: University of North Carolina Press, 1991).

8. Jill Jonnes, "New York Unplugged, 1889," *New York Times,* 13 August, 2004, A21. See also Essig, *Edison and the Electric Chair,* 136–37.

9. Tim Armstrong, "The Electrification of the Body at the Turn of the Century," *Textual Practice* 5, no. 3 (1991): 303–325.

10. Linda Simon, *Dark Light: Electricity and Anxiety from the Telegraph to the X-Ray* (New York: Harcourt, 2004).

11. Avital Ronell, *The Telephone Book: Technology, Schizophrenia, Electric Speech* (Lincoln: University of Nebraska Press, 1989).

12. David E. Nye, *Electrifying America: The Social Meanings of a New Technology, 1880–1940* (Boston: MIT Press, 1990).

13. Émile Durkheim, *Suicide* (New York: Free Press, 1951), and idem, *The Division of Labor in Society* (Basingstoke: Macmillan, 1984).

14. Quoted in Essig, *Edison and the Electric Chair,* 123.

15. Mary Wollstonecraft Shelley, *Frankenstein, or the Modern Prometheus* (London: William Pickering, 1993).

16. Wollstonecraft Shelley, *Frankenstein,* 24, 211, 38.

17. Author's introduction to the third edition, in Wollstonecraft Shelley, *Frankenstein.*

18. Essig, *Edison and the Electric Chair,* 42.

19. Kai Mikkonen, "Electric Lines of Desire: Narrative and the Woman's Body in Villiers de l'Isle-Adam's 'Future Eve,'" *Literature and Psychology* 44, nos. 1–2 (1998): 23–54.

20. Comte de Villiers de l'Isle-Adam, *L'Ève future* (1888; Paris : E. Fasquelle, 1902).

21. Mikkonen, "Electric Lines of Desire."

22. Stephen Hall, "Tesla: A Scientific Saint, Wizard or Carnival Sideman," *Smithsonian* 71 (June 1986): 120–131.

23. Essig, *Edison and the Electric Chair,* chapter 17.

24. In re Kemmler 136 U.S. 436 (1890).

25. Editorial, *New York Tribune,* 22 March 1889.

26. *Medical Record,* 24 November, 1888, quoted in Essig, *Edison and the Electric Chair,* 172.

27. For a fuller account, see Brandon, *Electric Chair,* 177–178.

28. "Far Worse Than Hanging," *New York Times,* August 7, 1890, 1. The following in-text quotes are from this source as well.

29. Brandon, *Electric Chair,* 182.

30. Brandon, *Electric Chair,* 170–171.

31. Quoted in "The Execution Protocol," *Economist,* 23 January 1993, 86.

32. See Robert Johnson, *Death Work: A Study of the Modern Execution Process* (Pacific Grove: Brooks/Cole Publishing, 1990).

33. Johnson, *Death Work,* 72.

34. Johnson, *Death Work,* 75.

35. Johnson, *Death Work,* 79.

36. Johnson, *Death Work,* 79.

37. Johnson, *Death Work,* 81.

38. Prison officer quoted in Johnson, *Death Work,* 92. This is consistent with the thinking of Durkheim: "[C]utting of the hair is a ritual act, accompanied by definite ceremonies . . . as soon as a man is dead they (the Aborigines) cut his hair off and put it away in some distant place." *The Elementary Forms of Religious Life* (London: George Allen and Unwin, 1915), 138.

39. Johnson, *Death Work,* 93.

40. Johnson, *Death Work,* 94.

41. Quoted in Stephen Kinzer, "Where the Big Attraction Is a Big-House Museum," *New York Times,* 15 October 2003, E1.

42. Quoted in Susan Blaustein, "Witness to Another Execution," *Harper's,* May 1994, 52–63.

43. S. Lehman, "A Matter of Engineering," *Atlantic Monthly,* February 1990, 26–29.

44. *Angels with Dirty Faces* (1938, Warner Brothers), director Michael Curtiz.

45. *Glass v. Louisiana,* 471 U.S. 1080 (1985).

46. Re Kemmler 136 U.S. 436 (1890).

47. Durkheim, *Elementary Forms,* 138.

48. The pivotal nature of these deaths is also attested by Austin Sarat, *When the State Kills* (Princeton: Princeton University Press, 2001).

49. Durkheim: "Human blood is so holy at thing that in the tribes of Central Australia, it frequently serves to consecrate the most respected instruments of the cult," *Elementary Forms,* 120.

50. David Byrd, "The Electric Chair on the Hot Seat," *National Journal* 20 (November 1999): 3416. The photographs can be seen in Sarat, *When the State Kills.*

51. "Dead Man Walking Out," *Economist,* 10 June 2000, 21.

52. "A Shocking Way to Go," *Time,* 21 May 1990, 33.

53. Quoted in Rick Bragg, "Florida's Messy Executions Put the Electric Chair on Trial," *New York Times,* 18 November, 1999, A14.

54. Sydney P. Greenberg, "Court Upholds Use of Electric Chair," *St. Petersberg Times,* 25 September 1999.

55. Wendell Smith, "Cruel and Unusual? Prison Editors Help Pull the Plug on an Electric Chair," *Columbia Journalism Review* (Sept.–Oct. 1991): 13.

56. Charles Perrow, *Normal Accidents: Living with High Risk Technologies* (New York: Basic Books, 1984).

57. Lehman, "A Matter of Engineering," 28.

58. Lehman, "A Matter of Engineering," 27.

59. *Trop v. Dulles,* 356 U.S. 86, 101.

60. Quoted in Henry Weinstein, "Ga. High Court Relegates Electric Chair to History," *Los Angeles Times,* 6 October 2001; Kevin Sack, "Supreme Court of Georgia Voids Use of Electrocution," *New York Times,* 6 October 2001, A8.

61. Jennifer Harry, "Nebraska Studies Execution Ruling," *Corrections Today* 64, no. 4 (2000): 14.

62. "Ashcroft's Last Stand," *Washington Post,* 18 November 2004, A39.

63. *Trop v. Dulles,* 356 U.S. 86 (1958).

64. See *Weems v. United States,* 217 U.S. 349 (1910).

65. *Furman v. Georgia,* 408 U.S. 238 (1972).

66. Claudia Wallis, "Too Young to Die," *Time,* 14 March, 2005, 40.

67. "High Court to Hear Challenge to Electric Chair," *Associated Press,* 18 April 2005.

68. Maria Glod, "Family's Killer Executed by Electrocution," *Washington Post,* 10 April 2003, metro B04.

69. Byrd, "The Electric Chair on the Hot Seat."

70. François Rochat and Andre Modigliani, "The Ordinary Quality of Resistance," *Journal of Social Issues* 51, no. 3 (1995): 195–211; and Hannah Arendt, *Eichmann in Jerusalem: A Report on the Banality of Evil* (New York: Viking Press, 1963).

71. Scott Christianson, "Going Up the River, for a Visit," *New York Times,* 21 January 2005, F1.

72. Martha T. Moore, "Town Wants to Open Sing Sing to Public," *USA Today,* 9 February 2005, A3.

73. Kate Stone Lombardi, "The Big House as Tourist Spot," *New York Times,* 8 April 2001, 14 WC, 8.

74. Moore, "Town Wants to Open Sing Sing to Public," A3.

75. Scott Christianson, "Sentenced to Tourism," *New York Times,* 6 February 2005, WC13.

76. "Up the River," *New York Times,* 9 January, 2005, WC14.

77. Durkheim, *Elementary Forms,* 137.

78. "Numbers," *Time,* 18 December 2000, 25.

79. Peter Carlson, "It's All in the Execution," *Washington Post,* 29 November 2004, C1–C2.

80. "Where the Big Attraction Is a Big-House Museum," E1. The uncomfortable association of electrocution with carnival found at the Texas Prison Museum is not as new as we might think. The coupling can be traced back to Edison himself and his public experiments, most particularly his increasingly desperate stunts to discredit AC. These culminated in the electrocution of Topsy, a rogue Coney Island Circus elephant, on January 4, 1903. Edison filmed the event and showed this widely.

81. Alain Jouffroy, quoted in George Plimpton, "Review: He Put the Camp in Campbell's," *Observer,* January 27, 2002, 5.

82. Peter Halley, "Fifteen Little Electric Chairs," in *Andy Warhol Little Electric Chair Paintings* (New York: Stellan Holm Gallery, 2001), quotations on 39, 43, and 43, respectively.

83. Robert Hughes, "A Caterer of Repetition and Glut: Andy Warhol, 1928–1987," *Time,* 9 March 1987, 90.

84. Eleanor Heartney, *Postmodern Heretics: The Catholic Imagination in Contemporary Art* (New York: Midmarch Press, 2004); and Jane Gaggett Dillenberger, *The Religious Art of Andy Warhol* (New York: Continuum, 1998).

85. Carol Kino, "Seeing and Believing," *Art in America* 90, no. 10 (2002): 148–153.

86. John Schwartz, "Noticed: It Growls, It's Creepy, It's at Your House," *New York Times,* October 6, 2002, sect. 9, 4.

87. At http://www.skullkingdom.com, accessed 14 April 2005.

88. "Welcome . . . to Pedro's Bloody House of Horrors," *Miami Herald,* 13 October 2003, E5.

89. Victoria Newton, "Madonna at Her Most Shocking," *Sun,* 20 May, 2004, 21.

90. The two lines on the Re-Invention Tour were first written in 2005, long before details of the Confessions tour were known. If we think of our interpretations of symbol systems as predictions of future symbolic activity, then Madonna's use of the crucifix can be understood as confirming the validity our hermeneutic frame.

91. *The Green Mile* (1999, Warner Brothers), directed by Frank Darabont.

92. David Ansen, "The Executioner's Song," *Newsweek,* 13 December 1999, 86.

93. See Heather Hicks, "Hoodoo Economics: White Men's Work and Black Men's Magic in Contemporary American Film," *Camera Obscura* 53 (2003): 27–57. Hicks insightfully decodes the religious and mystical elements of the film before going on to situate them within a critical discourse on race. Another reading of the film is provided by Austin Sarat in *When the State Kills.* Sarat correctly notes that themes of morality and individual responsibility are central and in this sense it is a conservative product. Curiously he does not seem to notice the genre of *The Green Mile*—perhaps horror, magic realism, mystery, or science fiction—or recognize that this makes it ideologically distinctive when contrasted to the more realist texts he also explores such as *Dead Man Walking.* Contra Hicks and Sarat, my position would be that *The Green Mile* is a deeply subversive film. It destabilizes authorized categories for thinking the electric chair.

94. Henri Hubert and Marcel Mauss, *Sacrifice: Its Nature and Function* (London: Cohen and West, 1964), quotation on 97.

95. Hubert and Mauss, *Sacrifice,* 98.

96. "Death, Purified," *New York Times,* 8 December 1982, A30.

97. "Death Purified."

98. Dan Balz, "Texas Executes Man by Drug Injection," *Washington Post,* 7 December 1982, A1, A8, quotation on A8, emphasis added.

99. "Three Hours in Missouri," *Economist,* 31 July 1993, 27, emphasis added.

100. For example, "Doctors and Death Row," *Lancet,* 23 January 1993, 209–10.

101. Lawrence D. Egbert, "Physicians and the Death Penalty," *America* 178, no. 7 (1998): 15–16.

102. "Unconstitutional? Lethal Injection," *Economist,* April 3 2004, 33.

103. Judith Graham, "Study: Lethal Injection Not Painless," *Chicago Tribune,* 15 April 2005, A1, A19, quotation on A19.

104. "Lethal Injections: Cruel and Unusual Punishment," *Gallup Poll Tuesday Briefing,* May 2004, 116.

Chapter Seven

1. I explore this idea further in *Why War?: The Cultural Logic of Iraq, the Gulf War and Suez* (Chicago: University of Chicago Press, 2005). Here I show that risk perceptions of foreign threats are shaped by the narrative genres through which world events are perceived by interested parties. The point is not that policy is "irrational" but rather that practical reason is a form of mythical thought.

2. Émile Durkheim, "Two Laws of Penal Evolution," in *The Radical Sociology of Durkheim and Mauss,* ed. Mike Gane (London: Routledge, 1992), 21–49.

3. See Jeffrey Alexander, ed., *Real Civil Societies* (London: Sage, 1996), also idem, *The Civil Sphere* (Oxford: Oxford University Press, 2006).

4. For another illustration of this point, see chapter 3 in Austin Sarat, *When the State Kills* (Princeton: Princeton University Press, 2001).

5. Erving Goffman, *Interaction Ritual* (Chicago: Aldine, 1967).

6. James Q. Whitman's *Harsh Justice* (Oxford: Oxford University Press, 2003) provides evidence on this point by showing the status of the self has long been a concern of penal legislators. In trying to explain American exceptionalism as manifest in a high imprisonment rate and the maintenance of the death penalty, Whitman argues that a "leveling up" of punishment in Europe saw efforts to preserve dignity become central there. By contrast, in the United States there was a leveling down, with harsh and humiliating punishments more common. His work captures some differences in mood but overstates the case. Respect for the individual has been built into the U.S. justice in various ways, and the imposition of degradation has been limited even here. This is really a situation of leaders and laggards, one hopes.

7. David Garland's *Punishment and Modern Society* (Oxford: Oxford University Press, 1991) is no exception here, the main thrust of his classic essay asserting that a little Foucault might go a long way to balancing out Durkheim's idealism.

8. Émile Durkheim, *The Division of Labour in Society* (1893; Basingstoke: Macmillan, 1984), quotation on 41.

9. On second thought there may be more to them than meets the eye. Parking tickets have become iconic of the perils and hassles of urban life. They are further caught up in mythologies relating to what Robert Merton called "ritualism," or the mindless bureaucratic mentality. Parking ticket stories told in friendship networks involve petty and inflexible officials who ignore common sense. Whether on the street or reading our letter at headquarters, these mean-spirited apparatchiks can be guaranteed to ignore our appeals about confusing or missing signage, faulty meters, or freak queues at the dry cleaners caused by a medical emergency. One might also reflect on the archetype of the sexy uniformed meter maid, a figure celebrated by the Beatles as "Rita."

10. Michel Foucault, *Discipline and Punish* (London: Penguin, 1975), 131.

11. Foucault, *Discipline and Punish,* 8–9, 13–14.

12. Foucault, *Discipline and Punish,* 136.

13. Ernst Kantorowicz, *The King's Two Bodies: A Study in Mediaeval Political Theology* (Princeton: Princeton University Press, 1957).

14. Foucault, *Discipline and Punish,* 29.

15. Foucault, *Discipline and Punish,* 29.

16. Foucault, *Discipline and Punish,* 73–103.

17. On this point see also Garland, *Punishment and Modern Society.*

18. Foucault, *Discipline and Punish,* 23.

19. Michael Walzer, *Spheres of Justice: A Defense of Pluralism and Equality* (New York: Basic Books, 1983).

20. Clifford Geertz, *The Interpretation of Cultures* (London: Hutchinson, 1975), quotation on 29.

21. David Garland, "Frameworks of Inquiry in the Sociology of Punishment," *British Journal of Sociology* 41, no. 1 (1990): 1–15, quotation on 9.

22. Garland, "Frameworks of Inquiry," 10.

23. Bryan Turner, *The Body and Society* (London: Sage, 1996), 173. See also Janet Semple, *Bentham's Prison* (Oxford: Clarendon Press, 1993); and Michelle Perrot, *L'impossible prison* (Paris: Éditions du Seuil, 1980).

24. Arpad Szakolczai, *Max Weber and Michel Foucault: Parallel Life Works* (London: Routledge, 1998).

25. Eric Paras, *Foucault* 2.0. (New York: Other Press, 2006), quotation on 95.

26. Richard Sennett, *Flesh and Stone: The Body and the City in Western Civilization* (New York: Norton, 1994), quotation on 26.

27. Michel Foucault, *Les mots et les choses* (Paris: Gallimard, 1966). This most Lévi-Straussian of Foucault's books speaks of the importance of representation and language in the organization of human activity. It diminishes the role of the human subject but does not subordinate knowledge to power in the process. Reworking this text would have provided another avenue into my book.

28. Foucault's late shift has often been misrecognized. Like Durkheim he did not directly disown his earlier work but simply moved on while pointing to broad thematic similarities. For example, the early phase of work on biopower continued the line of thinking found in *Discipline and Punish*. The later volumes on sexuality and care of the self had a different sensibility but were also tagged as social control products. This branding masked the transition from one mode of thought to another during the 1980s. In a sense it is only by looking closely at what Foucault wrote rather than taking him at his word that we can reconstruct the return of the subject and the formation of an ethical social theory.

29. Durkheim is now being seen as the point of origin for both structuralism and post-structuralism. See Smith and Alexander, "The New Durkheim," in *The Cambridge Companion to Durkheim,* ed. J. Alexander and P. Smith (Cambridge: Cambridge University Press, 2005), 1–37; and Alexander T. Riley, "Renegade Durkheimianism," in *The Cambridge Companion to Durkheim,* ed. J. Alexander and P. Smith (Cambridge: Cambridge University Press, 2005), 274–301.

Index